# *Varieties of Religious Invention*

# Varieties of Religious Invention

## *Founders and Their Functions in History*

*Edited by*

PATRICK GRAY

OXFORD
UNIVERSITY PRESS

OXFORD
UNIVERSITY PRESS

Oxford University Press is a department of the University of Oxford.
It furthers the University's objective of excellence in research, scholarship,
and education by publishing worldwide. Oxford is a registered trade mark
of Oxford University Press in the UK and in certain other countries

Published in the United States of America by
Oxford University Press
198 Madison Avenue, New York, NY 10016,
United States of America



Library of Congress Cataloging-in-Publication Data

Varieties of religious invention : founders and their functions in history /
edited by Patrick Gray.
p. cm.
Includes index.
ISBN 978–0–19–935972–1 (pbk. : alk. paper) —
ISBN 978–0–19–935971–4 (cloth : alk. paper) 1. Religions—History.
2. Religious leaders—History. I. Gray, Patrick, 1970–
BL430.V37 2016
206'.3—dc23
2015003223

1 3 5 7 9 8 6 4 2

Printed in the United States of America on acid-free paper

# *Contents*

# *Contributors*

**Måns Broo** (Ph.D., Åbo Akademi University) is Senior Lecturer in the Department of Comparative Religion at Åbo Akademi University, Finland.

**Liang Cai** (Ph.D., Cornell University) is Assistant Professor of History at the University of Notre Dame in Notre Dame, Indiana.

**Patrick Gray** (Ph.D., Emory University) is Associate Professor of Religious Studies at Rhodes College in Memphis, Tennessee.

**R. Kevin Jaques** (Ph.D., Emory University) is Associate Professor of Religious Studies and the founding director of the Islamic Studies Program at Indiana University in Bloomington, Indiana.

**Mark Leuchter** (Ph.D., University of Toronto) is Associate Professor of Religion and Director of the Jewish Studies Program at Temple University in Philadelphia, Pennsylvania.

**Nathan McGovern** (Ph.D., University of California, Santa Barbara) is Visiting Assistant Professor of Religious Studies at Dalhousie University in Halifax, Nova Scotia, Canada.

**Mark W. Muesse** (Ph.D., Harvard University) is Associate Professor of Religious Studies and Director of the Asian Studies Program at Rhodes College in Memphis, Tennessee.

**Gil Raz** (Ph.D., Indiana University) is Associate Professor of Religion at Dartmouth College in Hanover, New Hampshire.

# *Abbreviations*

Az — Abū al-Walīd Muḥammad b. ʿAbd Allāh al-Azraqī, *Akhbār Makkah wa mājāʾa fīhā min al-āthār*, ed. Rushdī al-Ṣālih Malḥas (Jiddah, Saudi Arabia: ʿAbd al-Maqṣūd Muḥammad Saʿīd Khūjah, 2005)

Biblical Texts:

| | |
|---|---|
| Gen. | Genesis |
| Exod. | Exodus |
| Deut. | Deuteronomy |
| 1–2 Sam. | 1–2 Samuel |
| 1–2 Kgs. | 1–2 Kings |
| 1–2 Chron. | 1–2 Chronicles |
| Jer. | Jeremiah |
| Ezek. | Ezekiel |
| Hos. | Hosea |
| Matt. | Matthew |
| Rom. | Romans |
| 1–2 Cor. | 1–2 Corinthians |
| Gal. | Galatians |
| Phil. | Philippians |
| Heb. | Hebrews |
| 1 Pet. | 1 Peter |

DZ — Kristofer M. Schipper and Franciscus Verellen, eds., *The Taoist Canon: A Historical Companion to the Daozang* (Chicago: University of Chicago Press, 2004)

*ER*$^2$ — Lindsay Jones, ed., *Encyclopedia of Religion*, 2nd ed., 15 vols. (Detroit: Macmillan Reference USA, 2005)

G — Alfred Guillaume, *The Life of Muhammad: A Translation of Isḥāq's* Sīrat Rasūl Allāh (Oxford: Oxford University Press, 1955)

IH ʿAbd al-Mālik b. Hishām, *al-Sīrah al-nabawīyah*, 4 vols., ed. Muṣṭafā al-Shaqqā, Ibrāhīm al-Ibyārī, and ʿAbd al-Ḥafīẓ al-Shalabī (Cairo: Muṣṭafā al-Bābī al-Ḥalabī, 1936)

N Gordon Newby, *The Making of the Last Prophet: A Reconstruction of the Earliest Biography of Muhammad* (Columbia: University of South Carolina Press, 1989)

Ṭ Abū Jaʿfar Muḥammad b. Jarīr al-Ṭabarī, *Tārīkh al- rusul wa'l-mulūk*, 16 vols., ed. M. J. De Goeje et al. (Leiden: Brill, 1879–98)

ZHDZ Zhang Jiyu 張繼禹, ed., *Zhonghua daozang* 中華道藏, vol. 8 (Beijing: Huaxia chubanshe, 2004)

*Varieties of Religious Invention*

# *Introduction*

*Patrick Gray*

THE STUDY OF religion generally or of particular religious traditions may be undertaken with any number of different aims and interests and operate in accordance with a variety of ideological assumptions and methodological principles. These factors influence the focus of any such investigation. One might approach the subject with special attention to doctrine, written texts, social organization, or ritual practice. Less orthodox is the literary approach taken by Gore Vidal in *Creation*, a sweeping historical novel that follows the travels of a fictional Persian diplomat in the fifth century BCE who narrates in first person his encounters with Confucius, Laozi, Mahavira, and the Buddha.[1] The protagonist also crosses paths with a young Socrates and, for good measure, claims Zoroaster as his grandfather. Vidal has to play fast and loose with the chronology to fit these luminaries into the life span of a single character. Scholars are well aware of his many shortcomings as a would-be historian of philosophy and religion, but a subtler point may escape notice. That Vidal makes the effort to include them in what he intends as a meditation on comparative religion—to be sure, a tendentious and highly imaginative one—is an indication of the hold such figures have on the popular imagination.

Perhaps the most common approach to the study of religion is a historical one that focuses on origins. And at the origins of the world's religions, one typically finds—or looks for—an originator. Because origins are

1. Gore Vidal, *Creation* (New York: Random House, 1981).

difficult to locate with precision, the identities of the responsible parties are frequently lost in the mists of time. Jack Stillinger describes the discomfiting experience of reading an anonymous text by likening it to a trip to an art gallery or the symphony without knowing the names of the artists or composers.[2] For many, thinking about religion is the same. The body needs a head, and it helps if the head has a recognizable face. Everyone who knows of Christianity, Islam, Confucianism, and Judaism recognizes Jesus, Muhammad, Confucius, and Moses. Yet their status and that of other "founders" has not gone contested: Does Paul, for example, deserve the credit—or, for Nietzsche and others, the blame—for founding Christianity? Is Laozi the father of Daoism, or should that title belong to Zhuangzi? Nor is it clear that "founders" function in analogous ways across these traditions: Why are Buddhists relatively disinterested in "the quest for the historical Buddha"? What assumptions are implicit in the claim that Hinduism is a tradition without a founder? The chapters in this volume do not provide systematic or comprehensive presentations of the careers and teachings of the so-called founders of the major religious traditions. Neither do they settle, once and for all, perennial arguments about the identity of the "true" founder of this or that religion. Rather, they attempt to understand what it means to think of someone as a "founder" at all and to reflect on the subtexts of such debates with reference to specific traditions as a prolegomenon to comparison.

Books describing the "invention" or "creation" of particular religions or of the category of religion in general have proliferated in recent years.[3] Jonathan Z. Smith's dictum that "Religion is solely the creation of the scholar's study" has achieved something akin to canonical status among

---

2. Jack Stillnger, *Multiple Authorship and the Myth of Solitary Genius* (New York: Oxford University Press, 1991), 186.

3. Lionel M. Jensen, *Manufacturing Confucianism: Chinese Traditions and Universal Civilization* (Durham, NC: Duke University Press, 1998); Derek R. Petersen and Darren R. Walhof, *The Invention of Religion: Rethinking Belief in Politics and History* (New Brunswick, NJ: Rutgers University Press, 2002); Russell T. McCutcheon, *Manufacturing Religion: The Discourse on Sui Generis Religion and the Politics of Nostalgia* (New York: Oxford University Press, 2003); Daniel Dubuisson, *The Western Construction of Religion: Myths, Knowledge, and Ideology*, trans. W. Sayers (Baltimore, MD: Johns Hopkins University Press, 2003); Tomoko Masuzawa, *The Invention of World Religions, or, How European Universalism Was Preserved in the Language of Pluralism* (Chicago: University of Chicago Press, 2005); Brian K. Pennington, *Was Hinduism Invented? Britons, Indians, and the Colonial Construction of Religion* (Oxford: Oxford University Press, 2005); Jason Ānanda Josephson, *The Invention of Religion in Japan* (Chicago: University of Chicago Press, 2012).

historians of religion.[4] Western scholars in particular are thought to be responsible for this creation. Daniel Dubuisson, for example, wonders whether the concept of religion is "wholly unique to Western civilization, one of its most original creations" and indeed "the West's most characteristic concept."[5] This creation does not appear to have occurred ex nihilo. It comes about in the nineteenth century with the emergence of liberal Protestant theology and the encounter with non-Western traditions that take place in the context of European imperial expansion. During this period, according to Tomoko Masuzawa, there seem to have developed "two typical, nearly requisite means of identifying an individual religious tradition as distinct, unique, and irreducible to any other: the naming of an extraordinary yet historically genuine person as the founder and initiator of the tradition . . . and the recognition of certain ancient texts that could be claimed to hold canonical status."[6]

Hinduism, of course, constitutes an apparent exception to this rule, which may explain why some scholars who study Hinduism have sounded a note of caution. David N. Lorenzen writes that what is now acknowledged as Hinduism takes a recognizable shape several centuries prior to the arrival of British colonizers and points out the fallacy of claiming that a thing—a religion, say, or a founder—cannot exist before the name for that thing has been coined.[7] To the question "Was Hinduism invented?" Brian K. Pennington gives a similarly negative answer. The claim that Hinduism is merely a modern invention is "tantamount to a theological statement about the normative constitution of religious identity," and this scholarly "appropriation of the authority to pronounce some version of a tradition an impostor," moreover, strikes him as "an illegitimate intervention of

---

4. Jonathan Z. Smith, *Imagining Religion: From Babylon to Jonestown* (Chicago: University of Chicago Press, 1982), xi.

5. Dubuisson, *The Western Construction of Religion*, 9.

6. Masuzawa, *The Invention of World Religions*, 132. Religion in this framework is, as Brent Nongbri observes, "anything that sufficiently resembles modern Protestant Christianity" (*Before Religion: A History of a Modern Concept* [New Haven, CT: Yale University Press, 2013], 157). John Bright illustrates (unwittingly) Masuzawa's point when he remarks with respect to Moses that "a faith as unique as Israel's demands a founder as surely as does Christianity—or Islam, for that matter. To deny that role to Moses would force us to posit another person of the same name" (*A History of Israel*, 3rd ed. [Philadelphia: Westminster, 1981], 127).

7. David N. Lorenzen, "Who Invented Hinduism?" *Comparative Studies in Society and History* 41 (1999): 630–59.

academic historiography into the sphere of religion itself, a sphere over which practitioners alone should have custody."[8]

While it is vitally important to register the role of nineteenth-century European scholarship in shaping popular and scholarly understandings of religion, it is thus possible to overcorrect for the problem. Preeminent individuals playing decisive roles in the birth and propagation of various religions are not purely figments of the modern imagination. Something as mundane as "The Vinegar Tasters" (三酸图), a popular motif in Chinese and Japanese scroll painting that features Confucius, Laozi, and the Buddha as representatives of the three major religious traditions of China, might suggest otherwise in that it predates the European engagement with Eastern religions by several centuries.[9] However one interprets the relationship between the three sages, they are clearly invoked as representatives of their respective traditions. Even earlier, legends from the second century CE describe the westward journey of Laozi, where he appears as an avatar of the Buddha and a reincarnation of Mani, the founder of Manichaeanism.[10] These and other examples give evidence of a rough parallelism among the roles played by these figures that is acknowledged by native observers and not simply imposed by Western scholars. Jason Ānanda Josephson has gone a step further, arguing that it was not Westerners but the Japanese who invented "religion" (*shūkyō*) as a means of accommodating Christianity and Buddhism in the course of elevating state-sponsored Shinto as a supra-religious national ideology.[11]

To recognize that "invention" may be a more apt term than "discovery" for what frequently happens when scholars attempt to describe religious traditions should not detract attention from the "creative" processes unfolding in the earliest stages of those traditions themselves. Furthermore, not all acts of invention are the same. A very real, very wide variety of invention is on display both in antiquity and in the modern period. One of the objectives of this volume is to take stock of this variety. The contributors

8. Pennington, *Was Hinduism Invented?*, 5.

9. See, e.g., Miyeko Murase and Judith G. Smith, *The Arts of Japan* (New York: Metropolitan Museum of Art, 2000), 246–47. On the "three teachings" discourse on which this decorative motif is based, see Michael Pye, "What Is 'Religion' in East Asia," in *The Notion of "Religion" in Comparative Research: Selected Proceedings of the XVI IAHR Congress*, ed. U. Bianchi (Rome: L'Erma di Bretschneider, 1994), 115–22.

10. Samuel N. C. Lieu, *Manichaeism in Central Asia and China* (Leiden: Brill, 1998), 112–14.

11. Josephson, *The Invention of Religion in Japan*, 94–98.

consider key texts, relevant contexts, and critical subtexts of scholarly and "popular" discourse about religious founders. Among the guiding questions addressed are the following five:

1. *Who is traditionally regarded as the founder, and what other "candidates" have been put forward? On what sorts of evidence and arguments do these claims rest?*

Insofar as it emphasizes orthopraxy over orthodoxy, for example, it is perhaps natural that the lawgiver Moses first comes to mind for Judaism—though pressed for a name, others might identify the fifth-century BCE scribe Ezra.[12] Muhammad's status raises different questions: Did he establish a religion, or something more comprehensive like a culture or a civilization? Is there a crucial distinction to be made in referring to the prophet as "the first Muslim" (Qur'an 6:14; 39:12) as opposed to "the founder of Islam"? Given that founders normally stand at the starting point, how does it complicate matters when Islam hails Muhammad not as the first but as the last of the prophets and implies in the Qur'an that individuals such as Abraham (3:67), Moses (7:143), and the disciples of Jesus (3:52) were proto-Muslims? Similarly, how should one understand the relationship between founder and founding when one recalls that Siddhartha Gautama is often regarded as the fourth or the sixth or the twenty-fifth "awakened one," and that Confucius emphasized that he was "a transmitter, not an innovator" (*Analects* 7.1)? Does it matter that Jesus "came not to abolish the law and the prophets . . . but to fulfill them" (Matt. 5:17) and thus may not have intended to start a new religion? To what extent are the putative founders part of the message rather than acting solely as messengers?

2. *To whom do these debates matter? Is debate more urgent or intense during particular time periods than at others?*

As one can tell from the reaction to the "Hagarism" theory—that what has been called Islam for over a millennium is actually a corruption of a quasi-Jewish messianic movement—these are not simply arcane squabbles

---

12. Bernhard W. Anderson, *Understanding the Old Testament* (Englewood Cliffs, NJ: Prentice-Hall, 1957), 453, refers to Ezra as "the father of Judaism." Another Moses—Moses Mendelssohn—trumps all other claimants if, as has been argued, he is responsible for "invent[ing] the idea of Jewish religion" (Leora Batnitzky, *How Judaism Became a Religion* [Princeton, NJ: Princeton University Press, 2011], 4, 13).

between scholars who spend all their time in the library.[13] To whom is it more pressing to determine how early Muhammad's *sunnah* was invested with special authority? What is one to make of changing attitudes about Confucius when one discovers that most Chinese today do not think of Confucianism as a religion?[14] Why did the nineteenth and twentieth centuries see such diverse writers as Mark Twain, Jeremy Bentham, and Mahatma Gandhi ascribe to the Apostle Paul a role in the origins of Christianity even more fundamental than that of Jesus? Whose interests were served by the depiction of the Buddha as an opponent of superstition, despite the fact that Buddhists in South and East Asia seemed to have little need for such a Buddha?[15] Why are practicing Daoists untroubled by the thought that Laozi may not have existed, especially when compared with practicing Christians, who tend to be scandalized by the same suggestion—however far-fetched it may be—when it comes to Jesus? To legitimate their authority, why did Levitical priests in the Second Temple period (515 BCE–70 CE) appeal to King David alongside, or even in place of, Moses?[16] When did Abraham score the hat trick of becoming the father of three faiths, a curious honor since neither Jews nor Christians nor Muslims typically refer to themselves as practitioners of "Abrahamic religions"?[17]

---

13. See the discussion surrounding Patricia Crone and Michael A. Cook, *Hagarism: The Making of the Islamic World* (Cambridge: Cambridge University Press, 1977).

14. Anna Sun, *Confucianism as a World Religion: Contested Histories and Contemporary Realities* (Princeton, NJ: Princeton University Press, 2013), 110–19. Consideration of Confucius as a religious founder appears to have started with the advent of Buddhism in China in the first century. Mark Csikszentmihalyi observes that comparison of Confucius to other founders becomes common among twentieth-century sociologists seeking to integrate China into cross-cultural typologies ("Confucius," in *The Rivers of Paradise: Moses, Buddha, Confucius, Jesus, and Muhammad as Religious Founders*, ed. D. N. Freedman and M. J. McClymond [Grand Rapids: Eerdmans, 2001], 298). The view that Confucianism may not be religion and that, at any rate, Confucius was not its founder is reminiscent of Voltaire's comment on the Holy Roman Empire, namely, that it was "neither holy, nor Roman, nor an empire."

15. Donald S. Lopez Jr., *The Scientific Buddha: His Short and Happy Life* (New Haven, CT: Yale University Press, 2012), 21–46.

16. Simon J. de Vries, "Moses and David as Cult Founders in Chronicles," *Journal of Biblical Literature* 107 (1988): 619–39.

17. See, e.g., Bruce Feiler, *Abraham: A Journey to the Heart of Three Faiths* (New York: William Morrow, 2002). Abraham's spiritual progeny is increased further by Frances Worthington in *Abraham: One God, Three Wives, Five Religions* (Wilmette, IL: Bahá'í Publishing, 2011). For a critical assessment of this classification, see Jon D. Levenson, *Inheriting Abraham: The Legacy of the Patriarch in Judaism, Christianity, and Islam* (Princeton, NJ: Princeton University Press, 2012), 173–214; and Aaron W. Hughes, *Abrahamic Religions: On the Uses and Abuses of History* (Oxford: Oxford University Press, 2012).

3. *When is "development" in a religious tradition perceived as "deviation" from its roots? To what extent is the founder assumed to define the "essence" of a religion?*

Protestant Reformers like Martin Luther and Matthias Flaccius believed that the church had undergone a "Great Apostasy" the further it strayed from the simple teachings of Jesus and extrapolated doctrines and institutions not found explicitly in the New Testament. At a different point on the spectrum is the Talmudic story of Moses being transported from his seat in heaven to the academy of Rabbi Akiba and understanding nothing the rabbi says (*Menachot* 29b). When a student asks about his reasoning, Akiba replies that it came from the law received by Moses at Sinai. Shocked but then pleased, Moses returns to heaven with the assurance that the eternal Torah remains alive in the world even as it bears little obvious resemblance to its original form. Along the same lines, would Laozi countenance the alchemical efforts of later Daoists to find elixirs of immortality in substances like cinnabar? To what extent, if at all, would he recognize, among other things, moral relativism, political anarchism, and even t'ai chi martial arts as logical developments of the *wu wei* philosophy? Are different attitudes about Laozi what distinguish early "philosophical Daoism" from later "religious Daoism," with its priests, temples, and rituals, or is this dichotomy a false one? Would Confucius look askance at the Neo-Confucianism that sought to synthesize Confucian ideas with Buddhist spirituality and Daoist cosmology during the Song Dynasty (960–1279 CE)—and should it matter to self-identified Confucians what Confucius might think? Would devotees of the Buddha agree with Gandhi's pronouncement that Buddhism "is a part of Hinduism" and that "Buddha did not give the world a new religion; he gave it a new interpretation"?[18] Is the image of Muhammad as "exemplar of humanity par excellence" essential to his status as a founder or is it incidental, appearing only later as part of Muslim efforts to present Muhammad as a prophet comparable or superior to Jesus?[19] Did Jesus and Muhammad both believe the world would end in their lifetimes, and are the true foundings of Christianity

18. In a speech at the Buddha Jayanti, Bombay, India, May 18, 1924.

19. Annemarie Schimmel, *And Muhammad Is His Messenger: The Veneration of the Prophet in Islamic Piety* (Chapel Hill: University of North Carolina Press, 1985), 235.

and Islam thus to be located in the attempts of their respective followers to come to terms with their "mistakes"?[20]

4. *In what ways do arguments about founders serve as a proxy for broader cultural, theological, philosophical, political, or ideological questions?*

How has the absence of a conventional founder factored into disagreements about the basic definition of Hinduism coinciding with the resurgent nationalism characterizing Indian politics over the last three decades?[21] Is Wahabbi criticism of Sufi devotional practices focusing on Muhammad theological or political in nature?[22] What motivations lie behind comparisons of, say, the Buddha and Jesus?[23] What changes have taken place between the Cultural Revolution, when "Criticize Confucius!" was used as the slogan for a Communist propaganda campaign, and the present day, when Beijing funds hundreds of Confucius Institutes around the globe, and what do they have to do with "Confucianity"?[24] How closely correlated is eighteenth-century anti-Semitism with the notion that Ezra is responsible for the founding of Judaism, understood as a legalistic and ethnically exclusive religion, and in what ways did the contemporaneous "invention of Jewish religion" during the German Enlightenment anticipate later debates about cultural assimilation, separation of church and state, and the scope of religious tolerance?[25] What is the agenda of the ninth-century Zen master Lin Chi when he advises, "If you meet the Buddha on the road, kill him," and how does it differ from that of authors who quote the same aphorism in arguing that

---

20. Stephen J. Shoemaker, *The Death of a Prophet: The End of Muhammad's Life and the Beginnings of Islam* (Philadelphia: University of Pennsylvania Press, 2012), 118–96.

21. See Brian K. Smith, "Questioning Authority: Constructions and Deconstructions of Hinduism," *International Journal of Hindu Studies* 2 (1998): 313–39.

22. John L. Esposito, *Islam and Politics*, 4th ed. (Syracuse, NY: Syracuse University Press, 1998), 37.

23. E.g., Thich Nhat Hanh, *Living Buddha, Living Christ* (New York: Riverhead, 1995). For Buddhists, according to Richard S. Cohen, the fact that the Shakyamuni was *not* unique is central to his status as a founder ("Shakyamuni: Buddhism's Founder in Ten Acts," in Freedman and McClymond, *Rivers of Paradise*, 133).

24. See Sun, *Confucianism as a World Religion*, 22, 91.

25. Bob Becking, *Ezra, Nehemiah, and the Construction of Early Jewish Identity* (Tübingen: Mohr Siebeck, 2011), 22; Batnitzky, *How Judaism Became a Religion*, 1–5.

"to turn the Buddha into a religious fetish is to miss the essence of what he taught"?[26] Why do Western scholars who specialize in Daoism sometimes show more zeal than self-identified Daoists in correcting the errors in popular presentations of Laozi and Zhuangzi?[27] When one hears that "Islam" emerged not during the Muhammad's lifetime but a few generations later, with the disappearance of the more ecumenical "Believers" movement and the revision of narratives about the prophet, may one wonder whether this is wishful thinking on the part of those who hope for the ascendancy of a more ecumenical Islam in the present?[28] What is at stake in making a distinction between "the Jesus of history" and "the Christ of faith"?

5. *What can be learned about a particular religion—or the category of religion in general—by contemplating it through the prism of its putative founders?*

Another way to put the question might be "What can be learned by thinking about how people think about them as founders?" Does consideration of these "founders" and the roles they play in popular and scholarly discourse contribute to the dismantling of the category of religion called for by Timothy Fitzgerald and others, or does it contribute in any way to its reclamation?[29] In what ways, if at all, does the convention of referring to religious traditions in the plural (Judaisms, Christianities, Hinduisms) change the equation? Is it necessary or possible or desirable to reconceptualize the notion of a founder so that it is useful in the study of individual traditions, or should it be abandoned? Is any disinterested study of these figures possible? Or must all comparison of, say, Jesus and Muhammad or Laozi and Confucius necessarily amount to an

---

26. Sam Harris, "Killing the Buddha," *Shambhala Sun* (March 2006): 73–74. Harris adds, "The wisdom of the Buddha is currently trapped within the religion of Buddhism."

27. E.g., J. J. Clarke, *The Tao of the West: Western Transformations of Taoist Thought* (London: Routledge, 2000).

28. Reviews of Fred M. Donner, *Muhammad and the Believers: At the Origins of Islam* (Cambridge, MA: Belknap, 2010) have raised this question.

29. Timothy Fitzgerald, *The Ideology of Religious Studies* (New York: Oxford University Press, 2000).

exercise in apologetics or inflict "epistemic violence" upon the subjects being studied?[30]

While the chapters assembled here do not answer all of these questions—as if any single volume could accomplish such a multifarious task, given the myriad historical, cultural, philosophical, ideological, and political issues involved—they explore the underlying concerns embedded in them from a variety of angles and provide crucial historical context for making sense of the problems they pose. Although the questions they address have generated fierce debate in the past as well as in the present, the authors do not engage in polemics. They write as observers of these debates, placing them in context and interpreting their significance rather than presuming to settle them. In some instances they put forward provocative theses that may not enjoy the unanimous assent of scholars in their respective fields, but in each case they describe the consensus that obtains, lay out the different positions available concerning the matter at hand, and suggest resources for those who want to pursue the subject in greater detail.

Mark Leuchter ("Finding Judaism's Founders") notes that the Jewish religious tradition readily identifies a handful of prominent candidates for the role of founder: the ancestor Abraham, the lawgiver Moses, King David, prophets like Isaiah and Jeremiah, and scribes like Ezra. Each of these is regarded as an important agent through whom the God of Israel established important social and religious ideas and institutions. Rabbinic lore contains extensive material about their contributions to the growth of Judaism, yet scholars have long recognized that the historical reality behind each of these "founders" presents a far more complicated picture than the tradition suggests. Narratives associated with each of these figures develop over a long period of time and represent diverse and often independent "foundings" of what would become Judaism, with each

30. Even if one regards all or most comparisons as apologetic in nature, this approach risks overlooking the variety to be found in such efforts, which may be directed at "insiders" or "outsiders." Charles S. Braden (*Jesus Compared: A Study of Jesus and Other Great Founders of Religions* [Englewood Cliffs, NJ: Prentice-Hall, 1957]), for example, is up to something very different from Denise Lardner Carmody and John Carmody (*In the Path of the Masters: Understanding the Spirituality of Buddha, Confucius, Jesus, and Muhammad* [New York: Paragon House, 1994]), Harold Rosen (*Founders of Faith: The Parallel Lives of God's Messengers* [Wilmette, IL: Bahá'í Publishing, 2010]) or the Marquis de Sade (in his 1782 *Dialogue entre un prêtre et un moribund*), who has a character say that "Jesus is no better than Mohammed, Mohammed no better than Moses, and the three of them combined no better than Confucius" in the course of characterizing all religion as fraudulent.

serving as a repository of the memories, experiences, values, and interests of the various authors behind the biblical texts that are invoked in different ways at different stages in later Jewish history. What Leuchter calls "the classical myth of Judaism's founding" is not easily reconciled with history, yet it would be a mistake to write it off as purely fictitious. Even if the patriarchs are literary constructs, they "resonate with real ancestral experiences rendered meaningful through their enshrinement in symbolic narratives."

Nathan McGovern ("The Buddha: Historicizing Myth, Mythologizing History") observes that Buddhism is unusual among Asian religions in the degree to which it actually fits the paradigm for a "religion"—a paradigm formulated by early modern scholars, who operated with tacitly Christian assumptions about what constitutes a religion—fairly well. This is in large part due to the fact that it was "founded" by an identifiable historical personage. The identity of the Buddha as a historical figure, however, is largely a construction of nineteenth-century Western scholarship, having as its basis a set of Western assumptions about the nature of history and religion. McGovern explores the Western scholarly construction of the "historical Buddha" out of a vast array of texts and traditions as well as its subsequent deconstruction, and then compares it to traditional Buddhist approaches to the Buddha and Buddhahood.

Liang Cai ("When the Founder Is Not a Creator: Confucius and Confucianism Reconsidered") begins with an awkward question: How did a failure in the political realm become a founder of the *ru* tradition that both existed before him and was once shared by all the elite? Scholars have puzzled over this conundrum for centuries. For example, whereas Hu Shi argues that Confucius was celebrated as the founder of *ru* tradition because he transformed the culture of a defeated dynasty from a subservient, parochial one into an energetic, universal school, Robert Eno argues that Confucius was a non-Chinese who revised a non-Chinese *ru* tradition to respond to the dominant Chinese culture. Lionel Jensen takes an even more radical approach, contending that there was no such thing as Confucianism until it was created by Jesuits in the sixteenth century and Chinese scholars in the early twentieth century. Although Jensen may be correct that the process of interpreting a tradition can be the very process of creating a tradition, Cai argues that he overlooks the transformation of Confucius wrought by Confucius's immediate disciples and scholars in the Qin and Han empires between the fifth and second centuries BCE. Due to its versatility, throughout history the *ru* tradition has allowed scholars and laypersons alike to transform Confucianism into a school of thought, a political agenda, a philosophical tradition, and a religion.

Gil Raz ("What Is Daoism and Who Is Its Founder?") reminds readers that only recently has Daoism been recognized as one of the world's major religions, having long been known in the West as a major Chinese philosophical tradition centered on Laozi and the ancient classic *Daode jing*. This religion emerged in the mid-second century CE, with the appearance of the divine form of Laozi to Zhang Daoling, who thus became the first Celestial Master. Subsequent scriptural revelations in the following centuries revealed higher realms of attainment from increasingly remote celestial sources, far surpassing the divine Laozi of the Celestial Master tradition. These revelations, received by different people at different times, led to the emergence of distinct and competing ritual traditions. By the fifth and sixth centuries these revelations were brought together in a variety of competing canons. It is from this complex dialectic of integration and contestation that the religion now known as Daoism emerged, with similar processes of revelation, integration, and contestation continuing through the following centuries. There remains great confusion regarding the definition and parameters of the term "Daoism," and the relationship between the ancient philosophical tradition and the religion. This confusion is not limited to Western scholarship but is also inherent in Chinese scholarship at least as early as the medieval period. Raz examines the ancient figure of Laozi, the rival lineages with their particular founders and fictive lineages, and the subsequent negotiations by which these various ritual traditions came to see themselves within a single tradition.

In my chapter ("Jesus, Paul, and the Birth of Christianity"), I briefly survey the roles played by Jesus in the history of Christianity: Son of God, a great moral teacher, the savior of humankind, and the incarnate Word, among many others. "Founder" is not among the titles assigned to Jesus in the Bible or in the classic creeds, yet most Christians of most times and places see nothing self-evidently problematic in regarding him as such. Especially but not exclusively during the Reformation, claims about Jesus and the senses in which scholars and adherents have variously regarded him as the founder intersect with arguments about the beliefs and practices of the early church and the extent to which these benchmarks confer legitimacy in the eyes of the faithful. The interplay of canon, historical reconstruction, and authority merit special attention in part because of

Christianity's self-understanding as a "religion of the book" and the heavy emphasis it has traditionally placed on the revelatory character of specific events within history. Assessments of Jesus's originality, for lack of a better word, have figured prominently due to the distinctive relationship between Christianity and Judaism. Since the Enlightenment, the Apostle Paul has assumed a large role in these debates. Instead of Jesus, some wonder, should Paul be regarded as the founder of Christianity? The assumptions at work in these ongoing and often acrimonious debates reflect as well as shape the cultural and institutional contexts in which they take place.

R. Kevin Jaques ("Muḥammad's Mission and the *Dīn* of Ibrāhīm according to Ibn Isḥāq") gives a close reading of a key text written during a dynamic period of debate over Muhammad's role as prophet in the first centuries after his death in 632. Central to these disagreements are different conceptions of prophecy and the role of the prophet. The earliest extant biography of Muhammad was written by Ibn Isḥāq during the last stages of the Abbasid Revolution (ca. 718–750). His *Sīrat Rasūl Allāh* (*The Biography of the Messenger of God*) presents Muhammad as a man chosen to reestablish a lost tradition of worship centered on the pilgrimage (*ḥajj*), to which Ibn Isḥāq refers as the *ḥanīfīyah dīn Ibrāhīm* (covenant of Abraham) and not as a new religion that came to be known as "Islam." When viewed within the larger religious milieu of the Persio-Mediterranean world, Ibn Ishaq's construction of Muhammad throws new light on controversies about the prophet that developed in the centuries that follow.

Mans Broo ("Hinduism and the Question of Founders") highlights the absence of a traditional founder as one reason for the great variety found within Hinduism. In orthodox Hindu circles, the Vedic texts enjoy preeminent authority. While modern scholars place the composition of the Vedas to the second millennium BCE, the orthodox Hindu position, first articulated by the ancient *mimamsaka* philosophers, is that the Vedas are eternal, otherworldly texts. These philosophers argued for the authority of the Vedas on the basis of their having no known authors. Not having a founder or an author, instead of being a weakness, has thus been regarded as a proof of the supra-human nature of a religion. While Hinduism per se does not have a founder, Hinduism is full of schools of thought (*sampradayas*) founded by (generally deified) human beings. As in many other religions, these founding figures are surrounded by myths and legends, and their teachings are accorded authority that, in practical terms, often supersedes that of the Vedas. Broo pays special attention to the interplay between these different attitudes toward "founders" and "foundings" within living Hindu traditions.

Mark W. Muesse ("Crossing Boundaries: When Founders of Faith Appear in Other Traditions") reminds us that while the principal significance of the individuals discussed in the preceding chapters is surely greatest within the traditions they have ostensibly founded, they often play important roles within traditions not their own. His brief survey reveals the wide range of functions these innovators and reformers serve for the adherents of other religions.

Each of the chapters stands on its own, but it is hoped that bringing them together in a single volume will, to borrow a phrase, make the familiar strange and the strange familiar. As the contributors survey the landscape shaped by a common set of concerns related to "founders," they not only provide an opportunity to map the contours within each tradition from a novel perspective but facilitate judicious comparison between traditions as well.

# I

# *Finding Judaism's Founders*

*Mark Leuchter*

## *Considering the "Classic" Myth of Jewish Founders*

IN UNDERGRADUATE COURSES dealing with world religions, Judaism is regularly taught according to the terms of its own mythology, or what some might call the "classic" myth of Judaism. That is, the Jewish people trace their collective roots to a common set of patriarchal ancestors—Abraham, Isaac, and Jacob, who initiated a community bound by kinship and the monotheistic belief in an omnipotent, universal God. The descendants of these ancestors endured centuries of slavery in Egypt, were redeemed by their deity through the agency of a figure named Moses, and were led by this same figure through the wilderness for an entire generation. During this time, the religious and social infrastructure of the nation was established through the giving of law at Mt. Sinai by the God of the ancestors, and on entry back into the ancestral land, priests and prophets led successive generations in their ongoing relationship with this God. This relationship between God and the Jewish people persevered through the rise and fall of monarchies, conditions of exile, and domination under foreign empires, sustained by the ancient practices and beliefs that had been established under divine auspices in the most ancient times. The foundations of Jewish belief, then, were drawn from the forebears who underwent these experiences, led by outstanding personalities whose deeds and teachings were commemorated in the pages of the Hebrew Bible and a detailed tradition of oral lore.

This understanding of Jewish foundations and founders is ultimately based on the image of the past preserved in the literature of the Rabbis, a movement of religious sage-scholars who formed the dominant ideological stream in Judaism from the end of the Roman era until the modern period.[1] For the Rabbis, all the ideas one encounters within the Hebrew Bible are essentially contemporaneous and equally binding for all time. As one important rabbinic text states: "There is no early or late in the Torah" (*Pesahim* 6b), which is to say that an early figure such as Abraham and a later figure such as Ezra are both Jews, practicing the same essential religion as the Rabbis, bound to the same covenantal terms and transmitting the same tradition to those who followed them. It is this concept of the distant past—a Judaism that is read into the narratives of major figures in the Hebrew Bible—that prevailed for most of the last two millennia.

## *The Classic Myth in Critical Perspective*

The problems with this view for the critical scholar, however, are manifold. While rabbinic tradition preserves much valuable information, this information is almost never without need of unpacking or decoding. Rabbinic texts are more interested in hermeneutics and other forms of intellectual modeling than in accurately reporting historical events or experiences.[2] Furthermore, the basic rabbinic texts were composed well before the Rabbis obtained widespread authority in the Jewish world; much of what they committed to text evidences attempts to shape memory and tradition to benefit their specific social location and interests, not that of most Jews.[3] As such, it is problematic to look to rabbinic texts for a transparent indication of Jewish origins or the ostensible founders of Jewish tradition.

Furthermore, the myth of foundations flattens what was a tremendously textured set of experiences characterizing Jewish history. The texts

---

1. Seth Schwartz notes that it is primarily following the Christianization of the Roman Empire throughout the fourth–fifth centuries CE that the Rabbis gained increasing religious and social influence throughout the Jewish world; see his discussion in *Imperialism and Jewish Society, 200 B.C.E.–640 C.E.* (Princeton, NJ: Princeton University Press, 2000), 240–74.

2. On the strong hermeneutical interest of rabbinic texts, see the general discussion by H. L. Strack and Günter Stemberger, *Introduction to the Talmud and Midrash* (Minneapolis: Fortress, 1996), 15–30. See also Mark Leuchter, "The Book of the Twelve and the Great Assembly in Rabbinic History and Tradition," in *Perspectives on the Formation of the Book of the Twelve*, ed. Rainer Albertz et al. (Berlin: De Gruyter, 2012), 337–52.

3. Schwartz, *Imperialism and Jewish Society*, 103–28.

of the Hebrew Bible attest to different worldviews, concepts of the divine, linguistic conventions, intellectual values, political leanings, and historical conditions spanning the antique Jewish world. The Jerusalem priesthood, for example, held up the Pentateuch (Genesis through Deuteronomy) as the definitive work of Scripture, with a variety of prophetic texts, historiographic works, hymns, and other literary collections playing a supporting role. All of these texts were arranged and taught in a manner that reified the priests' power as the mediators not only between God and the Jewish world but also between the Jewish world and the foreign empires who dominated them. Yet other groups existed simultaneously with rather different sets of religious priorities. Wisdom circles situated well beyond the Jerusalem priesthood, for example, produced alternative doctrines of sacred instruction (the book of Proverbs, for example) that challenged any monolithic understanding of God and history from the Jewish perspective. Though these works would eventually be incorporated into the Hebrew Bible, their earlier function was one that offered a potential disruption to the sense of Jewish social cohesion revolving around the teachings of the priesthood.[4]

It is also hard to pinpoint the time when one can begin speaking of Judaism in antiquity. The term "Judaism" itself grows out of Hellenistic references to a set of religious traditions and ideas sustained by an ethnic group (*ioudaioi* in Greek) with heritage bound to the geographical area where the kingdom of Judah was once located. If we define "Judaism" as a more mature form of traditions with ancient roots stemming from that region, revolving around the concept of a divine covenant with a monotheistic deity expressed through written revelation, then most scholars would agree that by the Persian period, there were early forms of Judaism that shared in the legacy of ancient Israel in a variety of ways.[5] Nevertheless, the further back one moves along a historical timeline, the more difficult it is to refer to residents of this area as "Jews" or to define

4. Gabriele Boccaccini, *Roots of Rabbinic Judaism* (Grand Rapids: Eerdmans, 2002), 103–11.

5. The groups associated with the successive returns from Babylon—especially under the activity of Ezra (ca. 458 BCE)—constitute the core community, for it is their literature which has survived most intact in the biblical record, and it is their parent community which remained in the eastern Mesopotamian Diaspora that provided the impetus for much of what eventually transpired in Jerusalem during the Persian period. See Peter R. Bedford, "Homeland: Diaspora Relations in Ezra-Nehemiah," *Vetus Testamentum* 52 (2002): 147–65.

the religious practices and beliefs of the area as "Judaism." Although the Rabbis assumed or promoted the view that the major figures in the Hebrew Bible were co-religionists, this was certainly not the case insofar as the lives of the biblical writers or audiences were concerned, or of the ostensible individuals who are depicted in the biblical text.[6]

Judaism (as known from the Persian period onward) was not a component of social identity in ancient Israel, that is, the culture that yielded the majority of texts in the Hebrew Bible. Identity was based in concepts for ancient Israelites that did not characterize the experiences or perceptions of early Jewish groups in the Persian period or beyond. Ancient Israelites were most self-consciously bound by geography and topology, the conduct of warfare, economic ties, agricultural conventions, and language, and these were by no means uniform in the earliest times. A systematic, common theology is not attested in sources relating to Israelite "national" identity, and nationhood itself is elusive in the context of a tribal society, the form of social organization that characterized early Israel. For many, the basis of national identity is found with the rise of a monarchic state in Israel under King David and his successor Solomon spanning the late eleventh and mid-tenth centuries BCE, and indeed, Jewish (and Christian) messianic principles are rooted in the memories of the Davidic monarchy. However, most of Israel's landed history (after David and Solomon) was marked by a divided monarchy, with two separate states boasting different political and religious systems (the northern kingdom of Israel spanning 922–721 BCE; the southern kingdom of Judah spanning 922–587 BCE).

From an inner-Israelite sociopolitical perspective, the northern tribes of Israel would hardly have considered themselves "Jews"—the word itself is derived from the name of the rival Judahite kingdom and culture to the south. This would have been an even greater problem before the tenth century BCE, for it appears that Judah was not even considered a genuine Israelite tribe until that point. It would only be during the reign of King Solomon that the wilderness of Judah would become more heavily populated. Before this time, Judah is essentially off the social map. The Song of Deborah in Judges 5 (dated by most scholars to a time before the tenth century BCE) bears witness to this, as it extols and harangues Israel's tribes for their respective participation in or evasion of battle—but makes no mention whatsoever of Judah. The narratives in the Book of Genesis

---

6. See especially Marc Zvi Brettler, "Judaism in the Hebrew Bible? The Transition from Ancient Israelite Religion to Judaism," *Catholic Biblical Quarterly* 61 (1999): 429–47.

regarding Judah as one of Jacob's sons most likely reflect a growing body of Judahite literary tradition from the monarchic period onward.

At any rate, "Israelite religion" as practiced within these kingdoms boasts some features that would survive into Judaism but had more in common with ancient Near Eastern religion typifying the cultures of neighboring nations. Archaeology and textual evidence within the Hebrew Bible indicate that ancient Israelites and the ancient Canaanites, Mesopotamians, and Syrians conceived of the cosmos in nearly identical terms. Epithets for YHWH,[7] Israel's patron deity, are nearly identical to epithets for deities in the Canaanite pantheon.[8] Unlike the Jewish belief in a single, universal God, Israelite religion was characterized alternately by polytheism, henotheism, and eventually monolatry well before genuine monotheism arose as a viable (let alone dominant or exclusive) standard of belief. YHWH stood at the center of Israelite devotion, but surrounding this deity was a consort (Asherah), a divine retinue (the heavenly Host), and an assortment of other lesser deities deriving from various family-based religious practices throughout the Israelite hinterland. Many narratives, hymns, and liturgical dramas within the Hebrew Bible draw from a stock of tropes common to the ancient world; the creation account in Genesis 1 is a well-known example of this, deploying terms and concepts derived from the old Babylonian epic known as *Enuma Elish*. Also, poems like the Song of the Sea (Exodus 15), Psalm 29, Psalm 68, and Habbakuk 3 are deeply indebted to Canaanite mythology.

A similar problem extends to the role of sacred text in classical Jewish thought and the realities of life in ancient Israel. The Rabbis imagined not only a complete written Pentateuch composed by Moses but also an oral tradition of exegesis accompanying it, with both traditions known to the religious leaders in Israel who followed after Moses. Yet even before the rise of critical scholarship, this view was not entirely accepted, and the last two centuries of research have demonstrated its historical inadequacies.[9] The tales of the prophets of Israel's monarchic period, for example, contain virtually no

---

7. Vocalized as "Yahweh." In English translations of the Hebrew Bible, the name YHWH is usually represented by the term "The Lord," a tradition that developed out of religious hesitance to pronounce the divine name.

8. C. L. Seow, *Myth, Drama, and the Politics of David's Dance*, Harvard Semitic Monographs 44 (Atlanta: Scholars, 1989), 11–54.

9. Rabbinic debate over Moses' authorship of the Pentateuch is attested in the Babylonian Talmud, where some rabbinic sages claimed that Moses could not have written the last several verses narrating his own death; those, they claimed, must have been written by his successor, Joshua (*Baba Bathra* 15a).

references to the Pentateuch. Indeed, these prophets often behave in a manner inconsistent with Pentateuchal law.[10] Most Israelites, moreover, were not only incapable of reading or writing but were in some instances even hostile to the notion of the written transmission of tradition.[11] The biblical texts that are datable to the monarchic era are usually regarded as written by scribes for an elite literati quite distinct from the general public.[12] Finally, while the Pentateuch does seem to have surfaced already during the Persian period as a national charter,[13] this was the end result of a long process of composition and redaction that began, at the earliest, in the late eighth century BCE—several centuries removed from the time when Moses would have lived.[14]

It would seem, then, that the classical myth of Judaism's founding figures and institutions is not easily reconciled with history if taken at face value. The myth first surfaces during the Persian and Hellenistic periods as the relics of Israelite religion were reassembled to create boundaries of a Jewish ethnicity within the context of international imperialism. A matrix of memory, mythology, and textual curricula formed the basis for identity and became the sacred history of the Jewish people; consequently, the major literary figures (some of them historical, some of them legendary) were adopted as the "founders" of Judaism within the living and enduring mythology. But while mythology cannot be taken as history, it can

---

10. The prophet Elijah, e.g., is reported to have conducted a sacrifice on Mt. Carmel in the northern kingdom of Israel sometime during the reign of King Ahab (mid-ninth century BCE). This contravenes the Pentateuchal law that one may only sacrifice in the one, single cult site chosen by God (Deut. 12:13–19). In the context of Ahab's reign (and from the perspective of the redactor of the Book of Kings), that site would be the Jerusalem temple, in the capital city of the southern kingdom of Judah. Elijah is either blissfully unaware of this law or engaged in a demonstrative campaign against it.

11. For an overview of literacy and its limits in ancient Israel, see Ian M. Young, "Israelite Literacy: Interpreting the Evidence," *Vetus Testamentum* 48 (1998): 239–53, 408–22.

12. See especially Karel van der Toorn, *Scribal Culture and the Making of the Hebrew Bible* (Cambridge, MA: Harvard University Press, 2007), 54–73.

13. See Alexander Fantalkin and Oren Tal, "The Canonization of the Pentateuch: When and Why?" *Zeitschrift für die alttestamentliche Wissenschaft* 124 (2012): 1–18, 201–12.

14. Scholars agree that it is nearly impossible to assign a specific date to the activity of the historical Moses, but most agree that he would have lived in the important transitional period spanning the Late Bronze Age to the early Iron Age, that is, from ca. 1250–1200 BCE. The pervasiveness of Moses as a founding figure in various biblical traditions affirms a memory of his activity from a very early era in Israel's cultural history; see Ronald Hendel, "The Exodus in Biblical Memory," *Journal of Biblical Literature* 120 (2001): 615–20.

never be fully dissociated from it. Historical experiences shape the manner in which mythology is formed and transmitted; embedded within it are some indications of genuine circumstances and reactions from real communities that can be quantified and examined.[15] The depiction of the patriarchs in Genesis, even if they are literary constructs, resonate with real ancestral experiences rendered meaningful through their enshrinement in symbolic narratives.[16] The laws ostensibly given at Sinai may date from centuries after the time of Moses, but the framers of these laws preserved a memory of Moses that was deemed suitable to associate with the purpose and function of these written legal collections. In short, these and other literary figures *within* the Hebrew Bible are avatars of genuine people and groups who stood *behind* the biblical traditions, which in turn formed the earliest mythologies of Jewish identity and history.

It is therefore a mistake to dismiss the rhetorical, the legendary, or the symbolic as purely fictitious. Judaism constructed its concept of foundations from the functional remnants of ancient Israelite history and religion that were made the subject of reflection, scrutiny, and interpretation by subsequent tradents. Disqualifying the conceptual relics bequeathed by those tradents is methodologically precipitous. It is those tradents, in fact, who constitute the real "founders" of Judaism by virtue of how they conceived and transmitted images of earlier Israel. What critical scholarship can do, then, is enter the myth of the founders as a system of embedded memories—an approach that is referred to as mnemo-historical, that is, a way of viewing texts or traditions as conditioned by memory and a way of determining how events and experiences are memorialized therein.[17] In what follows, we will consider three of the basic ideological institutions of Judaism preserved in the Hebrew Bible—(1) the ancestral concept of national kinship and divine patronage, (2) the tradition of law and legal instruction, and (3) the system of socioreligious ethics—that may be traced to ancient Israel and which are symbolically ascribed to

---

15. Zechariah Kallai connects this insight to the formation of historiography in ancient Israel ("Biblical Historiography and Literary History: A Programmatic Survey," *Vetus Testamentum* 49 [1999]: 345). It may also be applied to functional charter or foundation myths in early Judaism which eventually became normative under the influence of the Rabbis.

16. Ronald Hendel, *Remembering Abraham: Culture, Memory, and History in the Hebrew Bible* (Oxford: Oxford University Press, 2005), 31–55.

17. See Hendel, "The Exodus in Biblical Memory," 602–4, for a discussion of this methodology.

particular figures (the patriarchs, Moses, Aaron, the prophets, et al.).[18] Despite the symbolic dimensions of these ascriptions, the complexity of the tradents' lives and contributions as "founders" is powerfully attested and situates the myth within the tangible *realia* of experience.

## *The Ancestral Pioneers, Kinship, and the National Deity*

The figures of the Patriarchs in the Book of Genesis are tied to the memory of ancestors from the pioneering days of ancient Israel, a period that spanned the transitional period of the Late Bronze Age through the early Iron Age (ca. 1250–1100 BCE). It is during this time that the earliest communities identifiable as "Israelite" surface in the central highlands of Canaan. It is also during this period that we encounter the earliest nonbiblical reference to "Israel" as a people, namely, a brief passage in an inscription from the Pharaoh Merneptah commemorating his campaign through Canaan in 1209 BCE. According to the inscription, Merneptah boasts that "Israel is laid waste; his seed is naught." Thus *some* form of an Israelite people existed already by the end of the thirteenth century and was firmly entrenched enough in their land holdings to warrant the mention in Merneptah's inscription, dovetailing with the archaeological evidence for the appearance of Israel around this time as well.

There is general consensus that this earliest Israel emerged in response to a massive socioeconomic crisis in the thirteenth century BCE. This crisis saw the implosion of an imperial society dominated especially by Egypt, leading to the fraying of city-states throughout Canaan that had long relied on the stability of Egyptian hegemony. As a result, many groups appear to have taken flight from the lowland city-states to the

18. I purposefully exclude from discussion here the institution and legacy of kingship/monarchy. Though the majority of texts we consider here are either products of the monarchic era or strongly influenced by the impact of monarchy, kingship in the Hebrew Bible—and thus in early Judaism—is filtered through the sieve of prophetic and priestly literature, and it is this literature that formed the heart of rabbinic curricula. Moreover, with the brief exception of the Hasmonean rulers (ca. 150–63 BCE), Judaism proper was not characterized by rule under native kings but under foreign emperors. Indeed, even the Hasmoneans' claims to royal authority were significantly contested and seriously limited by the Greek and Roman imperial worlds surrounding it. Kingship/monarchy, then, is a subject and motif more than an enduring legacy within the social world of early Judaism; even important figures like David and Solomon (whose reigns left deep impressions on Jewish religion) are subjects of priestly-scribal characterization. It is therefore not through royal figures that Judaism's foundations were laid but through sacral and intellectual figures who, at best, anticipated a restored Davidic monarchy sometime in the distant future.

highland frontier of the central Canaanite hill country, a mostly unsettled wilderness that offered opportunities for a new beginning and, indeed, a new society.[19] The ancestors of early Israel were a melange of disaffected former lowland Canaanites and quasi-nomadic caravan groups from the east, both of whom settled the highland frontier to cope with the chaos and hardship brought on by Late Bronze Age socioeconomic fallout. Alliances between these groups were forged for the purposes of mutual self-interest, with kinships intertwined through intermarriage and cooperative land settlement and territorial defense.[20]

Most significantly, however, an intertwining of religious concepts accompanied this process. As the name Isra*el* implies, the earliest dominant deity in Israelite religion was El, a figure who stood at the head of the older Canaanite religious pantheon. This deity was appropriated by many of the early Israelite settlers but transformed from the chief deity of the city-state pantheons into the family deity of those Israelite kinship groups who had emerged from the lowlands. Indeed, there are persistent allusions to El as the "god of the fathers" in the patriarchal tales in Genesis, an echo of the role that this deity played among the leaders of the early highland pioneer families. However, the deity that eventually dominated on the pan-tribal, "national" level was YHWH—a desert warrior deity whose presence in Israelite religion can most likely be traced to those early Israelites with stronger ties to eastern caravan groups. Archaeological and epigraphical evidence within and beyond the Hebrew Bible points to such groups as already devoted to YHWH well before the beginnings of Israel.

It is likely, then, that both YHWH and El were simultaneously worshipped by Israel's ancestors as distinct deities, but a later biblical writer preserves some inkling of the manner in which the two were associated over time. Exodus depicts God saying to Moses, "I am YHWH; and I appeared to Abraham, to Isaac, and to Jacob, as *El Shaddai* (God Almighty), but by my name YHWH I did not make myself known to them" (Exod. 6:2–3). This verse, usually ascribed to a priestly author of the sixth century BCE, bears witness to the persistence of a tradition recalling the development of Israelite religion from an ancestral phase into a more mature, national faith. There is a recognition that the worship of El dominated in

19. Lawrence E. Stager, "The Archaeology of the Family in Ancient Israel," *Bulletin of the American Schools of Oriental Research* 260 (1985): 1–28.

20. J. David Schloen, "Caravans, Kenites, and Casus Belli: Enmity and Alliance in the Song of Deborah (Judges 5)," *Catholic Biblical Quarterly* 55 (1993): 18–38.

the days of the early ancestors, but the worship of YHWH eventually became the dominant form of national religious expression.[21] It is likely that the worship of YHWH spread across and eventually unified diverse lineages due to YHWH's role as a warrior deity. Early Israelite landholdings were in need of defense against a variety of hostile forces throughout the Late Bronze and early Iron Ages, and successful campaigns of defense would more naturally have been attributed to a warrior deity already worshipped by many early Israelite clans who contributed to the cause. Securing Israelite social space was understood as a sacral act, and this must have facilitated the equation between El and YHWH.

The patriarchal tales in Genesis brim with memories of these events. Indeed, the opening moment of these tales look back on the earliest days of settlement in a theologically charged but ideologically authentic manner:

> Now YHWH said to Abram: "Get thee out of thy country, and from thy kindred, and from thy father's house, to the land that I will show thee. And I will make of thee a great nation, and I will bless thee, and make thy name great; and make thee a blessing. And I will bless them that bless thee, and him that curseth thee will I curse; and in thee shall all the families of the earth be blessed." (Gen. 12:1–3)

In this brief passage, Abraham ("Abram," before his name is changed in subsequent chapters of Genesis) is told by God to break with convention, to sever ties with his own ancestral background, and to go to a new land. By so doing, a safe haven for social order will be established, fortunes will be found, and blessing will be secured. These verses are set within a narrative that, as we have already seen, cannot be taken as historically accurate. Yet the verses enshrine values that doubtlessly result from generations of reflection on the circumstances that secured Israel's existence in the highlands. Like the Abraham of Genesis 12:1–3, Israelites with roots either in lowland Canaanite culture or eastern caravan nomadism dissociated themselves from earlier ancestral convention, leaving the "houses" of their fathers to settle a new territory. Their survival in this new territory was understood and interpreted as evidence of blessing from a patron deity. If these conditions characterized the earliest days of Israelite life, it

21. Mark S. Smith, *The Origins of Biblical Monotheism* (Oxford: Oxford University Press, 2001), 140–46.

is not surprising that later generations developed a theology of ancestry eventually projected onto Abraham in Genesis 12. His story comes to represent the collective experience of the lineages that comprised the Israelite ethnos, bound together through devotion to YHWH.[22]

Finally, it is worth discussing the role of the ancestors in the formation of the Exodus ideology. In its current form, the Exodus tradition is imparted through the familiar tales in the Book of Exodus, and this tale incorporates a spectrum of memories spanning many centuries of west Semitic experiences with Egypt. But an even earlier Exodus tradition, one that predates the formation of the narrative in the Book of Exodus, may be identified with the experiences of the ancestors who pioneered the highlands. The defense of early settlements against hostile forces was interpreted in mythological terms as YHWH fighting battles on their behalf, with a mythic "Egypt" standing in as a symbol of the various enemies these pioneering communities faced. The setting of this material, such as the Song of the Sea in Exodus 15, within the Pentateuchal Exodus tale gave it a new meaning and conceptual context, but its initial function was to celebrate the founding accomplishments of the ancestors who, with YHWH's help, carved out a historical niche wherein Israel—as an extended kinship group—would flourish.[23] All subsequent concepts of nationhood are rooted in this most ancient liturgical model, which itself enshrines the foundational features of Israel's history in a manner that could be orally rehearsed and reexperienced through that rehearsal.

## *The Priesthood, Sinai, and the Legal Tradition*

Both in the Pentateuch and in post-biblical Judaism, the revelation at Sinai stands as the definitive moment when heaven and earth were joined through the communication of God's will as a tradition of legal instruction. A famous passage in the Mishnah (redacted ca. 200 CE) expresses this understanding in the most succinct and articulate terms:

---

22. A linguistic subtlety in the original Hebrew of v. 3 reinforces this; the phrase "in you all the families of the earth will be blessed" may also be translated "in you all the clans of the land will be blessed." The latter is suggestive of the Abraham traditions' galvanizing purpose in binding disparate highland lineage groups together in the memory of the Israelite writers who composed Genesis 12.

23. A majority of scholars views the Song of the Sea as among the oldest—if not *the* oldest—examples of biblical poetry, and it is typically dated to the mid-twelfth century BCE.

> Moses received *torah* from Sinai and transmitted it to Joshua; Joshua to the elders; the elders to the prophets; and the prophets handed it down to the men of the Great Assembly. They said three things: Be deliberate in judgment, raise up many disciples, and make a fence around the Torah. (Avot 1.1)

This text telescopes different social institutions and their role in the development and transmission of legal teaching (*torah*). Jurisprudence, at some level, was certainly cultivated by clan or village elders, preserved and promoted by the prophets, and eventually entrusted to the scribes associated with the Jerusalem temple of the Second Temple period (the "men of the Great Assembly"). What the passage omits, however, is the role of priests in the formation, transmission, and teaching of law. This omission probably indicates that the passage was written by proponents of a rabbinic culture that strove to supersede the priesthood that dissolved, as an institution, following the destruction of the Second Temple in 70 CE. Yet in most other parts of the Mishnah, the priesthood is the subject of much emphasis, and the earlier role of priests in the teaching of law is readily emphasized. This is not a rabbinic invention by any means but follows on well-established ancient conventions: in virtually all ancient Near Eastern civilizations, legal and intellectual authority rested first and foremost with priestly figures. It was the priesthood that was entrusted with the sacred texts of temple libraries, and it was priests who were charged with juridical initiative based on their expertise with these texts and their numinous contents.

Two biblical passages make abundantly clear that legal instruction and sacred text were matters of priestly jurisdiction:

> Then said they: "Come, and let us devise devices against Jeremiah; for instruction (torah) shall not perish from the priest, nor counsel from the wise, nor the word from the prophet." (Jer. 18:18)
>
> Calamity shall come upon calamity, and rumour shall be upon rumour; and they shall seek a vision of the prophet, and instruction (torah) shall perish from the priest, and counsel from the elders. (Ezek. 7:26)

Both prophets know and preserve close variants of an oral tradition that must have been current in their time (the early sixth century BCE) and which reflects the conventional role of established religious and political figures, including priests. Despite the very minor differences, Jeremiah and Ezekiel engage a slogan that affirms that legal instruction rests with the priesthood. If literacy was primarily limited to priests in ancient Israel, and if priests indeed held sway over legal instruction, it stands to reason that the legal collections in the Pentateuch were significantly shaped by Israel's priestly groups and survive due to the influence of these groups on the shaping of the Pentateuch more generally. While these laws are thus presented as being given all at once to Moses at Sinai, they reveal much about the history of the priesthoods that wrote and collected them.

There was a time when commentators looked at the laws of the Pentateuch as rooted in the reality of daily life in ancient Israel. But the discovery of law collections from the ancient Near East changed the way scholars understood the function of written law in antiquity. Contemporary scholars now view written law as an elite, learned pursuit, a platform for ideology and symbolic of the power of the temple institutions where the written collections were housed, taught, and preserved.[24] Rather than function as a basis for public policy, the study of law cultivated esoteric knowledge among the priesthood. These collections were understood as holy writs that evidenced the favor of the transcendent gods that was bestowed on the priesthood as their earthly representatives. The fact that these legal collections engaged seemingly practical matters of personal injury, property, inheritance, and the like simply demonstrated that all aspects of life were to fall under the jurisdiction of the priests with access to the law. The governance of the land would falter and fray without the integrity of the secret, holy knowledge these priests preserved.[25] Within this paradigm, the Sinai tradition was subject to reconception as diverse legal traditions were brought into conversation with each other by different priestly circles. The end result of this process was that the priesthood tracing its descent from Aaron—a priestly group that became increasingly powerful from the late pre-exilic through the Persian periods—receives rhetorical reinforcement and emerges as the ultimate guardians of Judaism's religious and political integrity.[26]

---

24. This does not mean that law was a completely utopian enterprise, only that it was a symbolic springboard for intellectual, political, and theological postulation that might relate in the abstract to practical social interaction; cf. Bruce Wells, "What Is Biblical Law? A Look at Pentateuchal Rules and Near Eastern Practice," *Catholic Biblical Quarterly* 70 (2008): 223–43.

25. Wells, "Biblical Law," 242–43.

26. James W. Watts, *Ritual and Rhetoric in Leviticus: From Sacrifice to Scripture* (New York: Cambridge University Press, 2007), 112–18.

Scholars have identified three major legal works that came to define the genre of law among the priesthoods in ancient Israel, all connected to the Sinai event. The first, usually regarded as the earliest, is known as the Covenant Code (or "the book of the covenant," Exod. 20:20–23:33; cf. 24:7). The Covenant Code presents the revelation at Sinai in terms very similar to the old Babylonian legal work known as the Laws of Hammurabi, a work that originated in the eighteenth century BCE but which was most likely introduced to Israelite audiences during the Assyrian conquest of the late eighth century. The Laws of Hammurabi were known to the author of the Covenant Code, who composed his work as a response to it, drawing from its language in a direct manner but formulating a distinctively Israelite parallel as a sort of protest against Assyrian cultural hegemony. The setting of this work within the Sinai narrative made a powerful statement that from the earliest days of the mythic past, Israel's intellectual and religious culture was every bit as sophisticated, powerful, and prestigious as the Mesopotamian culture that had come to dominate Israelite life. Israelite audiences might be political subjects to the Assyrians, but they remained in a binding relationship with their God YHWH who laid down the law long before the Assyrian conquest. The author of the Covenant Code was probably a priestly scribe recruited by the royal court in Jerusalem to construct a literary work that both competed and broke with the conventions of Mesopotamian law brought by the Assyrians, asserting (at least rhetorically) the independence of Israelite religion and culture.[27]

The next major legal collection associated with Sinai is found in the Book of Deuteronomy, which is set on the plains of Moab many years after Israel departs from Sinai within the chronology of the Pentateuchal narrative. Yet Deuteronomy is steeped in the Sinai tradition and presents itself as the sole legitimate way to understand the legal ideology associated with that tradition. Deuteronomy engages in a brilliant and complex strategy of exegesis, revision, and ultimately displacement, positioning itself as the only viable legal tradition whereby Israel's covenant relationship with God can be sustained and the import of the Sinai revelation can be fulfilled. In the rhetoric of Deuteronomy, the revelatory moment at Sinai

---

27. See the similar views of Lauren Monroe, who argues for a priestly scribe recruited two generations later during the reign of Josiah to write a narrative of the king's religious reforms (*Josiah's Reform and the Dynamics of Defilement* [New York: Oxford University Press, 2011]).

is extended through teaching and learning—exemplified in the book's own methods of legal interpretation. Deuteronomy appears to have been written well after the Covenant Code and uses the language of that older collection to reinterpret its contents. The "altar law" of the Covenant Code, for example, claims that altars can be set up "in every place" where, in the deity's words "I cause my name to be mentioned," that is, in any traditional sacred site (Exod. 20:24). Deuteronomy 12, however, reinterprets the language of this older law to legitimize only one sacred site—probably a reference to the Jerusalem Temple—saying that it is the only "place" where YHWH will "cause his name to dwell" (vv. 13–19).[28] This transformation of terms is found throughout Deuteronomy with regard to older legal traditions in the Covenant Code and elsewhere in the Hebrew Bible.

The authors of Deuteronomy were probably scribes from a Levite background, that is, a priestly caste with populist roots who sought to mediate between the old traditions of the hinterland and the preferences of the royal court in the late seventh century BCE.[29] For these authors, revelation was a continual process that only *began* at Sinai, demanding revision and reconstitution when history called for it. Proper priestly agency required the facilitation of these revisions in order to maintain the dialogue between Israel and their God. In theory, divine law was to be accessible to every Israelite: Deuteronomy states that every Israelite is to meditate upon the law and teach it to their children (6:5–9) and specifies that the divine word is "near" to every Israelite (30:11–14). The image contrasts sharply with the trend of legal texts remaining tucked away in the depths of a temple.

The third legal collection, and by far the most extensive, is the Priestly Code, a legal collection that spans Exodus 25–Numbers 10. This collection stems from scribes who were members of the Jerusalem priesthood, who knew the conventions of ancient Near Eastern law but who preserved social and cultic traditions particular to the function of the temple in Jerusalem, its ritual system, its calendar, and its concepts of holiness. Two compositional sources or layers are often identified within the Priestly Code. One is simply called the Priestly Torah (P), while the other is typically viewed as a subsequent expansion/commentary tradition and called the Holiness

---

28. For a full discussion, see Bernard M. Levinson, *Deuteronomy and the Hermeneutics of Legal Innovation* (New York: Oxford University Press, 1997), 28–38.

29. I discuss this in greater detail in *Samuel and the Shaping of Tradition* (Oxford: Oxford University Press, 2013), 13–21.

Source (H). Both P and H derive from Jerusalem priests, but while P focuses on the inner workings of ritual and priestly holiness, H emphasizes matters of social importance and expands holiness beyond the precincts of the sanctuary and its priesthood. In P, the priests are holy and maintain Israel's purity; in H, all of Israel is holy (though in different gradations), and all of Israel is responsible for maintaining those standards.[30]

The central repository of tradition for both sources is the Book of Leviticus. Both establish the essential relationship between ritual and society, and support the view that it is the Jerusalem priesthood that holds the most important of roles, namely, the maintenance of the sacrificial cult and standards of holiness for all of Israel. In both P and H strata in Leviticus, the Aaronide priesthood receives high honors, placing these priests at the heart of both the cultically centered and socially centered discourses on holiness. The shape of the Pentateuch itself indicates that Aaronide priests associated with the Priestly Code are probably the scribes who are responsible for the Pentateuch's final form. Deuteronomy is presented as an interpretation of the Priestly Code, but not a displacement of it. This mirrors the sacral hierarchy in the Persian period when Levite scribes were the teachers and interpreters of laws that were ultimately the province of the Jerusalem temple priests.

Much later, following the destruction of the Second Temple, the Rabbis would take it upon themselves to continue this tradition while simultaneously transforming it. They would serve both as stewards and interpreters of the old priestly law collections. For the Rabbis, as for the various priestly writers who formed these legal collections, law constituted a theoretical guide for social interaction both within the Jewish world and between Jewish communities and the larger world surrounding them, and a reflection of a deeper, universal truth expressing the otherwise incomprehensible nature and character of the divine.

## *The Prophets and Socioreligious Ethics*

The Mishnah places prophets within the spectrum of revelation and legal tradition, which is also rooted in the memory of genuine conditions. Prophecy as an institution is generally presented within the Hebrew Bible as a movement of spokespersons for the divine who—like the priests

---

30. See David P. Wright, "Holiness in Leviticus and Beyond," *Interpretation* 53 (1999): 351–64, for a concise and accessible overview of the differences between P and H.

teaching law—articulate God's will especially when the nation and its leaders need correction. The prophets are remembered in the Book of Kings, for example, as God's "servants," who were sent to inform a recalcitrant people that their actions had consequences (2 Kgs. 17:13, 23; 24:2). The various exiles suffered by Israel under Assyria (732–721 BCE) and Babylon (597–582 BCE) were understood as the fruition of this message, and the prophetic movement of the pre-exilic era became the subject of great study and speculation by those who endured the conditions of exile. Early Judaism of the Persian period would look back to the prophets of ancient Israel with special regard and elevate their message to a position of highest esteem, characterizing them as the purveyors of a divine word that was to serve as motivation for the reconstitution of the people under Persia (Ezra 1:1; 2 Chron. 36:22–23).

In the biblical tradition, Moses is credited with serving as the fountainhead of the prophetic movement. Prophecy is therefore rhetorically positioned as one of the foundational features of Israelite religion. Ascribing the roots of prophecy to Moses, however, is not entirely a matter of rhetoric. Moses is the eponymous ancestor of the Mushite priesthood, a line of priests that held a dominant position in the pre-monarchic period. In this early time, prophecy was a subset of priesthood; oracles were received and proclaimed by priests serving at various sanctuaries, and the Mushites certainly cultivated and promoted these experiences.[31] The transference of prophetic authority back to Moses in narrative traditions reflects, in part, the Mushite tradition of oracles. It would be only in the monarchic period that prophetic groups would arise independently of the major sanctuaries, many of which had fallen under royal jurisdiction. By this time, the association of prophecy with Moses was a well-established trend, and even non-Mushite prophetic figures aligned themselves with this practice, seeing themselves as servants following in Moses' footsteps.[32]

The Israelite prophets in the Hebrew Bible fall generally into two categories: the "pre-classical" prophets and the "classical" prophets, corresponding to the canonical literary division between "Former Prophets" (Joshua-Kings) and "Latter Prophets" (Isaiah-Malachi). The primary difference between these two categories is that the pre-classical prophets are those who often

31. On the origins of the Mushites and their ties to Moses, see Frank M. Cross, *Canaanite Myth and Hebrew Epic* (Cambridge, MA: Harvard University Press, 1973), 195–215.

32. Hosea, for example, aligns his social location with that of Moses (cf. Hos. 12:14). See also 1 Kings 19, where Elijah returns to Sinai in search of a Moses-like encounter with YHWH.

emerge as characters within narratives and who have no books preserving extensive collections of their oracles. Deborah (Judges 4–5), Samuel (1 Samuel), Nathan (2 Samuel 7; 12), Ahijah (1 Kgs. 11:29–40; 14), Elijah (1 Kgs. 17–2 Kings 2), Huldah (2 Kgs. 22:14–20), and others fall into this category. By contrast, the classical prophets are those whose words are ostensibly preserved in books bearing their names. Prophets such as Amos, Hosea, Micah, Isaiah, and Ezekiel fall into this category. The books bearing the names of these prophets are the written repositories of their oracles, though most scholars recognize that the contents of these books are amalgams of the words of these prophets and their interpretation and transcription by scribal disciples or by priestly scribes active in the nearby temples or sanctuaries where these prophets made their respective impacts.

The difference between the words of the prophets and scribes who developed their words is often difficult to determine. The tales of the preclassical prophets may well represent the contributions of the circles who shaped the teachings of their masters into narrative form. Similar problems are found with the classical prophets as well. Many of the classical prophetic books contain the essence of their namesakes' teachings and a number of oracles that may confidently be ascribed to them, but they also show signs of stereotyped literary formulation resulting from anonymous scribal interpolations. The Book of Isaiah, for example, contains the words of the prophet Isaiah himself, whose literary style and message is rather distinct from the contributions of the anonymous prophetic scribes whose words are also found within the book (especially in chapters 40–66). The Book of Jeremiah also contains blocks of tradition that clearly derive from different hands; the poetry is often ascribed to the prophet, while the prose material is regularly credited to later scribes.[33]

What all of these prophetic works have in common is an overriding concern with Israel's socioreligious ethics. The prophets concerned themselves with how Israel was to maintain their standing in the eyes of God by virtue of how they conducted themselves economically, ritually, and politically. Prophecy manifested itself both prescriptively and proscriptively: prophetic oracles would lay the foundations for how Israel was to carry on with the business of national life in concert with the principles that brought them into existence under God's favor. If these spheres of

33. This over-simplifies matters, though, since comparative evidence suggests that even the poetic forms of prophetic oracles were transcribed by secondary writers who could alter the original wording of the prophetic speaker.

conduct veered from those principles, the prophets did not hold back in voicing their criticism and offering severe condemnation. Despite the centuries separating many of the prophetic personalities appearing in the Hebrew Bible, this concern remains remarkably consistent.

Two examples will suffice to demonstrate this point. The first is found in 1 Samuel:

> Now therefore behold the king whom you have chosen, and whom you have asked for; and, behold, YHWH hath set a king over you. If you will fear YHWH, and serve him, and hearken unto his voice, and not rebel against the commandment of YHWH, and both you and also the king that reigneth over you be followers of YHWH your God; but if you will not hearken unto the voice of YHWH, but rebel against the commandment of YHWH, then shall the hand of YHWH be against you, and against your fathers. (1 Sam. 12:13–15)

Here the prophet Samuel has called Israel together to give his valedictory address as power is transferred to Saul, Israel's first king. Although the text itself may date from the late eighth or seventh century BCE, the narrative is set in the late eleventh century and authentically summarizes prophetic sentiments regarding the rise of kingship at that time. In this address, Samuel proclaims the terms under which monarchy may commence. Israel must remain true to the founding principles of Israelite society which sustained the relationship with their God, even with the shift to a dramatically new form of government that had by no means inspired confidence among Samuel and his supporters. Even at the moment when Israel demands kingship, Samuel responds with an oracle proclaiming the pitfalls of this office, and at Saul's coronation he delineates the rules and limitations of kingship (1 Sam. 8:11–18; 10:25). In 1 Samuel 12, we encounter the oracular definition of these terms as they relate to the entire nation and not just to the king himself. During this period of uncertainty, then, Samuel's oracle establishes ethical parameters to ensure that new and important social institutions correspond to the values that had maintained order and cultural continuity in earlier periods. If the nation were to falter in this ethical charge, they, and their king, would be "swept away" (12:25).

The second passage is found in the famous "Temple Sermon" offered by the prophet Jeremiah in 609 BCE:

> Thus say YHWH of hosts, the God of Israel: Amend your ways and your doings, and I will cause you to dwell in this place. Trust not in lying words, saying: "The temple of YHWH, the temple of YHWH, the temple of YHWH, are these." Nay, but if you thoroughly amend your ways and your doings; if you thoroughly execute justice between a man and his neighbour; if you oppress not the stranger, the fatherless, and the widow, and shed not innocent blood in this place, neither walk after other gods to your hurt; then will I cause you to dwell in this place, in the land that I gave to your fathers, forever and ever. (Jer. 7:3–7)
>
> Behold, you trust in lying words that cannot profit. Will you steal, murder, and commit adultery, and swear falsely, and offer unto Baal, and walk after other gods whom you have not known, and come and stand before Me in this house, whereupon My name is called, and say: "We are delivered," that you may do all these abominations? Is this house, whereupon My name is called, become a den of robbers in your eyes? Behold, I, even I, have seen it, saith YHWH. (Jer. 7:8–11)

Although this text is taken from a prophetic oracle rather than a prophetic narrative, it has much in common with 1 Samuel 12. Jeremiah delivered this oracle shortly after the unexpected death of King Josiah (1 Kgs. 23:29), which had left the nation in a state of great confusion and desperation; once again, then, prophecy surfaces during a time of social uncertainty. As the oracle indicates, this time was one that saw different corners of the population inappropriately emulating some institutions while neglecting others. Jeremiah's oracle is both prescriptive and proscriptive. The first canto affirms the ethical standards that will secure life in the land. The second canto, however, highlights the problematic over-emphasis on the Jerusalem temple cult and the national neglect of social and theological ethics—this is the type of conduct that incurs divine wrath and which will preclude the viability of the idyllic scenario enumerated in the first canto. Several years later, on the eve of the Babylonian Exile (587 BCE), Jeremiah would remind his audience that he, like all of God's prophets, had warned them to act ethically, but they "did not listen" (Jer. 25:3–7). For this reason, the exile from the land would be inevitable.

The prophetic tradition as a whole frames the monarchic period as an experiment in ethics, and one that resulted in failure but one that could teach the surviving community how to ensure a better future. The failures of monarchic society were already in prophetic sight in the pre-exilic period. This is evident not only within the oracles of Jeremiah that date from the closing decades of the monarchy but also within the laws of Deuteronomy. The Deuteronomic laws were penned by Levite scribes, but many scholars also see these scribes as deeply aligned with the prophetic movement and its critique of society.[34] Deuteronomy, in fact, couches its legal collection within the form of a prophetic pronouncement: the legal terms of Deuteronomy are set as part of Moses' own oral proclamation regarding tenable terms for Israel's life in the land, where monarchy is to be severely restricted (Deut. 1:9; 17:14–17) and true power is to rest with Levites and prophets (17:18–20; 18:15–18; 31:9–13) as the trustees of Israel's social and religious ethics. Deuteronomy opens the door to the entire prophetic tradition, with the divine word of every prophet providing examples of how Israel was to conceive of their theological and social roles within history and in the eyes of their deity. When Jews in the Persian period or later looked back at earlier days, they are refracted through the prophets' concept of ethics, which formed the ideological blueprint for a prosperous future.

## *Conclusion*

The founders of the institutions and traditions surveyed here remain largely anonymous, a principle that seems counterintuitive to the contemporary mind. Yet in antiquity, anonymity was a hallmark of authority. Scribes would often sign their names to documents they copied, but it is exceedingly rare to encounter notes, adjustments, comments, or interpretations in ancient prophetic, legal, or narrative texts that reveal the identities of the scribes who stand behind these secondary reflexes.[35] The claim of authorship on the part of these scribes would detract from the antique authority of what they were transmitting. So in the scribal construction of Israel's past, the anonymity of the scribes is not simply a matter of ancient convention but, indeed, a prerequisite for validation. A prophet's arguments for socioreligious ethical conduct could be extended to a different generation from that of the prophet himself, so long as the message was not diluted by the ego of the anonymous prophetic writer who inherited it,

34. Leuchter, *Samuel and the Shaping of Tradition*, 13–21; cf. Jeffrey C. Geoghegan, *The Time, Place, and Purpose of the Deuteronomistic History: The Evidence of "Until This Day"* (Providence, RI: Brown Judaic Studies, 2006), 149–52.

35. On scribal anonymity, see van der Toorn, *Scribal Culture*, 31–48.

added to it, and transmitted it. Symbolically, the prophetic tradition is transferred back to Moses as a sort of patron saint who founds the entire movement, but functionally it remained a public trust for those who counted themselves part of the prophetic legacy, available as a trove of ideas to be emphasized when society veers off course.[36]

This extends to the anonymity of the ancestors and the priests. By anonymizing the sacred deeds of the pioneering ancestors, a certain egalitarian ethic was advanced—the remembered merits of one ancestral figure could be broadly adopted and celebrated as evidence that God blessed the collective ancestors by transferring them to Abraham, Isaac, or Jacob. At least on paper, rank and privilege were sidelined in favor of a collective power structure claiming common ancestry. It is the same ethos found in the biblical law collections formed and preserved by the priests—they, too, remain mostly anonymous as they promote laws that safeguard against impulses to revert to practices common to the ancient Near East, maintaining the boundaries of a community whose members were all equally subject to the law.[37]

Certain trends can thus be discerned across diverse traditions that attest to shared biases and values deriving from quite an early point in time. This was no doubt sensed by the Rabbis of the Roman period who took stock of the literary relics of the past and stridently affirmed the commonality of experience and consistency of outlook that they read into these texts. Yet in so doing, they joined the anonymous founders who picked up the pieces of earlier cultures and rendered them mythically meaningful, transcending the temporal limitations of history. The authors of Deuteronomy emphasize that engaging the tradition of revelation at Sinai—a tradition that had been passed along from earlier generations—made the covenant with God immediate: "YHWH made a covenant with us at Horeb; it was not with our ancestors that he made this covenant but with us, all of us who are here, alive, today" (Deut. 5:2–3). From the perspective of Deuteronomy, the tradition may have derived from Sinai (here called Horeb), but it was actualized in the moment by contemporaneous

---

36. The emphasis on Moses in this respect reaches its apex in the closing of the Latter Prophets. The final verses of Malachi defer all attention to the *torah* (instruction) of Moses for the present age, in anticipation of a final day of judgment heralded by Elijah's return (Mal. 3:22–23).

37. This is the view of Joshua A. Berman, *Created Equal: How the Bible Broke with Ancient Political Thought* (New York: Oxford University Press, 2008), 51–108.

audiences and their commitment to it. The anonymity of the founders themselves allows for this to take place, for by abstracting the various ancient traditions from particular and definite individuals, a new generation of Israelites could "discover" them. In this sense, each successive generation of Israel served as the founders of their own religious identity by rehearsing, studying, and affirming it.[38] This concept becomes a defining myth in its own right as the literary relics of ancient Israelite religion became the constitutive blueprints for the Judaism of the Hellenistic, Roman, and ultimately the rabbinic ages.[39] The lines separating past and present, ancestor and descendant, and even teacher and pupil were blurred, one becoming the other as the connection between God, community, and history became regularly renewed.[40]

The foregoing discussion carries important implications for the way contemporary Judaism, in all of its diversity, might conceive of its own history and identity. Adherents of Orthodox Jewish tradition generally view the classical myth of Judaism's origins as inalienable truth and factually inerrant; on the other side of the spectrum are those Jews who disregard the bulk of Jewish theology and ritual tradition as antiquated, superstitious, or even the stuff of fantasy. A full reconciliation between these extremes is perhaps beyond the pale of possibility, but the issues addressed above suggest that a rapprochement is not. After all, Orthodox Jewish tradition has always held that the Bible should be read midrashically—that is, as a symbolic discourse that points to deeper meaning, and historical-critical analysis of these foundational texts affirms that this is indeed possible (albeit from a perspective not predicated on religious interest). Likewise, those who view the biblical text as disconnected from genuine history must consider that its symbolic function arises from a telescoping of authentic historical memory and experience. This carries obvious implications beyond intra-Jewish communal dynamics as well, especially in a global political culture currently characterized by disputes and debates that are regularly charged with religious rhetoric and agenda. The concepts and

38. See Jon D. Levenson, *Sinai and Zion: An Entry into the Jewish Bible* (San Francisco: HarperCollins, 1987) 18, for a similar view.

39. The Rabbis sound the same note in the Passover *hagaddah*, which commands all Jews to see themselves, and not only their ancestors, as part of the Exodus generation, effected through their participation in the Passover *seder* (ritual meal).

40. See especially the Talmudic tale in which Rabbi Akivah becomes the teacher of no less than Moses himself (*Menachot* 29b).

traditions that were textualized through the formation of the Hebrew Bible have much to teach about how communities countenance each other, negotiate with each other, and influence each other's development.

## *For Further Reading*

Cohen, S. J. D. "The Significance of Yavneh: Pharisees, Rabbis, and the End of Jewish Sectarianism." *Hebrew Union College Annual* 55 (1984): 27–53. An insightful study of the origins of the rabbinic movement. Most scholars see it arising from the closure of a long period of Jewish sectarianism marked by the destruction of the Jerusalem temple in 70 CE by Roman forces.

Dever, William G. *Who Were the Early Israelites and Where Did They Come From?* Grand Rapids: Eerdmans, 2003. An accessible survey of the archaeological record in relation to the Bible and what it suggests about the origins of Israel.

Halpern, Baruch. *David's Secret Demons: Messiah, Murderer, Traitor, King.* Grand Rapids: Eerdmans, 2001. Throughout this study, Halpern argues for an understanding of the biblical material about David as propagandistic in nature.

Knohl, Israel. *The Sanctuary of Silence.* Minneapolis: Fortress, 1995. The classic study of the concepts of holiness in Leviticus and their origins within the Jerusalem priesthood.

Leuchter, Mark. *Samuel and the Shaping of Tradition.* Oxford: Oxford University Press, 2013. Explores the ways in which the Samuel of the final form of the biblical narratives differs from Samuel of the sources "behind the text," where he is a figure who variously serves to highlight Israel's system of social ethics, to illustrate tensions within the priestly ranks, or to position prophets over monarchs as national authorities.

Meyers, Carol. *Discovering Eve: Ancient Israelite Women in Context.* New York: Oxford University Press, 1988. While the patriarchs receive most of the attention from biblical and ancient post-biblical writers, reflecting the male-dominated scribal cultures responsible for these works, Jewish tradition recognizes the role of the matriarchs Sarah, Rebecca, Rachel, and Leah. Meyers examines women's role in Israelite religion and ancient Judaism, revealing a more textured reality than what is indicated on the surface of the "classic" texts.

Smith, Mark S. *The Origins of Biblical Monotheism.* Oxford: Oxford University Press, 2001. A thorough examination of the polytheistic basis for what would later become monotheistic thought in ancient Israel.

2

# *The Buddha*

## HISTORICIZING MYTH, MYTHOLOGIZING HISTORY

*Nathan McGovern*

*Whether there is an arising of Tathāgatas or no arising of Tathāgatas, that element still persists, the stableness of the Dhamma, the fixed course of the Dhamma, specific conditionality.*

—PACCAYA SUTTA, Saṃyutta Nikāya 12.20[1]

THE ISSUE OF "founders" is important to the study of religion because debates over founders that take place within a religious tradition reflect contestation over the nature of that particular tradition. When such debates are found within modern scholarship, they reflect in a similar fashion the ideological assumptions and power structures that undergird the modern scholarly project of constructing "world religions" as parallels to Christianity. In this chapter, I argue that early modern scholarly debates about the Buddha as historical "founder" were part of a broader project of constructing Buddhism as a "world religion," and as such, the preoccupations of modern scholars vis-à-vis the Buddha have differed markedly from those within Buddhist traditions themselves. Nevertheless, increased recognition by scholars of the different assumptions underlying traditional discourses on the Buddha and Buddhas has led to an increased appreciation of these traditional discourses, as well as to a questioning of the assumptions that inform modern scholarship.

1. Bhikkhu Bodhi, trans., *The Connected Discourses of the Buddha: A Translation of the Saṃyutta Nikāya*, 2nd ed. (Boston: Wisdom Publications, 2005), 551.

Buddhism, more than any other non-Christian "world religion," fits the paradigm for a "religion" established by Christianity remarkably well. Indeed, the similarities between Buddhism and Christianity—and the doubt they sowed about Christianity's erstwhile claim to unique universality—played a pivotal role in the rise of the very concept of world religions in the nineteenth century.[2] As Måns Broo notes in his contribution to this volume, "What we call Hinduism . . . has no unified doctrine or system of belief set down in a creed or declaration of faith, no single system of soteriology, and no centralized authority or bureaucracy. Much of this variety stems from Hinduism having no recognized founder."[3] With Buddhism, however, in spite of its origins in a very similar context, we face none of these difficulties. The essential elements of the Buddhist Dharma, albeit with certain variations, are accepted by most Buddhists throughout the world. A common system of soteriology, consisting of escape from the cycle of rebirth, is also common, again with certain variations, to most Buddhist schools. And although Buddhism has never been as centralized as the Roman Catholic Church, it does, unlike many religious traditions, have an organized institution, the *saṅgha*, which has engaged in missionary activity and led to the spread of Buddhism far beyond its land of origin. One could indeed argue that, in contradistinction to Hinduism, these similarities with Christianity stem from Buddhism having a recognized founder, the Buddha.

That Buddhism was founded by a single historical person known as the Buddha has long been, and remains, uncontroversial in Buddhist Studies. Unlike the case of Christianity, moreover, there has been no attempt to elevate a later figure, analogous to Paul, as the "real" founder of Buddhism as an institutional religion.[4] This is likely because, at least according to our sources, the Buddha did in fact personally found the *saṅgha* as an institution, thus making him fit the unique role of "founder" even better than Jesus. There has been a trend in recent years, however, toward deemphasizing the importance of the Buddha as the founder of Buddhism. That is, while the historical existence of the Buddha and his act of founding the Buddhist *saṅgha* are recognized, the practical effect of this

2. Tomoko Masuzawa, *The Invention of World Religions* (Chicago: University of Chicago Press, 2005), 23–24.

3. Måns Broo, "Hinduism and the Question of Founders," this volume.

4. Cf. Patrick Gray's chapter on Christianity in this volume ("Jesus, Paul, and the Birth of Christianity").

man's life on the later development of Buddhism is reduced primarily to a rhetorical function. The significance of the historical Buddha lies not so much in what he actually did in attaining Awakening and founding the *saṅgha*, but in the usefulness of the Buddha in particular and Buddhahood in general as empty signifiers for articulating the worldviews, assumptions, and goals of various Buddhisms throughout history and around the world. In this way, Buddhist Studies has moved away from a literal reading of those Buddhist texts that portray the Buddha in his foundational role and toward a renewed interest in those aspects of the Buddhist tradition—arguably the more pervasive and influential—that deemphasize the uniqueness of the Buddha Śākyamuni and subsume him into a temporally cyclical and spatially infinite series of Buddhas who are all of a single type.

This chapter is divided into two parts. In the first part, I trace the history of "the Buddha" as a figure of interest to Western students of Buddhism, beginning with his establishment as a single, historical personage who founded a "religion" called "Buddhism," and then turning to the increasing recognition in the academic community that there is little that can be known about this person and about his life that matters for the subsequent development of Buddhism. In the second part, I trace the development of the concept of "Buddha" in the Buddhist tradition itself, with particular focus on the ways in which insider attention to the Buddha has differed markedly from the Western scholarly preoccupations that led to the establishment of the Buddha as founder of a world religion in the nineteenth century. Finally, I discuss the reasons that early scholarly work on the Buddha was so different from traditional attitudes toward the Buddha and how historians of religion can benefit from being more open to the seemingly unhistorical treatment given to a religious figure within a tradition.

## *The Buddha in Western Scholarship: Constructing and Deconstructing a Historical Figure*

Western Buddhist Studies followed an overall arc toward the establishment of the Buddha as a historical figure and founder of Buddhism, culminating in the late nineteenth century with the victory of Hermann Oldenberg's historicist school and continuing to hold sway well past the middle of the twentieth century. In the late twentieth century, Buddhist Studies were, like the rest of the humanities, deeply affected by a sudden burgeoning of interest in critical theory, which led to a total reevaluation of the discipline and a concomitant reaction against previous interest in the Buddha as a historical figure. In the following brief outline, I organize the history of Buddhist Studies in the West into four periods divided by four scholars who represent particular "turning points" in scholarly discourse on the Buddha: Eugène Burnouf, Hermann Oldenberg, Étienne Lamotte, and Gregory Schopen. I have chosen the first three of these scholars because their monumental contributions mark the end of a particular era in Buddhist Studies; the fourth, Gregory Schopen, stands as an early exemplar of the new trends that have emerged in the discipline since the 1970s.

## Locating the Buddha in Space and Time: Buddhist Studies before Burnouf

Europeans have been in contact with the story of the Buddha—although they did not know it—since the Middle Ages, when a legend about two Christian saints named Barlaam and Josaphat circulated throughout the continent. This legend was ultimately derived from the story of the Buddha and transmitted via the Islamic world.[5] Direct Western contacts with the Buddhist world began in the thirteenth century with papal envoys to the Mongol Khan and Marco Polo's journey to the court of Kublai Khan in China.[6] Nevertheless, several centuries passed before Europeans developed a clear picture of a single "religion" called Buddhism centered on the worship of a particular figure called the Buddha. In large part, this was surely due to a lack of interest by Westerners in developing a nuanced understanding of the differences between different Asians, all of whom they regarded simply as "heathens" or "idolaters." As late as 1614—four centuries after Marco Polo's journey and in the wake of many other European contacts with Asia—an anthropological work by Edward Brerewood divided religions quite neatly into four types: "Christianity, Mohametanism, Judaism and Idolatry."[7]

5. J. W. de Jong, "A Brief History of Buddhist Studies in Europe and America," *Eastern Buddhist* 7.1 (1974): 59. De Jong also discusses some scattered references to the worship of the Buddha from antiquity. This remains the most comprehensive history of Buddhist Studies yet written, and I rely heavily on it for my survey of scholarly treatments of the Buddha up to the 1970s. De Jong wrote this article just four years before the publication of Edward Said's *Orientalism* (1978), and his description of the field betrays no hint of the changes that were to come to Buddhist Studies in its wake.

6. De Jong, "A Brief History of Buddhist Studies in Europe and America," 61.

7. Jonathan Z. Smith, "Religion, Religions, Religious," in *Critical Terms for Religious Studies*, ed. Mark C. Taylor (Chicago: University of Chicago Press, 1998), 271.

Marco Polo himself had set the tone for early European descriptions of the Buddha by subsuming them into the catch-all category of "idolaters." In his description of Adam's Peak in Sri Lanka, he writes,

> And I tell you they say that on this mountain is the sepulchre of Adam our first parent; at least that is what the Saracens say. But the Idolaters say that it is the sepulchre of SAGAMONI BORCAN, before whose time there were no idols. They hold him to have been the best of men, a great saint in fact, according to their fashion, and the first in whose name idols were made.[8]

Here we see what would become a common theme: "Buddhists" as a distinct group are never referred to, but those in the vague category of "idolaters" are said to engage in the worship of a particular idol known by a particular name in a local language. Language barriers, in fact, appear to have played a significant role in delaying the European recognition of the pan-Asian worship of a single figure known as the Buddha. While scholars had begun to develop an awareness of this pan-Asian cult by the seventeenth century, in more popular circles there was still confusion as late as the early nineteenth century as to whether the various names under which the Buddha was worshipped in Asia really indicated forms of the same deity.[9]

Although by the end of the eighteenth century European scholars had become aware of the existence of a single religious tradition, dubbed Buddhism, that unified a number of "idolatrous" cults across Asia, there was no consensus for several more decades about the exact context in which it had arisen. In large part this was due to the vicissitudes of history: Buddhism had long since died out in India by the time European colonialists arrived, and the social and institutional knowledge needed for contextualizing Buddhism in its land of origin was unavailable. As Donald Lopez notes in his essay on the European "discovery" of the Buddha, scholars from the East India Company learned from Purāṇic texts that the Buddha

8. Henry Yule, trans. and ed., *The Book of Ser Marco Polo the Venetian concerning the Kingdoms and Marvels of the East*, 3rd ed., 2 vols., rev. by Henri Cordier (New York: AMS, 1986 [1926]), 2:316–17; cited by Donald S. Lopez Jr., "Buddha," in *Critical Terms for the Study of Buddhism*, ed. D. S. Lopez Jr. (Chicago: University of Chicago Press, 2005), 15.

9. Philip C. Almond, *The British Discovery of Buddhism* (Cambridge: Cambridge University Press, 1988), 9–10.

was the ninth incarnation of Viṣṇu. However, their Brahman informants appeared to be of two minds about the Buddha. Some held him to be a venerable figure who condemned the killing of cattle, and others condemned him as a heretic. To resolve this apparent contradiction, Sir William Jones postulated that there were two Buddhas: an early one who was the ninth incarnation of Viṣṇu and honored by Hindus as such, and a later Buddha who was an enemy of the Brahmans. He argued further that the former Buddha was not originally an Indian god but rather was imported from elsewhere. In making this argument, Jones pointed out that statuary depictions of the Buddha often gave him "crisp and wooly" hair like "Africans."[10] Both of these theories—that there were two Buddhas, and that one of them was originally of the "Negro race"—sparked decades of scholarly debate that would last until the middle of the nineteenth century.[11]

Resolution of these issues, though not absolute and certainly not immediate, was nonetheless effectively achieved with the publication of Eugène Burnouf's *Introduction à l'histoire du Buddhisme indien* in 1844. This incredibly influential book was based on a study of original Indian Buddhist texts discovered and sent to Burnouf by fellow British scholar Brian Hodgson, a novel development in the study of Buddhism that Burnouf portrayed as central to his thesis and to his understanding of the history of Buddhism. As Lopez and Buffetrille argue in the introduction to their recent translation of Burnouf's work, "Perhaps the most important sentence in the entire volume occurs on the first page of the foreword, where Burnouf declares that the belief called Buddhism is completely Indian, literally 'a completely Indian fact' (*un fait complètement indien*)."[12] For Burnouf, the discovery of Buddhist texts in the Indian language of Sanskrit confirmed once and for all that Buddhism was born in India, developed in India, and could be explained completely on Indian terms, without reference to outside influences or dubious theories about the Buddha's origins based on his hair.

10. Lopez, "Buddha," 16–17.

11. Almond, *The British Discovery of Buddhism*, 17–24.

12. Katia Buffetrille and Donald S. Lopez Jr., "Introduction to the Translation," in Eugène Burnouf, *Introduction to the History of Indian Buddhism*, trans. K. Buffetrille and D. S. Lopez Jr. (Chicago: University of Chicago Press, 2010), 14.

## Constructing the Historical Buddha: Buddhist Studies from Burnouf to Oldenberg

Eugène Burnouf's work marks a turning point in the Western study of Buddhism not only because Burnouf settled once and for all debates over the identity and land of origin of the Buddha, but also because of the means by which he did so: by exclusive resource to Buddhist texts. Unlike many earlier scholars who received information about Buddhism directly from Asian informants, Burnouf never traveled to Asia.[13] His insistence on the importance of studying Buddhism on the basis of its earliest texts led to what Philip Almond has called the "textualization" of Buddhism. Almond writes, "By the 1850s, the textual analysis of Buddhism was perceived to be the major scholarly task. Through the West's progressive ownership of the texts of Buddhism, it becomes, so to say, materially owned by the West; and by virtue of this ownership, ideologically controlled by it."[14] Whereas scholarly debates prior to Burnouf were driven by a proliferation of direct reports coming to Europe from different parts of Asia and sought to locate the Buddha geographically, those of the mid-nineteenth century were driven by the proliferation of Buddhist texts being sent back to Europe and sought to locate the Buddha textually. The debates of this period, in other words, were focused on whether the Northern Sanskrit sources, such as those studied by Burnouf in his *Introduction*, were earlier than the more recently discovered Pali texts being sent back from Sri Lanka and other countries of Theravāda Southeast Asia. Fundamental to this debate, of course, was the assumption that older texts were more reliable. The determination by the 1870s that the Pali texts were of greater antiquity solidified the importance of Pali studies for the textually mediated construction of a "pure" or "original" Buddhism.[15]

As textual studies began to proliferate in the mid-nineteenth century, a clearer picture of Buddhism emerged as an organized movement, originating in India, with a particular historical figure as its founder. In this context, the Buddha began to figure prominently in European discourses on the "great men of old." In a move that was to prove indicative of the motivations behind the entire project of Buddhist Studies in the nineteenth century, Western scholars began to superimpose a European religious narrative—namely,

13. Buffetrille and Lopez, "Introduction to the Translation," 7–8.

14. Almond, *The British Discovery of Buddhism*, 24.

15. Almond, *The British Discovery of Buddhism*, 28.

Protestantism's narrative of its own origins—onto the situation in early India. Philip Almond argues that in nineteenth-century England "it was perhaps inevitable that the Buddha, *qua* religious reformer, should be compared with Martin Luther, and that Buddhism should be compared with the Protestant Reformation."[16] Once it became established that Brahmanism predated Buddhism (in large part through Burnouf's analysis of Buddhist texts), it became easy to construct a narrative with the Buddha serving as the Luther of India.[17] The Brahmans were a priestly class associated both in ancient literature and in modern practice with ritual, and the Buddha in some sense rejected the "pretensions" of the Brahmans. This narrative served as an anti-Catholic polemic at a time when anti-Catholic sentiment in England was particularly high.[18] It also laid the basis for an Orientalist discourse in which Hinduism was painted in a negative light as an analogue to the "popery" of European Catholicism, and an essentialized portrait of Buddhism based on a selective reading of early texts was used to criticize by comparison both Hindu practice and the "degenerate" practices of contemporary Buddhists.

At the same time that the popular imagination in Europe was captivated with the emerging concept of the "historical Buddha" as an "Indian Luther," certain scholars went in the opposite direction, deemphasizing the Buddha as a historical figure and instead concentrating on "the Buddha" as a focus for intersecting mythological motifs. These scholars were in a certain sense continuing a trend, dating from the late eighteenth century, of identifying the Buddha with various mythological figures from outside India, perhaps most commonly the Germanic god Woden.[19] The Buddha in the pre-Victorian European imagination was

16. Almond, *The British Discovery of Buddhism*, 73.

17. Interestingly, Burnouf's firm conclusion on the basis of his study of the Hodgson Sanskrit manuscripts that Buddhism arose in a Brahmanical context was, in a sense, an accident. Although Burnouf did not realize it at the time, these texts were written much later than was generally supposed and reflected a retrospective projection of Brahmanical culture and ideology onto the past; see Johannes Bronkhorst, *Buddhism in the Shadow of Brahmanism* (Leiden: Brill, 2011), 168 n. 232.

18. Almond, *The British Discovery of Buddhism*, 73.

19. This (in retrospect) seemingly random association between the Buddha and Woden is based on philological carelessness and a coincidence. Early scholars frequently associated the Buddha with the planet Mercury because the Sanskrit name of the planet/god Mercury is *Budha*, superficially similar but etymologically unrelated to *Buddha*. Woden, the god of English *Wednesday*, or "Woden's Day," is frequently associated with Mercury, who in the Romance languages lends his name to Wednesday (e.g., *mercredi* in French). By the transitive property, then, Buddha = Budha = Mercury = Woden.

conceived of primarily as a mythological being, and it was only in the wake of Burnouf's *Introduction* and the concomitant textualization of Buddhism that the "historical Buddha" began to emerge.[20] Emile Senart, a French scholar who continued to take an interest in the Buddha as a mythological rather than a historical figure, was nevertheless influenced by the conclusive historical localization of the Buddha (or at least early Buddhism) in ancient India, and thus he based his analyses on the immediate Indian mythological context of early Buddhism rather than whimsical connections to far-flung countries and continents. In his *Essai sur la légende du Buddha* (1873–75), Senart argued that the Buddha's life story was simply a compilation and transformation of ancient Indian motifs centering on a solar deity.[21] In advancing this theory, Senart, a structuralist *avant la lettre*, did not deny that a historical Buddha existed, or even that the Sanskrit texts he favored as being mythologically richer were later than the Pali texts; rather, he saw in the story of the Buddha a single coherent system to be studied synchronically rather than diachronically.[22] The Dutch scholar Hendrik Kern took this argument a step further, arguing not only that the story of the Buddha was derived from ancient Indian solar mythology, but that it was wholly fabricated from ancient Indian solar mythology—that is, that the historical Buddha never existed.[23] Kern's more radical theory was never taken very seriously by the broader scholarly community, but Senart's was, and if it had become the paradigm for Buddhist Studies at the end of the nineteenth century, the field might have developed quite differently in the following decades.

Senart's approach did not become the standard for twentieth-century scholarship. This distinction falls to the German scholar Hermann Oldenberg, whose *Buddha: Sein Leben, seine Lehre, seine Gemeinde* was

---

20. Almond, *The British Discovery of Buddhism*, 56–60.

21. In advancing this theory, Senart was employing a method that had been pioneered in large part by Max Müller (de Jong, "A Brief History of Buddhist Studies in Europe and America," 79). Max Müller's comparative method, including the so-called sun myth, was published in 1856, but it was later mocked by the Reverend R. F. Littledale, who showed that by using Müller's own methods, one could "prove" that Müller himself is merely a solar myth. Both Müller's original essay and Littledale's rejoinder are published in F. Max Müller, *Comparative Mythology: An Essay*, ed. Abram Smythe Palmer (London: George Routledge, n.d.).

22. De Jong, "A Brief History of Buddhist Studies in Europe and America," 82.

23. De Jong, "A Brief History of Buddhist Studies in Europe and America," 79–80.

published in 1881. In this work, Oldenberg rejected Senart's "solar theory" and argued forcefully that the Pali texts were reliable and that they could be used to reconstruct the life of the historical Buddha. He thus established a diachronic "historicist" method rather than a synchronic method of mythological analysis, as the standard for Buddhist Studies for the next half-century.[24] In the course of solidifying the Buddha as a historical figure, however, Oldenberg also reined in popular speculation on parallels between the Buddha and Luther:

> People are accustomed to speak of Buddhism as opposed to Brahmanism, somewhat in the way that it is allowable to speak of Lutheranism as an opponent of the papacy. But if they mean, as they might be inclined from this parallel to do, to picture to themselves a kind of Brahmanical Church, which is assailed by Buddha, which opposed its resistance to its operations like the resistance of the party in possession to an upstart, they are mistaken. Buddha did not find himself in the presence of a Brahmanical hierarchy, embracing the whole people, overshading the whole popular life. . . . Thus Brahmanism was not to Buddha an enemy whose conquest he would have been unable to effect. He may often have found the local influence of respected Brahmans an obstacle in his path, but against this a hundred other Brahmans stood by him as his disciples or had declared for him as lay members. Here no struggle on a large scale has taken place.[25]

After Oldenberg's book was translated into English in 1882, the scholarly literature records repeated references to his work as having conclusively proven that the Buddha was not a social or political reformer. Almond argues that this rather dramatic change in scholarly opinion was "the result of an attempt to protect the Victorian Buddha from being perceived as an early proponent of those forms of socialism that were perceived by many as threatening the structure of English society from the beginning of the 1880s especially."[26] Regardless of the specific reasons

---

24. De Jong, "A Brief History of Buddhist Studies in Europe and America," 81–82.

25. Hermann Oldenberg, *Buddha: His Life, His Doctrine, His Order*, trans. William Hoey (London: Williams and Norgate, 1892), 170–72.

26. Almond, *The British Discovery of Buddhism*, 75.

that Oldenberg's argument became so widely accepted, the overall effect of his work was to solidify, in both the scholarly and popular imaginations of the West, the idea of the Buddha as a *unique* and *historical* figure. And although Oldenberg shot down the most common analogy to a Western religious "founder" in the nineteenth century, this at the same time freed the newly created historical Buddha to serve as the unique founder of his own religion, Buddhism.[27]

## Solidification of Buddhist Studies as an Independent Discipline: Oldenberg to Lamotte

For the first half of the twentieth century, the notion of the Buddha as historical founder of a unique "religion" called Buddhism remained relatively uncontroversial as the crystallization of Buddhist Studies as an independent field of study and the concomitant emergence of subspecialties within that field proceeded apace. The study of Tibetan Buddhism, Chinese Buddhism, Japanese Buddhism, and even modern Theravāda Buddhism as fields distinct from the study of Indian Buddhism all had their origins in this era, although their isolation from classical Indology has accelerated more in the late twentieth and early twenty-first centuries. I have chosen Monsignor Etienne Lamotte's 1958 *Histoire du bouddhisme indien* not so much as a turning point but as a culmination of this era, because it is one of the last attempts to produce a comprehensive history of Indian Buddhism on the scale of Burnouf's *Introduction* or Oldenberg's *Buddha*.[28] However, unlike Burnouf and Oldenberg, who engaged in numerous scholarly projects unrelated to Buddhism, Lamotte was very much a specialist in Buddhism and in fact the doyen of Buddhist Studies in his day. Likewise, in his *Histoire*, there is a certain confidence about the Buddha as a historical figure that is lacking in Burnouf's and Oldenberg's works. Whereas Burnouf and Oldenberg felt the need to defend at length their views about the historical reality of the Buddha and his context, Lamotte simply presents his life as a brief historical episode and then moves on to the nitty-gritty details of the centuries of Buddhist history that

---

27. Interestingly, comparisons of the Buddha vis-à-vis the Brahmans to Jesus vis-à-vis the Pharisees were far less common in the nineteenth century than comparisons to Luther vis-à-vis the Catholic Church (Almond, *The British Discovery of Buddhism*, 74–75).

28. One could also cite in this regard A. K. Warder's 1970 *Indian Buddhism*, which is broader in chronological scope but somewhat less encyclopedic than Lamotte's *Histoire*.

followed. In this way, he exemplified the trends toward specialization in Buddhist Studies and presaged—unintentionally—the paradigm shift in thinking about the Buddha that was about to come.

## Gregory Schopen and the Critique of Buddhist Studies as a Theological Project

The rise of critical theory in the humanities, and especially the publication of Edward Said's *Orientalism* in 1978, inaugurated a new era of critical self-reflection in Buddhist Studies that has had important implications for the way in which scholars now understand the significance of the Buddha to their field of study. Among the efforts of many scholars who have participated in this trend, the work of Gregory Schopen stands out. His 1991 essay "Archaeology and Protestant Presuppositions in the Study of Buddhism" is by far the most often cited exemplar of this new trend. Schopen contends that the way in which Buddhist Studies had been carried out up to that time was "decidedly peculiar."[29] By this he means that although nineteenth-century scholars had before them a wealth of evidence for the early history of Buddhism in India, they consistently privileged evidence drawn from scriptural texts over all other types of evidence, in particular the evidence provided by archaeological remains, art, and epigraphy. That is, they formed their reconstruction of early Buddhism on the basis of scriptural texts, and insofar as they considered other types of evidence, they interpreted these through the lens of the texts, even when there was a conflict between the two. Schopen argues that this "peculiar" state of affairs was the vestige of a Protestant theological project, namely, the Protestant tendency to locate "true religion" in scripture rather than in actual material practice, which could be easily dismissed as "corrupt."

This insight has implications far beyond a seemingly technical dispute over which forms of evidence to consider. As already noted, nineteenth-century Europeans had a tendency to read the rise of Buddhism through the lens of the Protestant Reformation. Although this overly simplistic narrative of Buddhist origins was quashed by Hermann Oldenberg before the end of the century, a set of assumptions clearly derived from Protestant Christianity continued to inform the scholarly study of Buddhism.

29. Gregory Schopen, "Archaeology and Protestant Presuppositions in the Study of Buddhism," in *Bones, Stones, and Buddhist Monks: Collected Papers on the Archaeology, Epigraphy, and Texts of Monastic Buddhism in India* (Honolulu: University of Hawai'i Press, 1997), 1.

Buddhism was studied primarily through its texts, with a clear preference for earlier texts over later texts, mirroring the Protestant insistence on basing its theology only on the Bible rather than later Christian writings. Scholars of Buddhism recognized early on that the picture of Buddhism they were reconstructing on the basis of textual study differed quite markedly from actual Buddhist practice in Asia. They attributed this discrepancy to "decadence," "decay," or "corruption" within the Buddhist tradition. This explanation reflected the Protestant rejection of all post-New Testament practice as "corrupt," but it also incorporated an Orientalist narrative that Asians were fanciful and over-imaginative, yet at the same time lazy and lacking in intelligence, and thus incapable of following the teachings of the Buddha "correctly."[30] Accordingly, early scholars of Buddhism tended to privilege the study of Theravāda Buddhism, which they considered the earliest and purest form of Buddhism—although the "Theravāda Buddhism" they studied was mostly a textual fabrication with little resemblance to actual practice in Sri Lanka and Southeast Asia.[31] At the same time, they were openly disdainful of Tantra and Tibetan Buddhism in general, which they dubbed "Lamaism" to indicate that they did not consider it truly Buddhist.[32]

Given this web of assumptions, the importance to the nineteenth-century scholarly project of constructing a historical Buddha and determining his teachings becomes clear. Just as Protestants went "back to the Bible" to learn the "true" Christian gospel and develop a relationship with God unmediated by the church, so too did European scholars look to the early Buddhist texts to learn the "true" teachings of Buddhism unmediated by corrupt Asian practice. The historical Buddha was important to this project in the same way that Jesus, as one who "lived as one of us," was to the Protestant project. As Richard King has argued, the *historicity* of the Christian gospel was an important facet of Christian apologetics even in antiquity, since it served to distinguish Christianity, as the "true"

30. For a discussion of the interaction between the textualization of Buddhism and Orientalism, see Almond, *The British Discovery of Buddhism*, 37–40.

31. On the many ways in which actual Theravāda practice often diverges from what one might expect from the Pali Canon, see Justin McDaniel, *The Lovelorn Ghost and the Magical Monk: Practicing Buddhism in Modern Thailand* (New York: Columbia University Press, 2011).

32. This disdain for Tantra can be seen, for example, in Burnouf, who characterizes the *tantras* as texts "for coarse and ignorant minds" (*Introduction to the History of Indian Buddhism*, 480).

and therefore "universal" religion, from the "myths" on which the various "religions" of ancient paganism were based.[33] As Buddhism came to be understood as a "world religion," in the same mold as Christianity, the textually reconstructed "historical Buddha" served the same role as Jesus to ground the "true essence" of that religion in history.

In light of the increasing self-reflexivity of Buddhist Studies scholars toward their own discipline, discussions of the "historical Buddha" and the "origins" of Buddhism have fallen decidedly out of favor, especially in the United States.[34] The discipline has become increasingly specialized, with studies focusing increasingly on Buddhist practice rather than doctrine, on countries other than India, and on later, even modern or contemporary, forms of Buddhism rather than early Buddhism. Nineteenth-century and early twentieth-century Buddhist Studies, which focus on ancient India, have been characterized as a "misguided quest for" or even "obsession with" origins, and attempts to study the historical Buddha are increasingly viewed (1) with suspicion, as reflecting this "misguided quest," and (2) as quixotic, since it is now generally recognized that little can be known about the historical Buddha. The Buddhist tradition itself, while quite concerned with the concept of "Buddha," had little interest in the Buddha as anything akin to the modern concept of a historical person, and thus there is little reliable evidence on which to reconstruct the historical Buddha's life.

## *The Buddha in the Buddhist Tradition: From Unique Legitimator to Universal Principle*

It is beyond the scope of this chapter to provide a comprehensive treatment of the Buddha in the Buddhist tradition. Instead, I focus on two countervailing approaches to "the Buddha." First, I consider briefly the use of the Buddha—that is, Śākyamuni—as a legitimating figure, both for the Dharma and the Vinaya. Second, I consider the development of the concept of Buddhahood from early Buddhism to the Mahāyāna. In both cases, I focus on the ways in which traditional Buddhist approaches to the Buddha are fundamentally at odds with the assumptions brought by

33. Richard King, *Orientalism and Religion: Postcolonial Theory, India and the "Mystic East"* (London: Routledge, 1999), 35–41.

34. This is less true in Britain, where some scholars are quite adamant in defending the possibility and importance of studying the historical Buddha; see, e.g., Alexander Wynne, *The Origin of Buddhist Meditation* (London: Routledge, 2007).

nineteenth-century scholars to their reconstruction of the historical Buddha. In particular, the use of the Buddha as a legitimator, while superficially resembling the biography of a historical figure, is based on assumptions other than those of modern historiography, and the increasing generalization of the concept of Buddhahood directly seeks to obviate the individuality of the Buddha as a historical figure in a broader cosmic narrative.[35]

## Legitimating the Dharma and Vinaya: The Buddha as Literary Character

It is not at all surprising that early European scholars would have felt confident in their ability to reconstruct the life of the historical Buddha given the way in which the Buddha is presented in especially the earliest Buddhist texts of the Pali Canon. In the majority of these early texts, the Buddha is the main character, and unlike some later texts, they present him in much the way that one might expect for the human founder of a religion. In the *Sutta Piṭaka*, he is presented mostly as teaching his own monks, answering questions posed by kings and other prominent laypeople, or debating doctrine with members of rival sects. Likewise, in the *Vinaya Piṭaka*, he appears as the arbiter of monastic law: the origin of each rule in the *pāṭimokkha* (the code of discipline for Buddhist monks and nuns) is explained with a backstory, in which a particular monk does something questionable, other monks or laypeople complain to the Buddha, and then the Buddha lays down a new rule to prevent such questionable behavior from occurring in the future. In both cases, the Buddha is often (though not always) presented in a way that is unmistakably human. Rather than performing miracles, he eats, sleeps, preaches, debates, and engages in the everyday regulatory work of a religious leader.

Increasingly, however, scholars have come to realize that the semblance of humanity does not suffice to make normative religious texts like those of the Pali Canon reliable evidence for reconstructing the life of a historical figure. No matter how "realistic" the portrayal of the Buddha in these texts might be, the purpose of these texts is not to record the life of the Buddha as a historical figure according to the modern standards of

35. While it is exceedingly difficult to determine precise datings for pre-modern Buddhist texts, there is a general consensus when it comes to the relative chronology of those discussed in this section.

historiography but rather to teach the Dharma. The folly of reading these texts as historical accounts can be seen in several ways. For example, while the Buddha is often presented "realistically" as a human being, this is not always the case. Although the Buddha does not often perform miracles in the Pali Canon, he frequently refers to his supernormal abilities (as in the *Sāmaññaphala Sutta*) and meets with various supernatural beings (as in the *Sakkapañha Sutta*, where he meets with the Vedic god Indra).[36] Just as scholars of Christianity have come to realize with respect to the gospels, so too have Buddhist Studies scholars realized that the "subtraction" method of reconstructing a historical biography by simply deleting the miraculous and supernatural is ultimately arbitrary. Doing so does violence to the texts and ignores the often ahistorical motivations that underlie the texts and unite their supposedly "natural" and "supernatural" portions.

Indeed, it is important to realize that the Buddha of the Pali Canon, even at his most "human" moments, is always fundamentally a *literary* character. Sarah McClintock, for instance, has argued that when read as a literary character, the Buddha of the Buddhist texts is a trickster figure whose actions embody the paradoxical state of the unconditioned.[37] Likewise, as Sakumar Dutt long ago argued, the Buddha of the Vinaya "is not any historical personage, but only the embodiment of a theory representing the formal source of all Buddhist laws and doctrines."[38] In other words, we can easily see by comparing the surviving versions of the Vinaya that the monastic code developed over time after the Buddha's death, but stories attributing the promulgation of all rules to the Buddha serve to further the legal fiction that the Buddha is the source of all monastic law. However impressed nineteenth-century scholars might have been by the "human" character of the Buddha they found in the Pali *suttas*, we now realize that reconstructing the life of the historical Buddha from such sources is next to impossible.

---

36. See also, e.g., the *Brahmanimantanika Sutta*, in which the Buddha engages in a contest of supernormal powers with Baka Brahmā.

37. Sarah L. McClintock, "Compassionate Trickster: The Buddha as a Literary Character in the Narratives of Early Indian Buddhism," *Journal of the American Academy of Religion* 79 (2011): 90–112.

38. Sakumar Dutt, *Early Buddhist Monachism* (London: Kegan Paul, Trech, Trubner, 1924), 28–29.

## "He Who Sees the Dhamma Sees Me": Subsuming "the" Buddha to Buddhahood

The use of the Buddha as a literary character to legitimize the Dharma and Vinaya may bear a superficial resemblance to historical biography, but another aspect of the way the Buddha is treated in the Buddhist tradition has no relation whatsoever to the modern concept of history. By this I refer to the subsuming of the historical Buddha into a whole lineage of Buddhas, a multitude of Buddhas, and ultimately an ever-expansive generalized concept of Buddhahood. Even today, the "mythologization" of Buddhahood and the proliferation of mythological Buddhas is often associated with later forms of Buddhism, in particular the Mahāyāna. In the nineteenth century, this perceived tendency in the Buddhist tradition away from the supposedly atheistic philosophy taught by its human founder toward a proliferation of mythological Buddhas and the "unscientific" cosmologies that came with them played into the Orientalist narrative that Buddhism in Asian practice, especially the Mahāyāna, was decadent and corrupt.[39] Nevertheless, many of these trends that early European observers noted disapprovingly in the Buddhist tradition have roots in pre-Mahāyāna Buddhism. In this section, therefore, I emphasize the continuity of the Buddhist tradition overall in subsuming the Buddha Śākyamuni's historical particularity to a generalized, cosmological regularity.

The earliest Buddhist tradition for which we have evidence is represented by the Pali Canon, which regards the Buddha Śākyamuni neither as a unique individual nor as the founder of Buddhism. The epigraph at the beginning of this chapter indicates that the operation of the Dharma was assumed to be completely independent of Buddhas and whether or not they arise in the world. In point of fact, however, Buddhas—in the plural—do arise, and they do so with a certain regularity. This is explained in detail in the *Mahāpadāna Sutta* (*Dīgha Nikāya* 14). In this *sutta*, the Buddha Śākyamuni uses his ability to see into the past to recount the lives of the past seven Buddhas. This *sutta* sets the precedent for the doctrine, which would become standard across Buddhist schools, that Buddhas arise periodically over the course of eons, discover the Dharma, teach it to their disciples, and institute a *saṅgha* to promulgate that teaching. In time, the *saṅgha* becomes corrupt, the teaching of the Dharma disappears from the earth, and a new Buddha arises to discover the Dharma and teach it

39. Almond, *The British Discovery of Buddhism*, 44–46, 90–93, 96–102.

once more. The Buddha Śākyamuni, according to this theory, is only one of an infinite string of Buddhas who have arisen and will arise in the world; in time, his teaching too will disappear, and the next Buddha, Maitreya, who is currently living his second-to-last life in Tuṣita Heaven, will be born as a human being to discover and teach the Dharma once more.

Aside from the fact that it introduces a whole host of Buddhas who, by the standards of modern historiography, are not "real," this doctrine is also ahistorical, even anti-historical, insofar as it seeks to obviate the uniqueness of the Buddha's life. The key theme in the *Mahāpadāna Sutta* is not simply that there have been many Buddhas before the current one, but that *their lives have all followed the same pattern.* All are born to either Brahman or Kṣatriya parents; all undergo virgin birth after descending from Tuṣita Heaven; their mothers all die seven days after giving birth; all are born with thirty-two marks of a Great Man; all are enlightened under a tree; all have a pair of chief disciples; all have a personal attendant; and so forth. Their lives differ only in the particulars of how many disciples they have and how many years they live, which follow the expansion and contraction of the universe.

One may protest that the *Mahāpadāna Sutta* is a relatively late *sutta* and thus does not represent the earliest teaching of Buddhism. And indeed, considering the argument presented in the previous section, there is no reason to believe that the historical Buddha actually taught his disciples about past Buddhas as this *sutta* claims. Nevertheless, we can be confident that the idea of previous Buddhas arose quite early in the Buddhist tradition since the Mauryan Emperor Aśoka refers in one of his edicts to enlarging a *stūpa* of the past Buddha Konakamuni (Konāgamana).[40] Aśoka lived during the third century BCE, possibly only a century or so after the Buddha, depending on how one dates the Buddha's death.[41]

The differences between Mahāyāna Buddhism and the "Mainstream" Buddhism that preceded it are often exaggerated.[42] Most of the key elements of Mahāyāna doctrine are already found in Mainstream Buddhist doctrine: the superiority of the *buddha* to the *arhat*, the *bodhisattva* vow,

---

40. John Strong, *Relics of the Buddha* (Princeton, NJ: Princeton University Press, 2003), 26.

41. On the controversy over the two traditional chronologies for the Buddha's life and the current scholarly trend toward a fourth-century dating for the *parinirvāṇa*, see Heinz Bechert, ed., *The Dating of the Historical Buddha*, 2 vols. (Göttingen: Vandenhoeck and Ruprecht, 1991–92).

42. I use the term "mainstream," as many scholars now do, to avoid the pejorative and etic term *Hīnayāna* ("Lesser Vehicle") and the imprecise term *Theravāda* (which refers to only a particular sect of early, pre-Mahāyāna Buddhism).

and the cultivation of "perfections" (*pāramitā*) by a *bodhisattva* over the course of innumerable lifetimes before attaining final Awakening in his last life. These are all found in standard accounts of the Buddha Śākyamuni's lives such as the Pali *Nidānakathā*, and thus they implicitly apply to all Buddhas past and future as well. The only innovation introduced by the Mahāyāna per se that distinguished it from Mainstream Buddhism is the idea that ordinary monks should strive not merely to become *arhats* in this life, but should embark on the *bodhisattva* path that will take innumerable lives and lead ultimately to full Buddhahood. As a sort of logical corollary to this doctrinal innovation, the idea of "cosmic" Bodhisattvas arose. These Bodhisattvas, of whom Avalokiteśvara, Mañjuśrī, and Kṣitigarbha are some of the more famous and popular examples, are so advanced on the *bodhisattva* path that they have transcended ordinary human existence and accumulated so much merit that they can provide aid to ordinary human beings who pray to them.[43]

Pure Land Buddhism, which superficially appears to expand the concept of Buddhahood greatly, can also be understood as a logical corollary of the Mahāyāna's call to embark on the *bodhisattva* path, and similarly shows continuities with earlier Mainstream Buddhist tradition. If the *bodhisattva* path is open to all beings, then Buddhahood cannot be such a rare thing, and there must be beings somewhere in the universe, even now, who have completed the path and attained full Buddhahood. Where are these Buddhas, given that early Buddhist tradition teaches that the next Buddha, Maitreya, will not arise for millennia, after the Dharma has died out? The Mainstream Buddhist tradition actually provides a ready answer, even if it does not find it necessary to engage in speculation about this specific question. According to the Abhidharma tradition, which is itself a systematization of information found in the *sūtras*, the universe is composed of innumerable "world-spheres" (*cakravāḍa*), each of which has its own Jambudvīpa and Mount Meru on Earth and its own gods in the heavens. As one progresses even higher in the cosmos, the world-spheres begin to meld together, and Brahmās who live in these higher realms rule over a multitude of world-spheres. Still higher are the "Pure Abodes" (*śuddhāvāsa*) where "non-returners" (*anāgāmins*) are reborn, and where they attain

43. On the current state of scholarly understanding of Mahāyāna origins, see Gregory Schopen, "Mahāyāna," in *Encyclopedia of Buddhism*, ed. R. E. Buswell Jr., vol. 2 (New York: Thomson Gale, 2004), 492–99.

Awakening without ever returning to the human realm.[44] These Pure Abodes appear to serve as a prototype for the Pure Lands, created by Buddhas such as Akṣobhya and Amitābha, into which Mahāyāna Buddhists hope to be reborn so that they can more easily attain Awakening.

Perhaps the most important innovation in thinking about Buddhas and Buddhahood was set in motion by the "Three Bodies" (*trikāya*) doctrine, which had its origins in Yogācāra philosophy and spread throughout the Mahāyāna as a whole. Even this doctrine is not entirely original, since it builds on the Mainstream Buddhist idea that the Buddha has two separate bodies: his *rūpakāya*, or material form, and his *dhammakāya*, or the Dharma itself.[45] There is thus a tendency, even in the early Buddhist tradition, toward conflating the particularity of a Buddha with the generality of Dharma. In splitting the *rūpakāya* into two bodies—the "Enjoyment Body" (*saṃbhogakāya*) and the "Transformation Body" (*nirmāṇakāya*)—the Yogācārins simply were exploring the consequences of their idealist philosophical principle that all phenomena are "mind-only" (*cittamātra*). Under this new scheme, the historical Buddha is no longer a "real" human being (if there even is such a thing) but rather a phantasm (*nirmāṇakāya*) created as a "skillful means" (*upāya*) by the Buddha's Enjoyment Body, which lives, fully Awakened, in a Pure Land. The Buddha Śākyamuni, in other words, did not really experience birth, attain Awakening, and then die; rather, he pretended to do these things in order to teach the Dharma to human beings.[46] This docetic understanding of the Buddha's life marks a key turning point in the tendency throughout the Buddhist tradition to deemphasize the particularity of the Buddha as a unique historical figure and subsume his very person into the eternal truth of Dharma.

Further developments in the concept of Buddhahood would continue along these lines. Worthy of mention here is the concept of *tathāgatagarbha*, or "Buddha Nature." According to this doctrine, the potential eventually to become a Buddha, an "embryo of the Tathāgata," within oneself is possessed by every being. This idea, which draws on the concepts of universal Awakening in the *Lotus Sūtra*, interpenetration in the *Avataṃsaka Sūtra*, and

---

44. Rupert Gethin, *The Foundations of Buddhism* (Oxford: Oxford University Press, 1998), 115–19.

45. Frank E. Reynolds, "The Several Bodies of the Buddha: Reflections of a Neglected Aspect of Theravada Tradition," *History of Religions* 16 (1977): 374–89.

46. Paul Williams, *Mahāyāna Buddhism: The Doctrinal Foundations*, 2nd ed. (London: Routledge, 2009), 179–82.

Mind-Only in the Yogācāra, would become tremendously influential in East Asian Buddhism, particularly within the Zen school, whose "just sitting" method of meditation is intended to help the practitioner realize that all things are intrinsically Buddha Nature.[47] Likewise, the theory of Awakening found in the Yoga Tantras builds on the doctrine of Mind-Only in Yogācāra philosophy to argue that it is not necessary so much to *attain* Awakening as to *realize* it by visualizing oneself as a fully Awakened Buddha.

With these latter-day Buddhist teachings, we see the trend of the Buddhist tradition brought to its logical conclusion. The historical Buddha in the early Mainstream tradition was subsumed into an ever-repeating type that recurs over and over throughout time. The Mahāyāna's advocacy of the *bodhisattva* path for all opened up new possibilities for this repeating "Buddha type," and Yogācāra philosophy in particular completely obviated the historical Buddha's "reality" with an idealist reformulation of Buddhahood. These developments opened the way for doctrinal speculation that further conflated Buddhahood, the Dharma, the cosmos, and our very selves.

## *Conclusion*

The development of the concept of the Buddha in the Buddhist tradition has been motivated by very different concerns from those that led to the construction of the historical Buddha by nineteenth-century Western scholars. On the one hand, the tradition used the Buddha as a literary character to embody and legitimize both the teachings of Buddhism and the regulations of the Buddhist monastic order. On the other hand, the tradition increasingly sought to assimilate the individuality, particularity, and historicity of the Buddha into an ever-expanding conception of Buddhahood characterized by regularity, universality, and timelessness. In both cases, one might say that concerns about the Buddha as a historical figure were overruled by concerns for promulgating the Dharma and emphasizing its universality.

But there is no reason to privilege the historical approach to the Buddha over traditional approaches to the Buddha in this way. After all, the modern historical approach to the Buddha was driven by a set of idiosyncratic assumptions derived from the particular history of religion in the West. Insofar as Christianity's polemic against paganism was based on a "historical" gospel, it created a dichotomy between "myth" and "history" that drove the

47. Williams, *Mahāyāna Buddhism*, 103–22.

focus on history in the first place. The Protestant theological project of returning to the pristine origins of the religion as reconstructed through the reading of early texts was paralleled by efforts to recover the person of the Buddha, using texts to form an idealized picture of the religion grounded in a newly constructed "historical Buddha." This "historical Buddha" functioned in nineteenth-century scholarship and popular literature, ironically, in much the same way as the Buddha of the early Buddhist texts, as a literary character to legitimize Buddhism as a "world religion," embedded within a network of Orientalist assumptions, practices, and power relationships. By embracing the Buddha fully as he is presented in the Buddhist tradition—as a man who legitimates that tradition, but also as a type who embodies an ideological project—we gain a more sophisticated understanding not only of the Buddhist tradition but also of the scholarly "traditions" that have shaped our understanding of Buddhism over time.

## *For Further Reading*

Almond, Philip C. *The British Discovery of Buddhism.* Cambridge: Cambridge University Press, 1988. Presents the thesis that "Buddhism" as a "world religion" was largely a creation of scholarly and popular discourse in Europe during the nineteenth century. Though often criticized for ignoring the agency of Asian Buddhists in this process, this book gives a good overview of nineteenth-century Western scholarship on Buddhism and its Orientalist and Protestant biases.

de Jong, J. W. "A Brief History of Buddhist Studies in Europe and America (Part I)." *Eastern Buddhist* 7.1 (1974): 55–106. The most comprehensive history written to date of the field of Buddhist Studies in the West. Focuses mostly on scholarship on Indian Buddhism and does not include scholarship from the last four decades.

Gethin, Rupert. *The Foundations of Buddhism.* Oxford: Oxford University Press, 1998. The best basic overview of normative non-Mahāyāna Buddhism written in English to date. Focuses on Pali texts but also makes reference to actual lived practice. Has a short chapter on the Mahāyāna.

King, Richard. *Orientalism and Religion: Postcolonial Theory, India and "The Mystic East."* London: Routledge, 1999. A book-length exploration of the interaction between Orientalist assumptions, Western assumptions about the nature of religion, and the study and representation of Indian religions in Western discourse.

Lopez, Donald S. Jr. "Buddha." In *Critical Terms for the Study of Buddhism*, edited by Donald S. Lopez Jr. Chicago: University of Chicago Press, 2005. A short article on the Western process of constructing the "historical Buddha," followed by a brief exploration of the contrast to the treatment of the Buddha in the Buddhist tradition itself.

Lopez, Donald S. Jr.. *From Stone to Flesh: A Short History of the Buddha*. Chicago: University of Chicago Press, 2013. A more extended, book-length treatment of the Western process of constructing the historical Buddha. Ends with Eugène Burnouf, the father of modern Buddhist Studies in the West.

Masuzawa, Tomoko. *The Invention of World Religions*. Chicago: University of Chicago Press, 2005. Presents the argument that the very idea of "world religions" is a recent, Western construction that ironically reinscribes a Christian theology of universalism within the language of multiculturalism.

Williams, Paul. *Mahāyāna Buddhism: The Doctrinal Foundations*. 2nd ed. London: Routledge, 2009. This remains the best, most comprehensive introduction to Mahāyāna Buddhism as a doctrinal system written in English to date. Focuses on Indian texts but also makes extensive reference to developments in Tibet, China, and beyond.

# 3

# *When the Founder Is Not a Creator*

## CONFUCIUS AND CONFUCIANISM RECONSIDERED

*Liang Cai*

CONFUCIUS DID NOT create Confucianism. Confucius himself is famous for saying, "I transmit but do not create; I trust and love the ancient way" (*Analects* 7.1). Yet Confucius has been regarded as the founder of the *ru* tradition since his lifetime. Whether or not one conflates *ru* with Confucianism, it presents a fascinating puzzle: how did a failure in the political realm become the founder of a tradition that both existed before him and was once shared by all the elite? This chapter considers the myths and realities connected with the figure of Confucius and proceeds to analyze the speculations and preoccupations of modern scholars in their attempts to reconstruct the history of the religion that bears his name. Lionel Jensen contends that there was no such thing as Confucianism until Jesuits in the sixteenth century and Chinese scholars in the early twentieth century manufactured it.[1] Jensen rightly demonstrates that the process of interpreting a tradition is the very process of creating a tradition, but this hermeneutic "invention" of Confucianism did not begin with the Jesuits. Confucius's immediate disciples and other scholars in pre-imperial and early imperial China (fifth century

1. Lionel M. Jensen, *Manufacturing Confucianism: Chinese Traditions and Universal Civilization* (Durham, NC: Duke University Press, 1977), esp. 3–28. See also Nicolas Standaert, "The Jesuits Did NOT Manufacture 'Confucianism,'" *East Asian Science, Technology, and Medicine* 16 (1999): 115–32.

BCE–second century CE) had by that time already wrought the transformation of *ru* into Confucianism.

## *Confucius and Ru* 儒

It is customary to call the followers of Mozi 墨子 (ca. 468–376 BCE) "the school of Mo" (*Mojia* 墨家) and the thought of Mozi "the teachings of Mo" (*Moxue* 墨學).[2] By contrast, although Mencius 孟子 (ca. 372–289 BCE) once used the term "the way of Confucius" (*Kongzi zhi dao* 孔子之道) and Xunzi 荀子 (ca. 312–230 BCE) used the term "disciples of Zhongni" (*Zhongni zhi men* [*ren*] 仲尼之門[人])—Zhongni being Confucius's personal name)—generally the rubric *ru* is employed to designate the thought of Confucius and his followers.[3] The earliest Chinese dictionary, the first-century CE *An Explication of Written Characters* (*Shuowen jiezi* 說文解字), defines *ru* as "gentle" and states that it is used in reference to "men of techniques."[4] Some scholars have examined the phonetic similarities between characters and redefined the composition of the etymological nucleus of the word, concluding that the character *xu* 需 is the original script for *ru*. This would indicate that *ru* is linked to those who have knowledge of astrology.[5] Others have attempted to identify the origin of the word in the oracle bones and argue that *ru* refers to those who have expertise in Ritual.[6] These claims sit comfortably with the discussions of *ru* in pre-imperial China.

---

2. Mozi was a prominent thinker active from the late fifth to early fourth century BCE. Attracting a large number of disciples, he was best known as the intellectual rival of Confucius and his followers.

3. Mengzi and Xunzi were two famous self-identified followers of Confucius in pre-imperial China. See D. C. Lau, ed., *A Concordance to the Mengzi* (Hong Kong: Commercial Press, 1995), 35; D. C. Lau, ed., *A Concordance to the Xunzi* (Hong Kong: Commercial Press, 1996), 25; D. C. Lau, *Mencius* (London: Penguin, 1970), 114; John Knoblock, *Xunzi: A Translation and Study of the Complete Work*, 3 vols. (Stanford, CA: Stanford University Press, 1994), 2:72; Ban Gu 班固, *Han shu* 漢書, 12 vols. (Beijing: Zhonghua shuju, 1962), 4:1701–85. See also Liu Xiang 劉向, "Qi lue" 七略, collected fragments in *Yu han shan fang ji yi shu* 玉函山房輯佚書, comp. Ma Guohan 馬國翰, 52 vols. (Changsha: Lang huan guan, 1883), 32:64.

4. Xu Shen 許慎, *Shuo wen jie zi* 說文解字 (Beijing: Zhonghua shuju, 1963), 162.

5. Zhang Taiyan 章太炎, "Yuan ru" 原儒, in *Zhang Taiyan zhenglun xuanji* 章太炎政論選集, ed. Tang Zhijun 湯志鈞, vol. 1 (Beijing: Zhonghua shuju, 1977), 489–94.

6. Xu Zhongshu 徐中舒, "Jia gu wen zhong suo jian de ru" 甲骨文中所見的儒, in *Xian Qin shi lun gao* 先秦史论稿 (Chengdu: Ba shu chubanshe, 1992), 302–5.

Two chapters in the *Mozi* 墨子—"Against *Ru*" and "Gong Meng"—bitterly attack the *ru*, whom Mozi accuses of being immersed in Ritual and Music.[7] One passage lists their faults in detail:

> [*Ru*] corrupt men with their elaborate and showy rites and music, and deceive parents with lengthy mourning and hypocritical grief. They propound fatalism, ignore poverty, and behave with the greatest arrogance. They turn their backs on what is important, abandon their tasks, and find contentment in idleness and pride.[8]

Mozi also questions the *ru*'s emphasis on the study of the *Songs* (*shi* 詩), pointing out that a man who spends all of his time in study has no energy left for farming, trading, and the like.[9] Interestingly, this attachment to the *Songs*, Ritual, and Music—the corrupt qualities of the *ru* in Mozi's eyes—were the very merits Xunzi attributes to this group. Xunzi argues that "the *ru* model themselves after the Ancient Kings; they exalt Ritual and moral principles." Furthermore, he continues, "Were *ru* to reside in this court, the government would become refined; were they to occupy subordinate positions, popular customs would be refined."[10] Xunzi also contends that a worthy man is not good at farming and trading but is capable of knowing people and placing them in their proper positions in a society. Clearly, although Mozi and Xunzi have diametrically opposed views, they are relatively consistent in their understandings of what the

---

7. It is not clear when received texts, such as the *Songs*, the *Documents*, and the three *Rites* canons took their respective written forms. Thus, when the pre-imperial thinkers make reference to "Songs," "documents," "ritual," and "music," it is difficult to discern whether they mean specific texts, oral accounts, or some combination of the written and unwritten sources. Recently excavated texts suggest that at least the *Songs*, the *Documents*, and the *Spring and Autumn Annals*, as well as commentaries on the *Spring and Autumn Annals*, had already been written down in the pre-imperial period. Hence, "songs" and "documents" here appear in the form of book titles, while "ritual" and "music" are capitalized, serving as generic terms. Nevertheless, the *Songs* and the *Documents* to which pre-Han thinkers make reference are not necessarily identical with the received versions of these two texts. Cf. Michael Nylan, *The Five "Confucian" Classics* (New Haven, CT: Yale University Press, 2001), 20.

8. Sun Yirang 孫詒讓, *Mozi xiangu* 墨子閒詁, 2 vols. (Beijing: Zhonghua, 2001), 1:291; Burton Watson, *Basic Writings of Mo Tzu, Hsun Tzu, and Han Fei Tzu* (New York: Columbia University Press, 1967), 127.

9. Sun Yirang, *Mozi xiangu*, 2:456.

10. Lau, *Concordance to the Xunzi*, 28; Knoblock, *Xunzi*, 2:70–72.

*ru* were, namely, a group of cultural experts dedicated to traditional Zhou culture (ca. 1050–256 BCE), conveyed by Ritual, Music, and the *Songs.*[11]

From this history it should be obvious that *ru* and "Confucianism" are not one and the same thing. There is nonetheless a long tradition among scholars to use Confucianism as the synonym of *ru* without distinguishing between them. One reason for this common practice is that the central term did not have a well-documented semantic history. The original meaning of *ru* is elusive but it first appears in the *Analects*, a collection of sayings attributed to Confucius and his disciples.[12] To one of these disciples Confucius says, "Be a gentleman *ru*, not a vulgar *ru*" (*Analects* 6.13). From statements such as this, it appears that Confucius likely thought of himself as a *ru*.[13]

Immediately after his death, people began to regard Confucius as the founder of *ru* tradition. This identification is reflected in Mozi, who remarks that Confucius's behavior casts doubt on *ru* and elsewhere is asked why he praises Confucius if he is a critic of *ru*.[14] For Mozi, then, *ru* and Confucius constitute a unified community. Praising Confucius as the perfect *ru*, Han Feizi 韓非子 (fl. 233 BCE) says that after the death of Confucius, *ru* separated into eight different factions. Whereas each faction embraced different doctrines, all claimed to carry on the true teaching of Confucius.[15] Han Feizi, like Mozi, identifies the *ru* community with followers of Confucius and the *ru* teaching with Confucius's

11. Benjamin Schwartz also points out that *ru* originally referred to the entire group of cultural experts in rites and in knowledge of the sacred literature (*The World of Thought in Ancient China* [Cambridge, MA: Belknap, 1985], 139).

12. The date of the *Analects* is debated; see John Makeham, "The Formation of *Lunyu* as a Book," *Monumenta Serica* 44 (1996): 1–24; and Bruce E. Brooks and Taeko A. Brooks, *The Original Analects: Sayings of Confucius and His Successors* (New York: Columbia University Press, 1996), 243–51.

13. D. C. Lau, ed., *A Concordance to the Analects of Confucius* (Taipei: Chinese Materials and Research Aids Service Center, 1966), 10; D. C. Lau, *Confucius: The Analects* (London: Penguin, 1979), 83.

14. D. C. Lau, ed., *A Concordance to the Mozi* (Hong Kong: Commercial Press, 2001), 66, 109.

15. Han Feizi 韓非子 was a thinker who is said to have studied with Xunzi, a follower of Confucius. His teaching, conventionally labeled legalism, presented a direct challenge to that of Confucius. See D. C. Lau, ed., *A Concordance to the Han Feizi* (Hong Kong: Commercial Press, 1995), 150.

teaching. In the Han dynasty, Confucius was explicitly celebrated as the forebear of *ru* tradition, just as Mozi was considered the founder of Mohism.[16]

However, *ru* were not always or necessarily associated with Confucius. To correct the modern (mis)identification of Confucianism with *ru*, scholars recently have taken pains to demonstrate that *ru* throughout Chinese history were a heterogeneous group of learned individuals with different intellectual orientations.[17] This twentieth-century "rediscovery" is supported by abundant evidence from pre-imperial and imperial China. Xunzi, for example, identifies the Duke of Zhou 周公 and Confucius as the great *ru*. The former helped to found the Zhou dynasty and predated Confucius by more than five hundred years. The *Kong Clan Anthology* (*Kongcongzi* 孔叢子), a collection compiled by Wang Su 王肅 (195–256 CE), includes an anecdote that documents this understanding of the relationship between Confucius and *ru*:

> The King of Zhao state 趙王 said to Zishun 子順, reputedly a sixth-generation descendant of Confucius, "I heard that since Zheng Kaofu 正考甫 [an eighth-generation ancestor of Confucius], there are *ru* following each other in the lineage of the Kong family. Confucius stressed the importance of this tradition and thereby became the great sage."[18]

*Ru* is thus a tradition that not only existed long before Confucius but also was widely carried on by a large number of people. In the *Zhuangzi* 莊子, a third-century BCE text important in the formation of the Daoist

---

16. *Lun heng suo yin* 論衡索引, ed. Cheng Xiangqing 程湘清 et al. (Beijing: Zhonghua shuju, 1994), 1545. See also *Han shu*, 30:1728.

17. E.g., John Dardess, *Confucianism and Autocracy* (Berkeley: University of California Press, 1983), 8–9; Nicolas Zufferey, *To the Origins of Confucianism: The ru in Pre-Qin Times and during the Early Han Dynasty* (New York: Peter Lang, 2003), 165–375; and Michael Nylan, "A Problematic Model: The Han 'Orthodox Synthesis,' Then and Now," in *Imagining Boundaries: Changing Confucian Doctrines, Texts, and Hermeneutics*, ed. Kai-wing Chow, On-cho Ng, and J. B. Henderson (Albany: State University of New York Press, 1999), 17–56. See also the pioneering work tracing the origin of *ru* by Zhang Taiyan, who shows that *ru* first serves as a generic term referring to men with special skills ("Yuan ru" 原儒, 1:489–94). For a critical treatment of Zhang Taiyin's interpretation, see Jensen, *Manufacturing Confucianism*, 151–270.

18. D. C. Lau, ed., *A Concordance to Kong Congzi* (Hong Kong: Commercial Press, 1998), 59.

tradition, it is said that Duke Ai of Lu 魯哀公 claimed that nearly all men in Lu dressed in *ru* costume.[19] While the descriptions of *ru* costume vary in different sources, they generally characterize this type of dress as an ancient style featuring a big-sleeved garment with a wide sash, a black hat called *Zhangfu*, and a pair of shoes with decoration in the front; the wearer is depicted holding a wooden tablet as a notebook. Confucius and his disciples were likely to dress themselves in the *ru* costume that appears to have distinguished them from their contemporaries, but Confucius denied that this particular style of dress had any special significance for him.[20]

Because of the heterogeneous nature of *ru* as a group, Xunzi took pains to differentiate Confucius from the petty *ru*. He celebrated Confucius as the great *ru* who, if he were successful in obtaining office, would unify the world; if unsuccessful, he would establish only a noble reputation. By contrast, Xunzi sharply criticized the petty *ru*, who in his view only invoked the ancient kings "to cheat the stupid and seek a living from them."[21]

Although many rivals of Confucius—such as Mozi, Zhuangzi, and Han Feizi—openly challenged his teaching, they were all immersed in the *ru* tradition. This is not surprising since *ru* learning, which involves study of both the *Songs*, the *Documents*, and the ancient ritual and music system, were the common heritage of the elite in the Zhou dynasty. Mozi and Confucius, though holding different political philosophies, are thought to have specialized in the same *ru* learning. A Han dynasty text praises them on the same grounds: "Confucius and Mo Di [Mozi] cultivate the methods of the previous sages, and penetrate the teaching of the Six Arts."[22]

---

19. See *Zhuangzi ji shi* 莊子集釋, compiled by Guo Qingfan 郭慶藩 and annotated and punctuated by Wang Xiaoyu 王孝魚, 4 vols. (Beijing: Zhonghua shuju, 1961), 3:717. For special costumes of *ru*, see Chen Lai 陳來, "Rufu, ruxing, rubian: Xianqin wenxianzhong ru de kehua yu lunshuo" 儒服儒行儒辨先秦文獻中儒的刻畫與論說, *Shehui kexue zaixian* 社會科學在綫 (2008.9): 239–47.

20. D. C. Lau, ed., *A Concordance to Liji* (Hong Kong: Commercial Press, 1992), 162–63.

21. Knoblock, *Xunzi*, 2:79–80.

22. Nevertheless, no one would identify Mozi as *ru* because he explicitly differentiated his own teaching from the *ru* tradition. As the ensuing discussion shows, the emergence of new thought helped to transform *ru* tradition from the common cultural heritage into a special school of thought. The Six Arts include the Five Classics and the *Music*, a canon that had long been lost. See D. C. Lau, ed., *A Concordance to the Huainanzi* (Hong Kong: Commercial Press, 1995), 77.

These two views—that *ru* tradition existed long before Confucius and that Confucius was the founder of *ru* learning—coexist in the ancient sources without any chronological gap. Modern scholars have puzzled over this paradox and have put forward fanciful theories to account for it. Hu Shi 胡适, a leading Chinese scholar in the first half of the twentieth century, argues that *ru* tradition was the cultural heritage of the defeated Shang 商 dynasty and that Confucius was a descendant of that defunct empire. More recently, Robert Eno claims that Confucius was a member of an ethnic minority who lived in a region surrounded by the prevailing Chinese culture and that *ru* learning was associated with that non-Chinese minority.[23] Hu Shi argues that Confucius was celebrated as the founder of *ru* tradition because he changed the conquered culture from a subservient, parochial one into an energetic, universal school; Eno, however, contends that Confucius revised the *ru* tradition to respond to the dominant Chinese culture.[24]

The dearth of sources encouraged the promulgation of these wildly divergent, even contradictory, conclusions. Lionel Jensen criticizes Hu Shi on the grounds that his construction of Confucius and *ru* is directly shaped by his concerns about the fate of Chinese culture in the early twentieth century when the Chinese faced encroachment by Western countries as well as Japan.[25] Similarly, Eno's construction of Confucius and *ru* resembles something like a psychological complex manifested by sinologists desiring to deconstruct the idea of an eternal and continuous Chinese culture put forward by the Chinese government.[26] As these reconstructions of the relationship between *ru* and Confucius suggest, the prejudices and predilections of individual scholars sometimes play as significant a role as objective and disinterested analysis of the primary sources.

In the ancient sources, *ru* are men specializing in the *Songs*, the *Documents*, the *Spring and Autumn Annals*, the *Rituals*, and the *Changes*, the

---

23. In Eno's thesis, the prevailing Chinese culture is represented by the culture of the Shang and Zhou dynasties ("The Background of the Kong Family of Lu and the Origins of Ruism," *Early China* 28 [2004]: 1–28).

24. Hu Shi, "Shuo ru" 說儒, in *Hu Shi Zuoping ji* 胡适作品集, vol. 15 (Taipei: Yuanliu Chuban, 1986), 99–159.

25. Jensen, *Manufacturing Confucianism*, 217–63.

26. See Li Ling 李零, "Xue shu 'ke suo wo': yi chang weirao Wu Hong xinzuo de taolun" 學術 "科索沃": 一場圍繞巫鴻新作的討論, *Zhongguo xue shu* 中國學朮 2 (2000): 217–28.

common cultural heritage of pre-imperial elites which has been known since the Han dynasty as the Five Classics.[27] Confucius taught the Five Classics to his disciples, and those who penetrated these traditions were celebrated as accomplished pupils.[28] Various thinkers in the Warring States period (475–221 BCE) were all steeped in these traditions, and the famous rivals of Confucius, such as Mozi, Han Feizi, and Chen Liang 陳良, are said to have directly studied with *ru*.[29] Not surprisingly, we find parallels between Confucius's teaching and that of his rivals, as their discussions also involved traditional values and practices such as benevolence (*ren* 仁) and righteousness (*yi* 義), rituals, and music. Similarities in their style of argumentation are common, as they all frequently cite historical precedents preserved in the *Spring and Autumn Annals* and the *Documents* to support their claims and employ verses in the *Songs* to illustrate their views.[30]

What differentiated Confucius from his rivals? Above all, it was their opposing attitudes toward the traditional culture. While Confucius openly announced himself as a carrier and defender of the old values and practices, his rivals put forward new political and social agendas based on their harsh attacks on that tradition. Whereas *ru* serves as a generic term designating men of letters and traditional learning, it is restricted to a particular school when contrasted with the emergent schools of thought. Both Mozi and Han Feizi studied with *ru* and widely cited the Five Classics when elaborating their own teachings, yet they were never called *ru* in our sources. Instead, their innovative doctrines transformed them into the leaders of rival schools that directly challenged the old *ru* tradition.

Insofar as new schools of thought all had a founding master, *ru* scholars needed a leader and a forebear to unify them, and their critics need

27. Scholars in pre-imperial China frequently mention these texts, regarding them as the core curriculum for elite education. They do not come into being as a fixed set, however, until the Han dynasty (Nylan, *The Five "Confucian" Classics*, 19–22).

28. *Shi ji*, 47.2436. Mozi praises Confucius for his expertise in *Songs*, *Documents*, Music, and Ritual (Lau, *Concordance to the Mozi*, 107). The relationship between Confucius and *Changes* has been debated by scholars since the Song dynasty. For a summary of the controversy and the studies of *Changes* in the Han dynasty, see Liang Cai, "Excavating the Genealogy of Classical Studies in the Western Han Dynasty (206 BCE–8 CE)," *Journal of the American Oriental Society* 131.3 (2011), 371–94.

29. Cf. Lau, *Concordance to the Huainanzi*, 228.

30. Michael Nylan, e.g., argues that there is very little difference between the teaching of Mozi and that of Confucius; cf. "Kongzi and Mozi, the Classicists (Ru 儒) and the Mohists (Mo 墨) in Classical-Era Thinking," *Oriens Extremus* 48 (2009): 1–20.

someone on whom to focus their attacks. Confucius became the choice. Mencius and Xunzi were great *ru* of the Warring States period, neither of whom had any direct connection with Confucius or his immediate disciples. But in order to defend *ru* teaching against rivals, both chose to be self-proclaimed followers of Confucius. As Mencius explained, "Do I love debate? I have no choice. Those who can reject the teachings of Yang and Mo are followers of the sage (Confucius)."[31]

Scholars in the Western Han dynasty (206 BCE–8 CE) understood the emergence of competing schools of thought precisely along these lines. Three treatises produced in early imperial China summarize the intellectual trends in the Warring States period: "Under Heaven" (*Tianxia* 天下) in the *Zhuangzi*, "Summary" (*Yaolue* 要略) in the *Huainanzi*, and "The Treatise on Literature and the Arts" (*Yiwenzhi* 藝文志) in *The History of Western Han* (*Hanshu* 漢書). They all regard the Five Classics as the common heritage, preserving the complete and perfect way. But this traditional learning needed to be both distinguished from and defended against various new teachings; therefore *ru*—in one sense, comprising experts on the Five Classics—was defined as a specific school of thought and Confucius named its spiritual founder. Ban Gu 班固 (ca. 32–92), a renowned historian of early imperial China, says that "*ru* scholars . . . immerse [themselves] in the words of the Six Classics, and pay heed to the values of benevolence and righteousness; they traced their ancestors back to Yao and Shun, followed the institutions established by King Wen and King Wu, and regarded Confucius as their founding master, thereby to add weight to their teaching."[32]

In fact, the dual roles of the rubric *ru* persist throughout Chinese history. On the one hand, *ru* serves as a broad category, referring to the classicists, or simply the men of learning in general. In this context, Confucius serves as an exemplary *ru*, and enjoys the reputation of "teacher and role model of all generations" (*wanshi shibiao* 萬世師表). On the other hand, when competing with rival voices—Yangzhu and Mohist thought of pre-imperial China, Buddhism and Daoism in the imperial era, and Christianity and the Western philosophical traditions of modern times—*ru*

31. Lau, *Concordance to the Mengzi*, 35.

32. *Han Shu*, 30:1728. Ban Gu spoke of the Six Classics because he included the canon of Music, which had been lost since the Han dynasty. On the change from Six Classics to Five Classics, see Nylan, *The Five "Confucian" Classics*, 20–21.

becomes a school of thought, a religion, or a philosophy, and Confucius becomes its founder.

Defenders of *ru* tradition, from Mencius and Xunzi of the Warring States period, to Cheng Hao 程顥, Chen Yi 程顥, and Zhu Xi 朱熹 of the Song dynasty (960–1279 CE),[33] to Kang Youwei 康有爲 and Tang Junyi 唐君毅 of modern China,[34] follow the same pattern. First, they are self-proclaimed followers of Confucius. Unlike other religious traditions, no organizational procedures ever existed to mark the membership of the *ru* group. For those who are educated in the Five Classics curriculum, whether and when to identify with Confucius is their personal choice.[35] Second, these scholars claim to rejuvenate the old *ru* tradition and spread the true message of Confucius in order to combat the rival doctrines. In the early twentieth century, for example, both to mimic Western countries and to respond to the widespread influence of Christianity in China, Chinese intellectuals reflected on the question of a national religion (*Guojiao* 國教) for the newly established nation-state. Taking Christianity as an example to follow and a rival with which to compete, a group of scholars mythologized Confucius as a "Christ" in Chinese civilization and reconstructed the *ru* tradition on a Christian-based model of what a religion should be. As Kang Youwei, a nationalist political thinker of the late Qing Dynasty, observed, "In the past, everyone in our country was immersed in Confucianism. Therefore while no one talked about Confucianism, Confucius' teachings were present . . . but nowadays circumstances are different; men must have desires for food and sex, therefore we have chosen *ru* not Buddhism. Men must respect

---

33. Daniel K Gardner, "Principle and Pedagogy: Chu Hsi and the Four Books," *Harvard Journal of Asiatic Studies* 44.1 (1984): 57–81; Jiang Yibin 蔣義斌, "Zhu Xi paifo yu chanjiu zhonghe de jingguo" 朱熹排佛與參究中和的經過, *Dongfang zongjiao yanjiu* 東方宗教研究 (1987.9): 145–67.

34. Chen Xiyuan 陳熙遠, "Confucianism Encounters Religion: The Formation of Religious Discourse and the Confucian Movement in Modern China" (Ph.D. dissertation, Harvard University, 1999), chapter 2; Chen Xiyuan 陳熙遠, "'Zongjiao'—yige Zhongguo jindai wenhua shi shang de guanjian ci" 宗教—一個中國近代文化史上的關鍵詞 ("Religion, a Key Term in the History of Modern Chinese Culture"), *Xin shixue* 新史學 13.4 (2002): 37–66. See also Ya-pei Kuo, "One Body with the People: Worship of Confucius in the Xinzheng Reforms, 1902–1911," *Modern China* 35.2 (March 2009): 123–54.

35. Even the most resolute defenders of *ru* teaching were often influenced by or immersed in other teachings. See Yu Yingshi 余英时, *Zhuxi de lishi shijie* 朱熹的歷史世界 (Taipei: Yun chen wen hua shi ye gu fen you xian gong si, 2003).

and honour their ancestors, therefore we have followed Confucius not Jesus."[36]

Not only has *ru* tradition been reconstructed into a school of thought, a religion, and a philosophy, but the *ru* community since the Han dynasty has also functioned as a political force.[37] Accordingly, not only was Confucius transformed into the founder of an intellectual tradition; he was also cast into a sage-king and a symbolic leader of the *ru* community in the political realm.

Confucius and his immediate disciples had powerful political ambitions, as did his self-proclaimed followers such as Mencius and Xunzi. They argued that *ru*, men who understood the knowledge of traditional culture and who embodied its virtue, should occupy important political positions. Holding a firm belief in his own capability, Confucius promised to accomplish great things in administering a state within three years (*Analects* 13.10). Likewise, Mencius identified himself as the savior of the chaotic Warring States period and Xunzi wrote lengthy essays advocating the political effectiveness of *ru*.[38]

Confucius, however, failed in pursuing his political dream, never achieving any prominent position. On the contrary, he and his disciples almost starved to death when searching for employment in self-exile from his home state.[39] It is said that some of Confucius's disciples were appointed as ministers and advisors of various states, but relevant sources to confirm this are scanty. While Mencius and Xunzi established their reputation in the intellectual world and are said to have been consulted by kings, neither was ever entrusted with political power. The frustrating fate of *ru* did not change when Qin 秦 (221–206 BCE), the first empire, was

36. Kang Youwei 康有爲, "Kong jiaohui xu yi" 孔教會序一 and "Kong jiaohui xu er" 孔教會序二, in *Kang Youwei zhenglun ji* 康有爲政論集, ed. Tang Zhijun 湯志鈞 (Beijing: Zhonghua shuju, 1981), 732–41, esp. 733. Jesuits in the sixteenth century followed a similar procedure to "manufacture" Confucianism, as Jensen shows. They rendered *ru* "the literati," as *ru* denoted general elites. At the same time, however, they used Christian criteria and categories to describe *ru* tradition, portraying it as the counterpart to Christianity in the East when presenting it to their Western audiences. See Jensen, *Manufacturing Confucianism*, 31–150.

37. See Liang Cai, *Witchcraft and the Rise of the First Confucian Empire* (Albany: State University of New York Press, 2013), esp. 113–86.

38. Lau, *Concordance to the Xunzi*, 24, 27–33.

39. Chen Ning, "Mohist, Daoist, and Confucian Explanations of Confucius's Suffering in Chen-Cai," *Monumenta Serica* 51 (2003): 37–54.

founded. Han scholars believed that the philistine Qin court burned books such as the *Songs* and the *Documents* and buried literati alive, a nadir in the history of the relations between rulers and *ru*.[40] After the founding of the Han, the situation seems to have improved. Shu Suntong 叔孫通, a *ru*, drew up a new set of protocols for the imperial ceremonies, propelling him to the center of the political stage and service as one of the Nine Ministers (*jiuqing* 九卿). Under Emperor Wu (156–87 BCE), a *ru* named Gongsun Hong 公孫弘 was appointed chancellor. These stories ignited *ru* passion and hopes for the future. According to Sima Qian 司馬遷 (145–87 BCE), the founding father of Chinese historiography, the literati in the whole country did what they could to follow these successful examples.[41]

The political achievements of a few *ru* in the Han empire depended on a range of contingent factors, however, and the advancement of the *ru* into the bureaucracy was far from certain. The central court was dominated by those with hereditary prestige and military accomplishments and by those adept in fiscal and legal affairs. The contemporary historian Sima Qian shows that only six out seventy-seven high officials during Emperor Wu's reign were called *ru* by their contemporaries. *Ru* were no more than a powerless faction in the upper level of officialdom. Knowledge of the Five Classics was despised as impractical and *ru* were perceived to be out of touch with everyday affairs and lacking an understanding of administration.[42] And although *ru* were a disadvantaged group in the political realm, they did not form an interest group and promote more *ru* to expand their power. Instead, the similar educational backgrounds of the *ru* made them regard each other as direct rivals and they often scrambled for political power at the expense of their fellow *ru*.

It was against this background that scholars in the Han dynasty transformed Confucius into an uncrowned king (*suwang* 素王) and called for a homogeneous and competitive Confucian community. In the Warring States period, there was already a voice that compared Confucius with a king. Gong Meng 公孟, for instance, states in the *Mozi*, "Confucius has an extensive knowledge of the *Songs* and the *Documents*, makes a scrutiny

---

40. This is a well-known story told by Han scholars, but its authenticity has been called into question; see Jens Østergård Petersen, "Which Books Did the First Emperor of Ch'in Burn? On the Meaning of *Pai Chia* in Early Chinese Sources," *Monumenta Serica* 43 (1995): 1–52.

41. *Shiji* 121.3116–17.

42. Liang Cai, *Witchcraft and the Rise of the First Confucian Empire*, 9–44.

of Ritual and Music, and understands thousands of things. Should Confucius be regarded as a sage-king, is this not treating Confucius as the Son of Heaven?"[43] Mencius was the first to explicitly claim that Confucius, by compiling the *Spring and Autumn Annals*, fulfilled the function of the Son of Heaven.[44] Following Mencius, Han scholars enthusiastically advocated the idea that Confucius created the *Spring and Autumn Annals* to convey the Way of the King, a statement that appears in almost every book produced in the Han dynasty since the second century BCE.[45] In the *Grand Scribe's Records* (*Shiji* 史記) written by Sima Qian, the Five Classics, once the common cultural heritage, were claimed to be the private teaching of Confucius, through which the sage set forth the Laws of the King (*wang fa* 王法). Through this identification of the Five Classics as the conveyor of the sage's message on rulership, Confucius—a man who had never achieved any political prominence in his lifetime—was transformed into an uncrowned king. The *ru*, who specialized in the Five Classics, became both the followers of Confucius and the most legitimate candidates for official positions.[46]

## *The Versatile Tradition of* Ru

Ruling elites in pre-modern China regarded *ru*/Confucians as political contenders. Scholars who study religion treat *ru*/Confucianism as a religion. Philosophers approach *ru*/Confucianism as a philosophy. Confucians are portrayed as politicians, thinkers, and classicists in different contexts. Self-proclaimed followers or rivals of Confucius are able to delineate the distinct identities of Confucianism partly because *ru* tradition itself is extremely flexible. Unlike Judaism and Christianity, Confucianism does not have one canon, but many. These canons—whether the Five Classics or the Four Books (see below)—are never closed in a strict sense nor do they enjoy a sacred status as does the Bible. Indeed, the Confucian

43. Lau, *Concordance to the Mozi*, 107.

44. Lau, *Concordance to the Mengzi*, 34.

45. Although Mencius was the first to attribute the *Spring and Autumn Annals* to Confucius and also compared him with the Son of Heaven, identifying Confucius as an uncrowned king did not become popular until the Han dynasty. See Liang Cai, "Who Said, 'Confucius Composed Chunqiu'? The Genealogy of the 'Chunqiu' Canon in the pre-Han and Han Periods," *Frontiers of History in China* 5.3 (2010): 363–85.

46. Liang Cai, *Witchcraft and the Rise of the First Confucian Empire*, 45–76.

canons have been constantly challenged, regularly undergoing revision to suit various purposes.[47]

In modern times, scholars still focus on different texts as representative of Confucianism. Hu Shi take the *Spring and Autumn Annals*, the *Changes*, and the *Analects* to represent the thought of Confucius, whereas Feng Youlan 馮友蘭, Hou Wailu 侯外廬, A. C. Graham, and Benjamin Schwartz take the *Analects* as the only reservoir of the sage's beliefs. Hu Shi, Feng Youlan, and Graham take the *Mencius*, the *Great Learning* (*Daxue* 大學), the *Doctrine of the Mean* (*Zhongyong* 中庸), and the *Xunzi* as the core texts of early Confucianism, whereas Hou Wailu excludes the *Great Learning* and Schwartz only briefly mentions the *Great Learning* and the *Doctrine of the Mean* when presenting the tradition. While Feng Youlan, Hou Wailu, and Graham barely discuss the Five Classics and their significance, Schwartz classifies the Five Classics as Confucian canons, though he does not examine their relationship to the Confucian tradition in any detail.[48]

These different treatments reflect the tension between the Confucianism manufactured in the Han dynasty and the one reinvented by the Song scholars. From early Imperial China until the Tang dynasty (618–907 CE), the Five Classics were taken as the carriers of Confucius's thought. But it is difficult to construct a single or coherent school of thought from those diverse texts, which consist of history, literature, ritual manuals, and divination. Represented by Zhu Xi 朱熹, a group of *ru* scholars of the Song dynasty elevated the *Analects*, the *Great Learning*, the *Doctrine of the Mean*, and the *Mencius*—known as the Four Books—as the core canons of Confucian tradition so as to construct a coherent cosmological and metaphysical system to compete with Buddhism. Zhu Xi's reinterpretation of Confucianism was institutionalized as the state orthodoxy when the Yuan court (1206–1368 CE) prescribed the Four Books as the core curriculum for the civil service examinations.[49]

---

47. Benjamin Elman, *A Cultural History of Civil Examinations in Late Imperial China* (Berkeley: University of California Press, 2000), 1–124.

48. Hu Shi 胡适, *The Development of the Logical Method in Ancient China* (Shanghai: Oriental Book Co., 1922), 2; Feng Youlan 馮友蘭, *Zhongguo zhexue shi* 中國哲學史, vol.1 (Beijing: Zhonghua shuju, 1961), 9; Hou Wailu 侯外廬, *Zhongguo sixiang tongshi* 中國思想通史, vol. 1 (Beijing: Renmin chubanshe, 1957), 4; Schwartz, *The World of Thought in Ancient China*, 57–66.; A. C. Graham, *Disputers of the Dao: Philosophical Argument in Ancient China* (La Salle, IL: Open Court, 1989), vii.

49. Elman, *Cultural History of Civil Examinations in Late Imperial China*, 1–65.

While this orthodoxy was supported by the imperial court until the early twentieth century, it did not prevent scholars from deconstructing Zhu Xi's paradigm of Confucianism. In the Qing dynasty (1644–1912 CE), the school of evidential scholarship (*kaozheng* 考證) employed philological methods to challenge the authorship of the *Great Learning* and the *Doctrine of Mean*, and explicitly called these texts forgeries.[50] Qing scholars identified themselves as the followers of Han *ru*, advocating a return to the Five Classics to explore the true message of Confucius.

Quarrels like those between Song and Qing scholars continue today. Intellectual historians present Confucianism as a textual and literary history that charts the imagination and creation of Confucius and Confucianism by anonymous authors and compilers. They reclaim the Five Classics as Confucius's legacy in early imperial China, reminding readers that the Four Books enjoyed a relatively low status at the formative stage of Confucianism. Textual studies demonstrate that the *Analects*—the allegedly authentic voice of Confucius—not only came into being several hundred years after his death but contains miscellaneous material shared by other contemporary textual traditions as well.[51]

Such efforts, however, cannot stop the philosophers from pursuing what they believe to be the true message of Confucianism. They explore the metaphysical, ontological, and ethical theories from Confucian canons like the *Analects* and the *Great Learning*, even though the authenticity of these texts has been called into question. This approach is understandable. While scholars motivated by patriotism feel an obligation to respond to Hegel's criticism that China failed to produce systematic philosophical thought, professors in departments of philosophy feel the urge to find a counterpart to the Western philosophical tradition in ancient China.[52] *Ru* learning—especially the

---

50. For the diverse opinions regarding the date and authorship of the *Doctrine of the Mean*, see Xu Fuguan, "Zhongyong de diwei wenti: jin jiuzheng yu Qian Binsi xiansheng" 中庸的地位問題: 謹就正於錢賓四先生, in *Xueshu yu zhengzhi zhijian* 學術於政治之間, vol. 2. (Jiulong: Nan shan shu wu, 1976), 322–38. For debates regarding the date and intellectual affinities of the *Great Learning*, see Xu Fuguan, *Zhongguo renxing lun shi: Xian Qin pian* (Taipei: Commercial Press, 1978), 231–44.

51. See Makeham, "The Formation of *Lunyu* as a Book," 1–24; Bruce E. Brooks and Taeko A. Brooks, *The Original Analects: Sayings of Confucius and His Successors* (New York: Columbia University Press, 1996), 243–51. Oliver Weingarten, "Textual Representations of a Sage: Studies of Pre-Qin and Western Han Sources on Confucius (551–479 BCE)" (Ph.D. dissertation, University of Cambridge, 2009).

52. See Homer Dubs, "The Failure of the Chinese to Produce a Philosophical System," *T'oung Pao* 26 (1929): 96–109; Tang Junyi 唐君毅, Mou Zongsan 牟宗三, Xu Fuguan 徐復觀 et al., "Wei Zhongguo wenhua jinggao shijie renshi xuanyan" 為中國文化敬告世界人士宣言, in *Dang dai xin ru jia* 當代新儒家 (Beijing: Sanlian shudian, 1989), 15–18.

version contained in Zhu Xi's Four Books—provides both a precedent to follow and the raw materials with which to reconstruct a tradition.[53]

## *Why Choose Confucius as the Founder?*

The diverse content of *ru* tradition allows later scholars to present it as a collection with a distinct identity. But why has Confucius been chosen as its founder? Confucius never claimed for himself divine origin, nor did he claim to be a savior in the chaotic times or to possess any power to alleviate human suffering.[54] He did not think of his own teaching as special or unique, let alone sacred. Rather, he explained his versatile ability as a result of dealing with the hardships of life when he was young and portrayed himself as a man who liked learning and teaching. Confucius pursued employment in various states but, having no success, ended up dying in obscurity.[55] People once laughed at Confucius, comparing him to a homeless dog whose owner had died. Rather than feeling offended, Confucius happily embraced it as his self-image.[56]

But this "loser" in the political world was quickly celebrated as a sage by his contemporaries. His disciples praised him, saying that no one could attain his level, "just as the heaven cannot be reached through climbing ladders" (*Analects* 19.25). Likewise, "the worthiness of other people is like hills, which can be surpassed," but "Confucius is like the sun and moon, which no one is able to surpass" (*Analects* 19.24). Rivals of Confucius, though criticizing his teachings, regarded him as the most significant figure in the intellectual world, whose stories were shared lore, widely cited and reworked by the educated men in the pre-Han and Han eras.

How can a man without prominent social status exert such a profound influence? The conventional view holds that Confucius was the first

53. Tu Wei-ming, *Humanity and Self-Cultivation: Essays in Confucian Thought* (Berkeley: Asian Humanities Press, 1979), 5–16, 35–57; John H. Berthong, *Transformations of the Confucian Way* (Boulder, CO: Westview, 1998); Liu Shu-hsien, *Understanding Confucian Philosophy: Classical and Sung-Ming* (Westport, CT: Greenwood, 1998).

54. Not until the Han dynasty, in an apocryphal text, did Confucius become an astral deity with a miraculous birth; see Michael Nylan and Thomas Wilson, *Lives of Confucius: Civilization's Greatest Sage through the Ages* (New York: Doubleday, 2010), 67–100; and Lionel M. Jensen, "Wise Man of the Wilds: Fatherlessness, Fertility, and the Mythic Exemplar, Kongzi," *Early China* 20 (1995): 407–37.

55. Nylan and Wilson, *Lives of Confucius*, 1–28.

56. Li Ling, "The Explanation of 'Sang Jia Gou' [The Homeless Dog]," *Contemporary Chinese Thought* 41.2 (2009): 43–53.

independent teacher who spread aristocratic education to commoners. Confucius claimed that he would teach anyone, regardless of background. He was said to have taught about three thousand students, among whom seventy-two penetrated the Five Classics.[57] To break down the barrier between the aristocracy and the commoners, Confucius revised the connotation of *junzi* 君子. Whereas *junzi*—literally "son of a lord"—refers to the nobility in its original sense, Confucius reinterpreted *junzi* to refer to moral men. This revolutionary innovation posits that everyone is able to become a *junzi*, and only those with high morality should be called *junzi* and thereby enjoy political power and social privilege.

Confucius not only gave commoners hope of sharing the political power with aristocrats, but he also showed his followers the way to an aesthetic manner of living. He reworked the traditional ritual, transforming it into a generic term prescribing the appropriate behavior in changing situations. He instructed his disciples to follow the ritual in every aspect of life, just like a dancer performing according to choreography.[58] He created a community that "starts with the *Songs*, establishes themselves by Ritual, and becomes complete through Music" (*Analects* 8.8).

Without a doubt, Confucius attracted followers throughout his lifetime. But the conspicuous success of this community was due not only to the innovation Confucius brought to the tradition but also to its special organizational structure.[59] An anecdote from the *Analects* (16.13) provides a glimpse:

> Cheng Kang asks Boyu [the son of Confucius], "Did you receive different teachings [from the master]?" [Boyu] replies, "No. Once [my father] stood alone and I ran across the yard. [He] asked,

57. *Shiji* 47.1938.

58. Robert Eno, *The Confucian Creation of Heaven: Philosophy and the Defense of Ritual Mastery* (Albany: State University of New York Press, 1990), 30–63.

59. The organizational structure of the community led by Confucius has not yet been fully investigated. Both Mark Lewis and David Elstein notice the father-son relationships between Confucius and his disciples but do not further pursue the subject. Lionel Jensen explores this feature of Confucius's community in more detail, contending that Confucius's disciples instead of his biological descendants served as the master's intellectual heirs. See Mark Edward Lewis, *Writing and Authority in Early China* (Albany: State University of New York Press, 1999), 53–97; David Elstein, "Friend or Father? Competing Versions of Master-Student Relations in Early China" (Ph.D. dissertation, University of Michigan, 2006), 19–67; Lionel M. Jensen, "The Genesis of Kongzi in Ancient Narrative: The Figurative as Historical," in *On Sacred Grounds: Culture, Society, Politics, and the Formation of the Cult of Confucius*, ed. T. A. Wilson (Cambridge, MA: Harvard Asia Center, 2002), 175–221.

"Have you learned the *Songs*?" I replied "Not yet." "If you don't learn the *Songs*, you cannot make a speech." [So] I returned and studied the *Songs*. The other day, [my father] stood alone again, and I ran cross the yard. [He] asked, "Have you learned the Ritual?" I replied, "Not yet." "If you don't learn the Ritual, you cannot establish yourself." I returned and studied the Ritual. I heard about just those two things. Cheng Kang returned, happily saying, "I asked one question but learned three things. I heard the *Songs*, heard the Ritual, and heard that the master kept a distance from his own son."

Because Cheng Kang, a disciple of Confucius, wanted to learn whether the master gave secret teachings to his own son, Boyu recalled private meetings between him and his father. Interestingly, it was not a basic routine for Confucius to spend time only with his family. Boyu had a personal conversation with his father because he ran into him and, at that moment, Confucius happened to have no companions. This suggests that the master must have lived his life largely with his disciples. This communal living is further confirmed by the fact that when Confucius chose self-exile and wandered from state to state seeking employment, several of his close disciples followed him.

Cheng Kang is happy that Confucius kept a distance from his own son. Yet this mentality is difficult to comprehend, especially when one considers that Mencius, in order to defend *ru* teaching, attacks Mozi's doctrine of "making no discrimination in loving people." Mencius despised those who believed that "a man's love toward his brother's son is as much as his love toward his neighbour's son."[60] Cheng Kang's happiness about the master's treatment of his own son is understandable only if Confucius had transformed his community of learning into a family lineage, taking his disciples, especially close ones, as his own sons. In fact, invoking the father-son relation to bind master and disciples together is a salient feature of Confucius's community of learning.

Confucius said openly that Yan Hui 顏回 regarded him as his own father, and that he would regard Hui as his own son (*Analects* 11.11). This father-son relation was not merely lip service but shaped their lives and death. When Yan Hui dies, his biological father asks Confucius for money

60. Lau, *Concordance to the Mengzi*, 30.

to buy a vault and Yan Hui's classmates take care of Hui's funeral. As is well known, the deaths of Yan Hui and later of Zilu 子路 lead to the emotional collapse of Confucius, who cries "Heaven is destroying me, Heaven is destroying me" (*Analects* 11.9). It was Confucius's disciples who assumed the role of sons at the end of the master's life. In the records, it is his disciples, not members of his own biological lineage, who attended to Confucius on his deathbed, took care of his funeral, and resided near his tomb to perform the three-year mourning service.[61] The three-year mourning service is a ritual Confucius strenuously advocated for one's parents. Although this practice might have originated within an older tradition, no extant sources show that it was ever implemented before Confucius's time. But his disciples performed it for their dear master, an action that not only declared Confucius to be their spiritual ancestor but became the symbol of his community of learning in both the pre-imperial and imperial periods.[62]

Confucius's undisputed reputation in the intellectual world resulted primarily from the attention his community of learning successfully drew from their contemporaries. While the lore of the master and his immediate disciples has been widely circulated since their lifetime, the social organization and the communal life they initiated did not survive. It is said that after the death of Confucius, some of his disciples wanted to serve You Ru 有若, who behaved just like Confucius, as their new master. But this proposal was rejected because Zengzi 曾子 argued that no one could ever compare with Confucius.[63] Throughout the history of Confucianism, no institutionalized ceremonial rites have ever been formulated for "baptizing" a Confucian. Without a clear boundary between followers and non-followers of Confucius, it thus becomes a personal choice for one to decide when and under what circumstances to identify oneself with the sage and in what manner to defend his teaching.

---

61. Cf. Jensen, "The Genesis of Kongzi in Ancient Narrative," 181–82.

62. For discussion of the three-year mourning services, see Keith N. Knapp, "The *Ru* Reinterpretation of *Xiao*," *Early China* 20 (1995): 195–222; Keith N. Knapp, *Selfless Offspring: Filial Children and Social Order in Early Medieval China* (Honolulu: University of Hawaii Press, 2005), 31–50; Xu Zhongshu 徐中舒, *Xian Qin shi lungao* 先秦史論稿 (Chengdu: Bashu shushe, 1992), 306–7; and Fang Shuxin 方述鑫, "'Sannian zhisang' qiyuanxinlun" 三年之喪" 起源新論, *Sichuan daxue xuebao* 四川大學學報 119 (2002.3): 98–103.

63. Lau, *Concordance to the Mengzi*, 29.

## *Conclusion*

Confucianism does not promise personal salvation in the afterlife or the salvation of the world at some future time. Although Confucius receives sacrifices from the imperial families from the Han dynasty onward, the sage is almost always presented as a human, not as a divine being. Even those who try to mythologize his birth and life seldom attribute any magic power to Confucius, and he is never portrayed as efficaciously interfering with this world. Therefore, questions such as whether Confucius created the *ru* tradition seldom engage the general public. Instead, arguments concerning the founder of this tradition have more typically served as a proxy for broader intellectual, political, or ideological questions. In pre-imperial and early imperial China, scholars who endeavored to defend the traditional elite values elevated Confucius as the founder of *ru* learning so as to compete with newly emerging schools of thought. Scholars with political ambitions transformed Confucius into an uncrowned king who led the *ru* community so as to legitimate their aspirations for political power. In Song China, Confucius became an exponent of truth who sanctioned *ru* learning as a better cosmological and metaphysical system than the Indian-imported Buddhism. In the twentieth century, Confucius became the symbol of the nation and Confucianism the quintessence of Chineseness so as to bind the affections of the people to the nation and safeguard the national heritage against Western culture.[64] Throughout Chinese history, there has been no institutional authority to arbitrate the "true" and "false" doctrines of the sage. Confucius, along with the rest of the *ru* tradition, has become a free-floating signifier, opening endless possibilities for groups and individuals to reconfigure Confucianism as they see fit. Contemplating Confucianism through the prism of its putative founder thus sheds new light on the various thinkers who produced these multifaceted images of Confucius, hermeneutically reinventing an old tradition in order to address the intellectual and social concerns of their own times.

---

64. Ya-pei Kuo, "In One Body with the People: Worship of Confucius in the Xinzheng Reforms, 1902–1911," *Modern China* 35.2 (March 2009): 123–54; Ya-pei Kuo, "Redeploying Confucius: The Imperial State Dreams of the Nation, 1902–1911," in *Chinese Religiosities: Afflictions of Modernity and State Formation*, ed. M. Yang (Berkeley: University of California Press, 2008), 65–84; and Vincent Goossaert, "1898: The Beginning of the End for Chinese Religion?" *Journal of Asian Studies* 65.2 (May 2006): 307–35.

## *For Further Reading*

Cai, Liang. *Witchcraft and the Rise of the First Confucian Empire.* Albany: State University of New York Press, 2014. Cai demonstrates how *ru* successfully transformed itself from an intellectual force into a political one and how scholars of the Han empire refashioned *ru* tradition into what is now recognized as Confucianism.

Chin, Annping. *The Authentic Confucius: A Life of Thought and Politics.* New York: Scribner, 2007. A book-length biography of Confucius in which Chin attempts to recover an image of the historical Confucius on the basis of available sources.

Eno, Robert. *The Confucian Creation of Heaven: Philosophy and the Defense of Ritual Mastery.* Albany: State University of New York Press, 2013. Eno examines the concept *tian* (Heaven) in early *ru* tradition. Appended to this goal is a more speculative description of the social and theoretical project of the *ru*, a project which Eno argues is centered around the performance of ritual.

Goldin, Paul. *Confucianism.* Berkeley: University of California Press, 2011. Goldin explores the major thought and concerns of Confucian canons, such as the *Analects*, the *Mencius*, the *Xunzi*, the *Great Learning*, and the *Canon of Filial Piety*.

Jensen, Lionel M. *Manufacturing Confucianism: Chinese Traditions and Universal Civilization.* Durham, NC: Duke University Press, 1997. Jensen demonstrates how Jesuits in the sixteenth and seventeenth centuries and Chinese scholars in early twentieth century "recreated" Confucianism.

Knapp, Keith N. *Selfless Offspring: Filial Children and Social Order in Early Medieval China.* Honolulu: University of Hawaii Press, 2005. Knapp provides a broad picture of filial devotion—a core value in early Confucianism—as a set of evolving and gendered ritual, political, and social practices in early medieval China (100–600 CE).

Nylan, Michael, and Thomas Wilson. *Lives of Confucius: Civilization's Greatest Sage through the Ages.* New York: Doubleday, 2010. Nylan and Wilson present six carefully selected and distinctive perspectives to illustrate the multifaceted images of Confucius throughout history.

Van Norden, Bryan W., ed. *Confucius and the Analects: New Essays.* Oxford: Oxford University Press, 2002. An anthology of essays exploring the *Analects* via literary, philological, historical, and philosophical approaches, with an excellent annotated bibliography of works on Confucius and the *Analects*.

# 4

# *What Is Daoism and Who Is Its Founder?*

*Gil Raz*

> *The learning of contemporaries is mostly shallow. They only recite the Daode and do not know about the Perfect Scriptures, so they say Daoism arose from Zhuang Zhou and began with [Laozi].*[1]

WHO IS THE founder of Daoism? The answer depends on one's definition of Daoism. Identifying the founder of any religion is a difficult task, and posing this question perhaps says more about the preoccupations, concerns, and misconceptions of modern Western audiences than about the historical developments of the religions themselves. Nevertheless, the question concerning the founder of Daoism is further compounded by the problematic understanding of Daoism: Is it a religion? Is it a unitary tradition? When did it first appear? Who are the major figures in this tradition? Is there a founder of Daoism? Indeed, is it even possible for it to have a founder?

Before seeking a founder, we first need to establish what we mean by the term "Daoism" and whether it is a unitary tradition that may indeed have a founder. "Daoism" in English and other European languages has three distinct yet related connotations. These reflect Chinese usages, but there are at least two Chinese terms one may translate as Daoism, as well as several specific labels we may include within the category Daoism. First, the term is loosely applied to any Chinese artifact, poem, story, practice, or person who is closely associated with nature. Second, it is applied

1. *Seven Slips from the Bookcases in the Clouds* (*Yunji qiqian* 雲笈七籤) DZ 1032: 3.3b.

to a philosophical trend in early China, conventionally associated with a set of texts dating to the fifth and fourth centuries BCE. Third, it is applied more specifically to a communal religious tradition that appeared in the second century CE and continues to flourish today. The first usage of Daoism is far too general to serve any meaningful function. The second and third meanings, however, are far more difficult to disentangle. We must remember, however, that the philosophical tradition was not labeled as such by its contemporaries. Rather, this textual tradition was retroactively constructed and named during the Han dynasty (207 BCE –220 CE). There is little evidence of any social context to the various texts now associated with this tradition. The religious tradition, on the other hand, labeled itself Daoist soon after its emergence in the second century (see below).

Daoism has long been known in the West as one of the major philosophical traditions of ancient China. This tradition is often defined as centered on the classic *Daode jing* 道德經 (*Scripture of the Way and the Power*) attributed to the ancient sage Laozi 老子. A second text associated with this tradition is the slightly less known eponymous work by Zhuangzi 莊子. Only recently has Daoism also been recognized as one of the world's major religions, but the history, parameters, and contours of what the label Daoism refers to remain obscure, not just to the general public but to scholars of Chinese religion as well.

One of the major problems in understanding the history of Daoism is the relationship between the so-called philosophical texts of the Warring States era and the Daoist communities that appeared five centuries later. These texts, and especially the *Daode jing*, were inspirational to these Daoist communities. The cosmology developed in these texts, and the practices associated with it, remain at the core of Daoist practice. Most important, and most germane to the topic at hand, the emergence of these communities was closely associated with the deification of the mysterious sage Laozi, the purported author of the *Daode jing*.

The problem of defining the tradition of Daoism and identifying its founder, however, is not limited to contemporary Western misunderstanding of Daoism but was already current in medieval China. The epigraph with which this chapter began is among the opening lines of a text entitled "Origins of Daoism" (*Daojiao suoqi* 道教所起) from the imperially sponsored encyclopedia *Seven Slips from the Bookcases in the Clouds* (*Yunji qiqian*), compiled by Zhang Junfang 張君房 and presented to Song emperor Ren in 1027. It is thus a history of Daoism written from the perspective of the

Daoist orthodox priesthood as it wished to be understood by the imperial court. These lines from "Origins of Daoism" show that Daoists of the era were already at pains to distinguish their practices and texts from the better-known ancient classics. The key term in this passage is "Perfect Scriptures" (*zhenjing* 真經), which refers to a specific set of texts that appeared at the beginning of the fifth century CE. The appearance of these scriptures, however, was not a unique event. Rather, their appearance should be understood as one of several revelations of Daoist scriptures between the second and fifth centuries CE.

In turn, these textual revelations need to be placed within the larger framework of religious developments in China during this period. This was an era of political and social turmoil as the long-lasting Han dynasty collapsed, to be followed by almost four centuries of political fragmentation, invasion, and conquest by non-Chinese peoples. It was during this time that Buddhism became integrated into Chinese culture and society. Scholars recognize this era as the formative period of Daoism, although the communities and religious groups that came into being during this period may have called themselves by several different names.

The problem of defining Daoism is our first task. All religions are difficult to define, as any concise definition will inevitably lead to reification and objectification that will often obscure and occlude the sociohistorical reality of lived religion. In Daoism, this problem is compounded by the social and historical intricacies of the religion, which developed in medieval China and remains a living religion today. The next section investigates the relationship between the ancient figure of Laozi and the religious communities that appeared in the second century. I then turn to the appearance of competing revelations and rival lineages with their particular founders and fictive lineages, and the subsequent negotiations by which these various ritual traditions came to see themselves within an emerging single tradition: Daoism. Finally, I return to the basic question: What is Daoism and who is its founder?

These questions stem to a large extent from the Western conceptualization of religion as it developed during the late nineteenth and early twentieth centuries. As Tomoko Masuzawa shows, this time marked the emergence of "two typical, nearly requisite, means of identifying an individual religious tradition as distinct, unique, and irreducible to any other: the naming of an extraordinary yet historically genuine person as the founder and initiator of the tradition . . . and the recognition of certain ancient texts that could be claimed to hold a canonical status."[2] Masuzawa shows that these two criteria, founder and canon, led to particular formulations of the category of religion, and in particular to the establishment of the modern label of "world religions." She correctly critiques these formulations as constructing and reifying a particular notion of religion, which bear little resemblance to the sociohistorical realities of specific traditions.

It is intriguing, however, that medieval Daoists were also preoccupied with similar issues, albeit for different reasons. On the one hand, "Origins of Daoism" argues against the then-common misconception of identifying the founder of Daoism with one or two ancient figures. On the other hand, this text indicates that this misconception stems from not recognizing the correct canonic basis for the religion: the so-called Perfect Scriptures. The preoccupation with founders was not limited to medieval Daoists but extended to several medieval Chinese religious traditions that invested much effort and ingenuity at crafting complex genealogies for their particular teachings.[3] The discourse of lineage in Chinese religions, and throughout Chinese culture, stems from the fundamental importance of genealogical imagination in early Chinese mythology and cosmology.

## *Definitions of Daoism*

At the core of Daoism is the ancient notion of *dao* 道, the Way. On the one hand, this term referred to a path to follow and a method for practice. In Daoism, however, *dao* has a far more complex significance, as it comes to refer to the fundamental process of existence. These two meanings can be glimpsed by contrasting passages from Confucius's *Analects* and the *Daode jing* attributed to Laozi.

In a famous passage, Confucius tells his disciple Master Zeng 曾子, "My way has a single thread through it." Master Zeng concurs. After Confucius leaves the room, the other disciples inquire of Master Zeng what Confucius meant. Master Zeng replies, "The Master's way is simply dutifulness and empathic understanding."[4] The word "way" is used here to

2. Tomoko Masuzawa, *The Invention of World Religions: Or, How European Universalism Was Preserved in the Language of Pluralism* (Chicago: University of Chicago Press, 2005), 132.

3. Among the best known of such creative efforts are the transmission narratives constructed by the Chan tradition, better known in English as Zen.

4. On the various interpretations of this important passage, see Edward Gilman Slingerland, *Confucius Analects: With Selection from Traditional Commentaries* (Indianapolis: Hackett, 2003): 34–35.

refer to the totality of Confucius's teaching, and more precisely to correct ways of behavior. Although the precise connotation of these may be difficult, the point is that Confucius's way can be summarized in words.

This use of *dao* can be contrasted with the opening of the received version of the *Daode jing*:

The way that can be spoken of is not the constant way;
The name that can be named is not the constant name.

These lines seem to critique precisely the use of "way" seen in Confucius. If one can define and talk about a particular way, then it is not the ultimate way. As the second line hints, moreover, the word "way" is only a provisional label for the ultimate entity, which is ineffable, formless, and beyond all linguistic and logical distinctions. The text goes on to discuss the *dao* as prior to heaven and earth, the mother of all things. All natural processes emanated from the *dao*, which is therefore the primordial impetus and continuing process by which the cosmos operates. Daoists seek to align themselves, as individuals and as communities, with the basic cosmic patterns of transformation. By uniting with the process of change, a person may not only gain health but may indeed rise beyond the limits of time and space and ascend to the heavens and live as an immortal within the limitless way. While this perception of *dao* may suffice for understanding the philosophical basis of the Daoist tradition, it is far too vague to serve as a social category and offers little help in determining the contours of the religion.

Most important, in recent years as several manuscript versions of the *Daode jing* have been discovered, there is growing scholarly agreement that (1) the *Daode jing* as we know it is a product of a century of compilation, editing, and redaction, and that (2) there is no single author responsible for the text.[5] That is, there was no individual author named Laozi who produced it. This developing understanding of the history of the *Daode jing* is of course contrary to the traditional understanding of the text, at least since the Han era.

While early texts such as the *Daode jing* and *Zhuangzi*, dating to the fifth and fourth centuries BCE, were obviously important for the development of

5. There is an enormous bibliography devoted to these discoveries and their implications for understanding the *Daode jing*. See, e.g., Edward L. Shaughnessy, "The Guodian Manuscripts and Their Place in Twentieth-Century Historiography on the *Laozi*," *Harvard Journal of Asiatic Studies* 65 (2005): 417–57.

Daoism, they are by no means the only sources for the religious tradition that now bears the name Daoism. Several other traditions current during the Warring States and Han, including *qi* cultivation techniques, royal and imperial ritual, Buddhist discourse and practices, local cultic and shamanic practices, and a variety of healing and divinatory traditions, were all incorporated in various ways into the emerging religious tradition we call Daoism.

The social history of the religion begins with the appearance of several new religious movements and communities in the mid-second century CE. Among the best known of these are the Way of Great Peace (*Taiping dao* 太平道) and the Way of the Celestial Master (*Tianshi dao* 天師道). The latter is said to have been established following the appearance in 142 CE on a mountaintop in Sichuan of the divine form of Laozi, who bestowed on Zhang Daoling 張道陵 the title of Celestial Master as well as a new textual corpus according to which Zhang organized the new religious community. Subsequent scriptural revelations in the following centuries revealed higher realms of attainment from increasingly remote celestial sources, far surpassing the divine Laozi of the Celestial Master tradition. Such revelations, received by different people at different times, led to the development of distinct and competing ritual traditions. It is during this time that the aforementioned Perfect Scriptures appear. During the fifth and sixth centuries these various revelations were brought together in a variety of competing canons. From this complex dialectic of integration and contestation, the religion we know as Daoism emerged. Similar processes of revelation, integration, and contestation continued through the following centuries, with a major flurry of activity in the tenth to twelfth centuries. Not surprisingly, there remains great confusion regarding the definition and parameters of the term Daoism, and the relationship between the ancient philosophical tradition and the religion.

## *First References to Laozi and Daoism*

By the beginning of the Han dynasty, several versions of the *Daode jing* were in circulation showing a complex process of composition and redaction. These variant texts were probably associated with narratives regarding authorship and transmission, but none of these have survived. The earliest extended references to Laozi as the author of the *Daode jing* and to a term we may translate as Daoism are in the *Annals of the Historian* (*Shiji* 史記),

the first official history of China compiled by Grand Historian Sima Qian and presented to the throne in 104 BCE. Modeled on standard biographies, the text opens with a record of Laozi's place of origin and family lineage, which are creative fictions. This section also states that Laozi served as archivist in the Zhou palace and continues with two narratives that were especially important in the development of the Laozi mythology.[6]

The first story recounts the clearly apocryphal and anachronistic encounter between a young Confucius who seeks the elder sage Laozi. Confucius questions Laozi about ritual, and Laozi dismisses this query as "of no benefit to the body." As Confucius departs he comments to his disciples, "When it comes to a dragon, I cannot understand how it rides the wind and clouds and ascend into the heavens. Today I saw Laozi, and he is like a dragon!"

The second narrative describes the writing of the *Daode jing* by Laozi:

> Laozi cultivated the way and virtue (*dao de*), his teaching was to make one's vocation self-concealment and namelessness. He lived in the Zhou for very long. When he saw the Zhou's decline, he departed. As he reached the Pass, the Pass Keeper Yin Xi said: "You are going into hiding, I urge you to write a book for me." Laozi therefore wrote a book in two parts, discussing the meaning of the way and virtue in a little over five thousand words and left. No one knows his end.

Sima Qian then links Laozi to various ancient figures and mentions that he may have lived to be two hundred years old. Careful historian that he is, Sima Qian concludes by stating that "in this generation, no one knows whether this is true or not. Laozi was a mysterious gentleman."[7]

This biography reveals that by the early Han, Laozi was already perceived as a mythical figure, with a growing set of legends accruing around his name. Indeed, as there are no extant contemporary records that refer to him, there are grave doubts about the historical existence of Laozi. Nevertheless, the two passages mentioned above served as a basis for much

6. *Shiji* 63.2140–43. For translation and discussion of the text, see A. C. Graham, "The Origins of the Legend of Lao Tan," in *Lao-Tzu and the Tao-Te-Ching*, ed. Livia Kohn and Michael Lafargue (Albany: State University of New York Press, 1998), 23–40; and Mark Csikszentmihalyi, *Readings in Han Chinese Thought* (Indianapolis: Hackett, 2006), 96–104.

7. *Shiji* 63.2142.

later elaboration and development of mythology about Laozi. The label "like a dragon" was borrowed for a large hagiography of Laozi compiled in the early eleventh century.[8] The narrative about the "urging" of Laozi to write the *Daode jing* became the standard story, and Yin Xi, the Pass Keeper, was also accepted as a Daoist sage, and texts attributed to him soon began to circulate.[9]

The *Annals of the Historian* also includes the earliest reference to a collective tradition using the term *daojia* 道家 which one may translate as Daoism, although it is better understood as "traditions of the *dao*." This term appears in the essay "Essential Points" (*Yaozhi*), composed by Sima Tan 司馬談 (d. 110 BCE), Sima Qian's father, and included in the final chapter of the *Annals of the Historian*. Sima Qian's decision to incorporate his father's essay into this chapter probably reveals not only his filiality but also his own identification with its intellectual premises. In the essay, Sima Tan categorizes the diverse traditions of practice current in the Warring States period and early Han under six rubrics: *Yinyang* 陰陽 (technical experts in a variety of mantic traditions), *Ru* 儒 (known to us as Confucians), *Mo* 墨 (the Mohists), *Fajia* 法家 (Legalists), *Mingjia* 名家 ("Terminologists"), and *Daojia* (or *Daode* 道德). Sima Tan celebrates the *daojia* as the supreme tradition as it adapts the best of all the rival traditions and is thus able to cohere with the *dao* itself:

> The Daoist tradition enables man's numinous essence to be concentrated and unified, so as to move in unison with the formless, and to provide adequately for the myriad things. As for its methods, it follows the great compliance of the Yin-yang specialists, picks out the best of the Confucians and Mohists, and adopts the essentials of the Terminologists and Legalists. It shifts with the times and changes in response to things. In establishing customs and carrying out affairs, there is nothing it is not suitable for. It is simple to grasp and easy to hold onto; there is much achievement for little effort.[10]

---

8. *Youlong zhuan* 猶龍傳 DZ 774; cf. Livia Kohn, "Youlong zhuan," in *The Encyclopedia of Taoism*, ed. Fabrizio Pregadio (London: Routledge, 2008), 1187–88.

9. Livia Kohn, "Yin Xi: The Master at the Beginning of the Scripture," *Journal of Chinese Religions* 25.1 (1997): 83–139.

10. *Shiji* 130.338–92; *Han shu* 62.2710. For discussion of this text, see Gil Raz, *The Emergence of Daoism: Creation of Tradition* (London: Routledge, 2012), 7–8.

The term *daojia* was later adopted as a bibliographic category in Ban Gu's 班固 (32–92 CE) bibliographic treatise, used as a collective term for thirty-seven different texts.[11] We may therefore credit Sima Tan and his son Sima Qian, the great historians of the early Han, with the creation of the category Daoism, as well as with the construction of the figure of Laozi.[12]

Sima Tan and Sima Qian, however, were not the only agents involved in crafting the figure of Laozi during the early Han. Their efforts may in fact be due to the development of a tradition named Huang-Lao, named for Huangdi, the Yellow Emperor, and Laozi. This tradition, which was very influential in the late third and early second century BCE, remains somewhat mysterious. This term shows up in several late Warring States and Early Han texts. It seems to refer to intellectual trends that combined esoteric mantic and healing practices, labeled Yellow Emperor teachings, with the political thought of the *Daode jing*. This synthesis seems to have produced several quite different, and seemingly contradictory, offshoots. For example, the legalist treatise *Hanfeizi* includes the earliest commentaries on the *Daode jing*, and its author, Han Feizi (c. 280–233 BCE), is said to have been influenced by Huang-Lao teachings.[13] Alongside the emphasis on law as a cosmic principle, however, other aspects of this tradition emphasize healing and longevity practices. Harold Roth summarizes the basic concerns of this tradition under three headings: (1) cosmology—based upon *dao* as the dominant unifying power in the cosmos; (2) self-cultivation—the attainment of *dao* through a process of emptying out the usual contents of the mind until a profound state of tranquility is achieved; and (3) political thought—the application of the cosmology and methods of self-cultivation to the problem of rulership.[14]

---

11. *Han shu* 30.1729–32.

12. A. C. Graham, *Disputers of the Tao* (La Salle, IL: Open Court, 1989), 370–82, summarizes the issues related to classification and "schools" during the Han. On Sima Tan's "invention" of schools, see Mark Csikszentmihàlyi and Michael Nylan, "Constructing Lineages and Inventing Traditions through Exemplary Figures in Early China," *T'oung Pao* 89 (2003): 59–99; Kidder Smith, "Sima Tan and the Invention of Daoism, 'Legalism,' *et cetera*," *Journal of Asian Studies* 62.1 (2003): 129–56; and Sarah A. Queen, "Inventories of the Past: Rethinking the 'School' Affiliation of the *Huainanzi*," *Asia Major*, Third Series 14.1 (2001): 51–72.

13. *Shiji* 63.2146. Han Feizi's biography follows that of Laozi in the *Shiji*.

14. Harold Roth, "Some Methodological Issues in the Study of the Guodian Laozi Parallels," in *The Guodian Laozi—Proceedings of the International Conference, Dartmouth College, May 1998*, ed. Sarah Allan and Crispin Williams (Berkeley: Society for the Study of Early China and the Institute of East Asian Studies, University of California, 2000), 84.

However uncertain the category of Huang-Lao may be, it seems closely related to the so-called Jixia 稷下 academy established by King Wei of Qi (r. 357–320 BCE) by the gate to his capital. While this was not an academic institution in the modern sense of the term, it was a gathering place for many intellectuals and practitioners in the third century BCE. Most important, several teaching lineages that continued into the Han were defined as Huang-Lao. For example, the early Han lineage based around the Yue 樂 family, which was the most important lineage associated with the transmission of Huang-Lao practices during the Han, was linked to several leading politicians and scholars in Qin and Han.[15]

This Huang-Lao lineage may have been a fictive construction by Sima Qian who set up this tradition as a counterpoint to the decline of the moral authority of the Confucians.[16] Whatever the term Huang-Lao may have meant for Sima Tan and Sima Qian, it was soon accepted as referring to an actual way of practice. By the Eastern Han (first–second centuries CE) we find numerous references to practitioners of Huang-Lao. It seems likely that the term referred to a combination of esoteric practices. It carried religious overtones, as practitioners of Huang-Lao, including emperors, were also often described as antagonistic to local ecstatic cults, and particularly to the bloody rites and extravagant offerings they demanded.

For example, Emperor Huan, who had in 165 CE sponsored imperial rites to the deified Laozi, is described as "serving the Way of Huang-Lao and completely destroying all local shrines."[17] A second-century memorial by Xiang Kai 襄楷 criticizing the religious activities of emperor Huan also states that the deities revered were Huang-Lao and Buddha.[18] Huang-Lao

15. The biographies of the Yue clan are in *Shiji* 80. On the possible relationship of this family to the emerging Daoist lineages of the third century, see Gil Raz, "Creation of Tradition: The Five Numinous Treasure Talismans and the Formation of Early Daoism" (Ph.D. dissertation, Indiana University, 2004), 228–38.

16. Csikszentmihàlyi and Nylan, "Constructing Lineages and Inventing Traditions through Exemplary Figures in Early China," 23–30.

17. *Houhan shu* 76.2470; see also *Houhan shu* 7.314. Of the four variant descriptions of this ritual, two refer to the deity Huang-Lao as an object of reverence: (1) *Houhan shu* 7.313, 316 and *Houhan ji* 22.12a refer to Laozi; (2) *Dongguan Hanji* 3.1.31 and *Houhan shu* 7 refer to Huanglao; (3) *Houhan shu* 7.320 refers to Buddha and Laozi; (4) *Houhan shu* 60 refers to Buddha and Huanglao. See, Anna Seidel, *La Divinisation de Lao Tseu dans le Taoisme des Han* (Paris: EFEO, 1969), 48.

18. *Houhan shu* 30B.1082. Doubt has been cast on the authenticity of this memorial by Jens Østergård Petersen, "The Early Traditions Relating to Han Dynasty Transmission of the Tai ping jing," *Acta Orientalia* 50 (1989): 131–51.

and Buddha are linked together even earlier, in what is currently the earliest historical reference to Buddhism in China. In a report dating to 66 CE, the King of Chu, Liu Ying 劉英, is said to have "cherished the teachings of Huang-Lao and performed fasting and sacrifice to the Buddha" at his capital Pengcheng.[19] Reports of practitioners of esoteric arts as well as literati reveal a wide adherence to Huang-Lao, without specifying the referent or content of such a statement. Zhang Jue, the leader of the Way of Great Peace, is said to have revered the Way of Huang-Lao, taught his followers to kneel and confess their transgressions, and effectively healed the sick with talismanic water.[20]

To summarize, while a text entitled *Daode jing* clearly existed by the end of the third century BCE and may have already been associated with an author named Laozi, it is only in the early second century CE that this text was codified and the biography of its author developed. However, Sima Qian, the author of the first biography of Laozi, admits that there is little factual basis for the narratives collected in the biography. Nevertheless, Sima Qian and Sima Tan appear to have adhered to certain traditions which they labeled *daojia* and Huang-Lao, both of which are closely related to the emerging tradition of Daoism. While the social reality these labels are supposed to reflect is difficult to comprehend based on the evidence, it is nonetheless clear that during the four centuries of the Han the figure of Laozi was transformed from a mysterious ancient philosopher to an increasingly mythical figure. This transformation was completed during the second century CE, as Laozi was now perceived as a cosmic figure, equivalent to the *dao* itself.

## *Deification, or Dao-ification, of Laozi in the Late Han Dynasty*

The next stage in the developments we are tracing occurred in the second half of the second century CE and is closely related to the apparent decline of the Han dynasty and a growing sense of eschatological dread. It is in

19. *Houhan shu* 42.1428.

20. *Houhan shu* 71.2299. This movement is also known as the Yellow Turbans. For the religious practices of this community and their relationship with the Celestial Masters, see Howard Levy, "Yellow Turban Religion and Rebellion at the End of Han," *Journal of the American Oriental Society* 76 (1956): 214–27; Paul Michaud, "The Yellow Turbans," *Monumenta Serica* 17 (1958): 47–127; and Ōfuchi Ninji 大淵忍爾, *Shoki no Dōkyō* 初期の道教 (Tokyo: Sōbunsha, 1991), 13–35, 77–133.

this context of cosmological, political, and religious tension that we find the appearance of radically new religious movements, and among these new communities the religion we call Daoism developed. The best known of these new religious communities is the Way of the Celestial Master (*Tianshi dao* 天師道), and despite evident vicissitudes and changes it remains a living tradition today. The current sixty-fifth Celestial Master is based in Taiwan, while a "stand-in" Celestial Master is based in Longhu shan (Dragon-Tiger Mountain) in Jiangsu province, the base of the Celestial Master lineage since the seventh century.[21] The origins of this community are traced within its own scriptures to the revelation of a divine form of Laozi, called Most High Lord Lao (*Taishang laojun*), given to Zhang Daoling in 142 CE on Mt. Heming in Sichuan.

The significance of this revelation needs to be understood within the context of a religious change during the Latter Han which reflected a new perception of the ancient quest for transcendence, that is, of attaining physical unity with the *dao* and thus transcending the limits of mundane time and space. This change led to the rise of new cultic sites centered on individual practitioners who had attained transcendence. These sites became cultic centers, which were distinct from the traditional shrines and temples to local gods. These new sites were dedicated to individuals whose escape from the mundane world paradoxically made them foci for succor and beneficence for local communities. Many of these sites, including the cult to Laozi, were designated and supported by the imperial court. Laozi, however, was not unique in having attained the *dao*.

Alongside the Celestial Master documents discussed below, two documents, that are almost contemporary with Lord Lao's revelation to Zhang Ling, show that there was general acceptance of Laozi's identification with the *dao* extending from the imperial court to the lowest classes on the margins of the empire. The former is exemplified by the Imperial Inscription to Laozi erected in 165 CE by Han Emperor Huan, while the latter is exemplified by the *Scripture on Transformations of Laozi* (*Laozi bianhua jing* 老子變化經).[22] The latter document is the sole record of a Daoist community contemporary with the Celestial Master community,

21. This division within the current Celestial Master lineage is due to the political situation following the Communist revolution in China.

22. *Laozi bianhua* jing, Dunhuang manuscript S. 2295; published in Ōfuchi Ninji 大淵忍爾, *Tōnko dōkyō* 敦煌道經; 2 vols. (Tokyo: Fukubu shoten, 1978), 1:324, 2:686; *Zhonghua daozang* 中華道藏, vol. 8 (Beijing: Huaxia chubanshe, 2004), 181. See Raz, *Emergence of Daoism*, 26–32.

which is otherwise unknown. It presents Laozi as coeval and identical with the *dao*: "sometime existent and sometime absent, he is prior [to all things]; and when formed is human." Laozi thus participates in the cosmogonic process. Laozi, in fact, is not a mundane human but a manifestation of the *dao*, who "borrowed physical form in mother Li, and within her womb transformed his body" (line 6). After listing nine alternative names and forms of Laozi (lines 30–38), the text continues by listing several manifestations of Laozi in which he appeared in different bodies and names to serve as counselor to sage rulers, beginning with the Three Sovereigns and Five Emperors of ancient myth and extending forward in time to the Han. Most important, the text then claims a recent set of manifestations occurring between 132 on Mt. Pianjue Ming and 155 on Mt. Bailu. A final transformation will occur thirty years after the manifestation on Mt. Bailu where, it is claimed, a temple will be erected, and Laozi will become a Celestial Preceptor 天傅. The repeated appearances of Laozi in different bodies and the repetition of the phrase "after death I live again" seem to imply that leaders of this group claimed to be actual manifestations of Laozi, who inhabits their physical bodies. The external form of the individual leader was thus unimportant. Most significant is the political message of this text, which reflects the eschatological dread of the period. Laozi, having personally "initiated the offices of the Han, by changing form" (line 76) will now personally "turn the cycle and smash the Han regime." He will choose the "good people" who will be saved from the coming calamities.

It is precisely this type of eschatology, claiming the imminent end of the cosmic cycle embodied by Han and salvific expectations of a savior who will deliver his selected people from the coming catastrophe, that link this text with both the Daoist texts of the following centuries and with the Imperial Inscription erected in 165 CE at Ku in Chen county, identified as Laozi's birthplace since Sima Qian's time, at the behest of Han Emperor Huan 桓 (r. 147–167) to commemorate imperially sponsored rites to Laozi held at Ku and at the Imperial court.[23] The inscription begins by recapitulating Laozi's human biography as it had become accepted in the Han, elaborating on the narratives already mentioned by Sima Qian. To be sure, the reader encounters a numinous figure. However, whatever mythical, remote, and extra-human elements this inscription contains, its portrayal of Laozi remains that of a

23. *Houhan shu* 7.316, 324; cf. Seidel, *Divinisation de Lao Tseu*, 122–28. The inscription is translated in Csikszentmihàlyi, *Readings in Han Chinese Thought*, 105–12.

successful adept, and not a divine entity distinct from humanity. In fact, this description of Laozi does not provide a more divine image than the hagiographic portrayals of other adepts who had attained transcendence. Moreover, the practices by which Laozi attained unity with the *dao* are similar to practices mentioned in other contemporary biographies and inscriptions. The final lines of the inscription refer once more to Laozi's practices:

Unifying his radiance with sun and moon, merging with the five planets,
Entering and exiting the Cinnabar Furnace,
ascending and descending from the Yellow Court,
Turning away and abandoning popular vulgar customs,
He conceals his effulgent spirits and hides his form,
Embracing the primordial, his spirits are transformed,
He inhales and exhales the ultimate pneumas.

The emphasis here is on the accomplishment of perfection through practice. Some of these practices, or very similar variants, are found in several Daoist texts. Phrases referring to unifying and merging with the sun and moon and the stars are not metaphoric, nor are they references to divine qualities. Rather, these are references to meditative practices by which adepts absorbed the solar, lunar, and astral essences.

The representation of Laozi in the Imperial Inscription contrasts sharply with the image of Laozi presented in the nearly contemporaneous *Scripture on the Transformations of Laozi*, which describes Laozi as the physical manifestation of the *dao* descending in human form to the world. The Imperial Inscription stresses the humanity of Laozi and emphasizes the practices by which he attained perfection and ascended to the *dao*. This is not surprising in that the Inscription presents the imperial view of Laozi, a vision of an adept of superior quality and attainment, whom the emperor claims as a model for his own personal practice. The emperor's motivation is described in the inscription:

The Imperial Highness, revering Virtue and exalting the Way,
Ingesting the vast radiance, contemplating his spirits and nourishing his form,
He set his intention on ascending to the clouds.

He therefore fixed his mind on the Yellow Emperor and matched tallies with the High Ancestor.
Seeing Laozi in his dream he revered and offered him worship.

While we may see Emperor Huan simply as a sincere seeker of transcendence requesting further instruction in the practices he has already begun to follow, we must also interpret the Imperial Inscription within the larger context of Laozi cults. The insistence on the humanity of Laozi who ascended to the *dao* by the very practices now followed by the emperor, should be seen as counteracting potentially rebellious ideas, such as the messianic message of the *Scripture on the Transformations of Laozi.* As we turn to the depictions of Lord Lao in the texts of the Way of the Celestial Master, we will see that while Lord Lao is a physical manifestation of the *dao,* he does not dwell within the body of the Celestial Master. And rather than calling for rebellion, the Celestial Master always seeks to emulate Laozi's example and become counselor to a sage ruler.

## *Way of the Celestial Master*

Most scholars today agree that the social history of the religious community we call Daoism began with the community of the Celestial Master. While the texts of this community date the origins of the community to the revelation of Lord Lao to Zhang Ling, historical references to the early community reveal a far more complex historical development.[24] The historical origins of the community remain somewhat unclear, but the centrality of Laozi to this new communal religion is undisputed. The actual sociohistorical developments are of less relevance to the concerns of this essay than the image of the community, and especially of Lord Lao, presented in its canonic texts.

At the core of this new community was a set of practices and beliefs that marked it as a harbinger of a new type of religion. These practices and ideas remain central to Daoism and thus help in defining Daoism as a wholly new, even revolutionary, religion in medieval China. Several of these new notions were shared by other contemporary communities of practice, such as the Great Peace (*Taiping*) movement, indicating that the second half of the second century was a crucial period in the history of Chinese religion.

---

24. For details, see Raz, *Emergence of Daoism,* 22–25.

First, this community explicitly rejected sacrificial rites, which were the core ritual practices in both the imperial ritual system and the ancestral cult. Second, the community thus rejected the traditional pantheon as flesh-eating, blood-drinking demons. Instead, the community instituted a new pantheon of deities that were perceived as pure emanations of the *dao*, arrayed in a bureaucracy modeled on an idealized imperial bureaucracy that extended into the heaven, the earth, and the waters. These could only be approached through the ritualized presentation of petitions, which combined meditative visualization techniques with the codified, bureaucratic imagination. The Celestial Master community redefined *dao* as an ethical and moral entity, which manifests in form as Lord Lao, who promulgated a set of ethical and moral standards. Adherence to these standards determined health and illness. Illness was thus defined not as a physical ailment that could be treated by traditional medical procedures but as a moral offense against the *dao* that could only be treated by religious means, beginning with confession of sins and ingestion of talismanic water imbued with ashes of burnt amulets, and the presentation of petitions. All these religious codes, communal structure, and rituals were considered to be revelations transmitted by the Most High Lord Lao.[25]

Among the main rites of the community was a communal recitation of the *Daode jing*. The earliest extant texts of this community include a commentary to the *Daode jing* entitled *Xiang'er Commentary to the Laozi*, which reveals something of how the Celestial Master community understood the ancient classic and its author:

> The One disperses its form as pneuma and gathers its form as the Most High Lord Lao, whose permanent rule is on Mount Kunlun. . . . Now that the precepts of the *dao* are spread abroad to instruct people, those who keep the precepts and do not transgress them have maintained unity. Those who do not practice the precepts will lose this Unity.[26]

---

25. Terry Kleeman, "Daoism in the Third Century," in *Purposes, Means and Convictions in Daoism: A Berlin Symposium*, ed. Florian C. Reiter (Wiesbaden: Harrassowitz Verlag, 2007), 11–28; Terry Kleeman, "Community and Daily Life in the Early Daoist Church," in *Early Chinese Religion, Part 2: The Period of Division (220–589)*, ed. John Lagerwey and Lü Pengzhi (Leiden: Brill, 2010), 395–436.

26. The translation is that of Stephen Bokenkamp, *Early Daoist Scriptures* (Berkeley: University of California Press, 1997), 89.

Here the unitary *dao* is described as having two complementary aspects, formless and formed. In the former, the *dao* is simply *qi*; in the latter, the *dao* is Lord Lao. The passage continues by shifting the discourse from the abstract cosmology of the *dao* to the mundane set of religious injunctions, the precepts of the *dao*, by which the members of the community are to regulate their lives. Keeping the precepts is equated with maintaining unity, that is, preserving the original integrity of the psycho-physical components of the human person. Death is defined as the loss of this unity. Adherence to the precepts thus ensures continued health in this life. Moreover, this was also a salvific promise, as maintaining unity ensured a resumption of life as "chosen people" after the rest of humanity would perish in the imminent catastrophe.[27]

The oblique references in the *Xiang'er Commentary* are developed into a coherent history of the community presented in *Commands and Admonitions for the Families of the Great dao* (*Dadao jia lingjie* 大道家令戒 年), another of the earliest texts of the Celestial Master community.[28] Composed in 255 CE, this text is in the voice of Zhang Lu, the third Celestial Master, and describes the history of the community, beginning with the formless *dao* itself.[29] Recapitulating some of the earlier narratives discussed above, this text also mentions the descent of the *dao* in human from "to act the teacher of the thearchical kings, but they were unable to revere and serve it."[30] All human misery and history is in fact due to "loss of faith with the *dao*." The text then shifts to more recent history, recounting—albeit not quite accurate historically—a series of revelations and transmissions of the teachings of the *dao*. The first instance is transmission of the *dao* of Great Peace upon the sage Gan Ji at the end of the Zhou.[31] The next instance is the *dao* itself "born through transformation" and transmitting the text of the Five Thousand Characters (*Daode jing*) at the western pass. This is of course a retelling of the ancient narrative of Laozi, who is now said to be an incarnation of the *dao*. Next, we are told of the *dao* going

27. Bokenkamp, *Early Daoist Scriptures*, 102, 135.

28. *Zhengyi fawen tianshi jiaojie kejing* 正一法文天師教戒科經 DZ 789.

29. On the dating of the text, Zhang Lu's death, and the significance of the revelatory voice, see Bokenkamp, *Early Daoist Scriptures*, 150–54.

30. Bokenkamp, *Early Daoist Scriptures*, 168.

31. On the complex mythology associated with the *dao* of Great Peace, see Grégoire Espesset, "Editing and Translating the Taiping Jing and the Great Peace Textual Corpus," *Journal of Chinese Studies* 48 (2008): 469–86.

west and teaching the "barbarians." In this teaching, the prohibitions were "extremely severe," including celibacy, absolute non-violence, and vegetarianism.[32] This is an allusion to Buddhism or, more precisely, to the medieval notion of "conversion of the barbarians," in which Buddhism was seen as a teaching by Laozi fit only for the barbarians but not for the Chinese. None of these teachings were followed correctly by humanity, and so the *dao* reappeared as Lord Lao and bestowed the Way of Covenantal Authority of Correct Unity (*zhengyi mengwei* 正一盟威) upon Zhang Daoling, the first Celestial Master.[33]

The most interesting aspect of this narrative is that Daoism is here perceived as an eternal teaching emanating from the *dao*, which intervenes in human history by appearing in successive human forms and bestowing particular teachings suitable for specific historical moments and people. The teaching of the Celestial Master, or the Way of Correct Unity, is thus the most recent, most appropriate, and truest teaching.[34] However, all other teachings, including Buddhism, are subsumed within the larger category of the *dao*. Laozi, the transmitter of the *Daode jing*, is seen as a specific manifestation of the *dao* but is superseded by the Newly Appeared Lord Lao. While scholars may explain Lord Lao as a further development in the changing imagination of Laozi, from the perspective of the Celestial Master community Lord Lao is a distinct manifestation of the *dao*, much greater in status and providing a much higher teaching.

During the waning years of the Han dynasty, as the imperial power declined following the Great Rebellion of 184 CE, the Celestial Master community managed to establish itself in the Hanzhong region on the border of modern Sichuan and Shanxi provinces where it conducted itself in accord to the communal guidelines for thirty years under the leadership of Zhang Lu, the third Celestial Master. This era was idealized in later writings. The Celestial Master community, numbering in the tens of thousands, was moved from Hanzhong and resettled in the region near the capitals Loyang and Chang'an, and further north in Ye. The establishment of the Wei dynasty ushered in the era of the Three Kingdoms (220–265), and the Celestial Master community extended its full support

---

32. Bokenkamp, *Early Daoist Scriptures*, 169–70.

33. Bokenkamp, *Early Daoist Scriptures*, 171.

34. *Zhengyi*, sometimes rendered as "Orthodox One," is one of the preferred names used by the community to describe itself.

to the Wei as explicitly stated in the *Commands and Admonitions for the Families of the Great dao*.[35] In the following decades the religion of the Celestial Master community spread through the north and was adopted by many of the elite families of society. Despite this seeming social success, the cohesion of the original community was broken, as the supremacy of the Zhang family was eclipsed, and several lineages of Celestial Master priests competed for royal and social support.

## The Perfect Scriptures of the Numinous Treasure

The social and political turmoil that accompanied the decline and collapse of the Han continued into the era of the Three Kingdoms as internecine warfare continued for the next few centuries.[36] For a very brief time, the realm was reunited under the Western Jin dynasty (265–317), which also soon collapsed due to internal conflicts and military pressure from nomadic peoples. North China was finally conquered in 317, causing the Jin court accompanied by hundreds of thousands of refugees to flee south, where it established the Eastern Jin (317–420). The succeeding two centuries are known as the era of the Northern and Southern dynasties, in which north China was ruled by a succession of non-Chinese regimes, while the southern coastal region was ruled by successive Chinese dynasties. This era ended with the reunification of the realm by the Sui dynasty in 589.

Alongside the changes caused by the arrival of the Jin court and its attendants in the south, there were also critical developments in the history of Daoism. As elsewhere in China, the southern coastal region had its own religious traditions. Many of these practices overlapped with the mantic, mediumistic, healing, and exorcistic traditions from which the Celestial Master tradition adopted its practices. Moreover, the southern traditions were focused on the quest for transcendence and shared many of the philosophical underpinnings of the Celestial Master tradition. Unlike the Celestial Master community, however, the southern traditions seem to have been focused on individual attainment. The social and political competition between the northern émigré who dominated the Eastern Jin court and the local elite was soon translated into the spiritual

35. Bokenkamp, *Early Daoist Scriptures*, 180.

36. Mark Edward Lewis, *China between Empires: The Northern and Southern Dynasties* (Cambridge, MA: Harvard University Press, Belknap Press, 2011), 31–53.

realm, where the libationers who came with their northern patrons competed with the local adepts and practitioners for support and patronage. This spiritual contestation led to the emergence of the way of Supreme Clarity (*Shangqing* 上清).[37] The texts and practices of this lineage were revealed to Yang Xi 楊羲 (330–386), a medium in the service of the Xu family, a family of the old southern elite. These revelations for the most part occurred in the Xu family compound on Mt. Mao; hence this tradition is also known as Maoshan Daoism. The *Shangqing* texts were revealed to Yang Xi by several "Perfected" practitioners who have ascended to the highest celestial realms far beyond the attainment imagined by the Celestial Master community. These texts exhibit a complex response to the challenge posed by the texts and practices of the Celestial Master tradition. Rather than simply rejecting these practices, the *Shangqing* texts absorb these practices and assert their own supremacy.

Laozi does not play an important part in these revelations, as he is considered to represent a lower level of practice. We can observe this strategy in two biographical accounts that circulated among the *Shangqing* practitioners.[38] The first is from the biography of Hua Qiao, a medium who served the Xu family before Yang Xi. The biography begins by stating that the Hua family had for generations served the profane gods. Hua Qiao was highly susceptible to possession and often dreamed that he traveled and feasted with the spirits, dreams so vivid that he would wake up drunk and vomit. For several years the spirits demanded that Qiao recommend talented people to serve at the infernal bureaus. Qiao recommended more than ten people, all of whom died. When Qiao feared that he himself would become a target, he turned his back on the vulgar gods and "enter[ed] the *dao*." He approached the local libationer, who initiated him into Celestial Master Daoism. The offending spirits soon stopped bothering him. After a few years of following Celestial Master practice, he began receiving visitations from two celestial beings, who introduced him to new teachings.

The text is important for what it reveals about the various traditions competing for support in south China at the time, and how the Shangqing revelation co-opts and suborns these traditions within their own teachings. We see at first a complete rejection of local religion, here described

37. Michel Strickmann, "The Mao Shan Revelations—Taoism and the Aristocracy," *T'oung Pao* 63 (1977): 1–64.

38. *Ziyang zhenren neizhuan* 紫陽真人內傳 DZ 303: 18a5–10.

as causing demonic possession and death. Hua Qiao turns to the local libationer who is a Celestial Master priest. Initiation into the Way of the Celestial Master suffices to stop the demonic incursions. However, Hua Qiao soon receives new revelations from two Perfected men, described as extraordinary in appearance. These two men, Zhou and Pei, visit him repeatedly and yet are never seen or heard by anyone else. These two Perfected reveal esoteric teachings that are said to match and supersede the *Daode jing* and the precepts of the Daoists—probably referring to the Celestial Master tradition—as well as the arcane teachings of the Han mantic arts.

We see a similar strategy in the biography of Wei Huacun, the female libationer who thirty years after her death became the main instructor of Yang Xi. Lady Wei was born in north China to an elite family and was swept up in the great migration south following the conquest of the north.

> In her youth she read Lao-Zhuang and set her intention on transcendence. Her practices included ingesting sesame power and *fuling* pills and breath control. She wanted to live in seclusion, but her parents refused and when she was twenty-four they forcibly married her off to Liu Wen of Nanyang, clerk at the Grand Guardian office.

Huacun soon bore her husband two sons, thus fulfilling her social function. When they reached maturity, she was free to turn to her solitary cultivation practice. After three months she was visited by five Perfected persons who began a program of teaching and transmission of practices and texts. These Perfected visited her daily, and yet her husband never saw or heard a thing. After moving south, her experiences intensified, until finally when she was eighty-three, one of the Perfected presented her with two elixirs. Having taken these elixirs, "after seven days a whirlwind chariot descended to carry her up. She transformed her body by 'borrowing' a sword and departed."

Having died in the mortal realm, Wei Huacun now embarked on an even more profound course of teachings under the tutelage of the Perfected, including Zhang Daoling, who transmitted to her various instructions. After sixteen additional years of training and study she ascended to the highest court of the supreme purity heaven where she received the title Original Creator of the Purple Void and appointed as superior perfected

Director of Destinies.[39] It is from this lofty post that she descended to Yang Xi, to present him with the *Shangqing* teachings.

This biography shows that the *Shangqing* revelations placed the ancient texts of Laozi and Zhuangzi at the lowest level of teachings. In this case they mark Wei Huacun's precocious interest in seeking transcendence. While many of the various Perfected encountered by Wei Huacun, as well as Hua Qiao, are adopted from earlier mythologies and narratives, they do not include Laozi or Zhuangzi. On the other hand, among the eschatological scriptures of the *Shangqing* revelations we find the *Annals of the Lord of dao, Sage of the Latter Heavens of Shangqing*, which is a hagiography of a savior figure named Lord Li, who represents a complex reworking of the mythology of Lord Lao of the Celestial Master tradition.[40] The Shangqing scriptures reveal a Daoist tradition that did not trace its origin to Laozi and which placed the Celestial Master teachings at a preliminary stage of studying the *dao*.

About a generation after the *Shangqing* revelations, a new set of revelations appeared in the same southern region and among the same group of elite families. The scriptures transmitted in these revelations are known as Numinous Treasure (*Lingbao* 靈寶). These are the Perfect Scriptures mentioned in the essay "Origins of Daoism" from which the epigraph at the beginning of this chapter was taken. Although they appeared in the early fifth century, the *Lingbao* scriptures claimed to have been revealed on earth about two centuries earlier, and thus earlier than the *Shangqing* scriptures. The *Lingbao* scriptures, moreover, describe their own history as coeval with the cosmos itself. They claim to have originated at the very separation of the primordial *dao* and to have emanated as cloudlike graphs composed of the primordial *qi*, before the appearance of heaven and earth.[41] The mundane *Lingbao* scriptures that appeared in the human realm are perceived as transcriptions, or traces of the primordial graphs. Rather than referring to the mundane *Lingbao* scriptures, "Origins of Daoism" is referring to the primordial Perfect Scriptures, which of course

39. *Taiping guangji* 太平廣記 58.380–386; cf. Edward Schafer, "The Restoration of the Shrine of Wei Hua-ts'un at Lin-ch'uan in the Eighth Century," *Journal of Oriental Studies* 15 (1977): 24–137.

40. See Bokenkamp, *Early Daoist Scriptures*, 339–62.

41. These graphs are akin to written Chinese characters but in a more ethereal form. On the complex cosmological descriptions in the *Lingbao* scriptures, see Raz, *Emergence of Daoism*, 152–69.

placed them far earlier than any other teaching. The cosmogonic function of the Perfected scriptures can be explained by the developing cosmology associated with talismans, scripts, and texts, but claims to temporal antecedence were also motivated by the continuing debates among the various Daoist lineages regarding their primacy. The *Lingbao* scriptures, however, were also asserting their primacy against the Buddhist tradition.

The *Lingbao* scriptures are known for incorporating Buddhist cosmology, practice, and discourse such as the notion of "universal salvation." Large sections of the *Lingbao* scriptures, furthermore, were directly copied from Buddhist sutras.[42] Yet it is important to understand that this incorporation of Buddhist elements was motivated by a rejection of Buddhism as foreign to China. The *Lingbao* authors thus realized the popularity of specific Buddhist notions but rejected the Buddhist institutional presence and sought to replace it with their own Buddho-Daoist synthesis.[43] Laozi appears in the cosmological speculations developed in these texts, often in reformulations that are complex interweavings of narratives about the Buddha with the earlier narratives about Laozi described above.

Most important for our purposes is that there are two basic transmission narratives in the *Lingbao* scriptures. The fifth-century catalogue of the *Lingbao* scriptures, compiled by Lu Xiujing 陸修靜 in 437, divides them into two groups.[44] The first group is defined as "ancient scriptures of the Celestial Worthy," while the second group is described as "new scriptures that provide precepts, essential instructions, and explanations for correct practice that had been received by Transcendent Duke Ge."[45] The former group of texts is heavily indebted to Buddhist cosmology while the latter group is clearly based on Celestial Master material. The Celestial Worthy is the highest deity in the Lingbao pantheon, the first of the three Pure Ones that emerged from the primordial *dao*. The Celestial

42. Erik Zürcher, "Buddhist Influence on Early Taoism: A Survey of Scriptural Evidence," *T'oung Pao* 66 (1980): 84–147.

43. Stephen Bokenkamp, "The Silkworm and the Bodhi Tree: The Lingbao Attempt to Replace Buddhism in China and Our Attempt to Place Lingbao Taoism," in *Religion and Chinese Society*, ed. John Lagerwey, vol. 2 (Hong Kong: Chinese University Press, 2004), 317–39.

44. This catalogue survives as copied into Song Wenming's 宋文明 (fl. 549–551) *Tongmen lun* 通門論, also known as *Lingbao jing yishu* 靈寶經義疏, preserved as Dunhuang manuscripts P.2861B and 2556 (published in Ōfuchi, *Tonkō dōkyō*, 725–34; ZHDZ 5:509–18).

45. P.2861, ZHDZ 5:510b, 510c; Ōfuchi Ninji 大淵忍爾, "On Ku *Ling-pao-ching*," *Acta Asiatica* 27 (1974): 33–56.

Worthy is thus a timeless entity. Transcendent Duke Ge, on the other hand, is Ge Xuan (traditional dates 164–244), the grand-uncle of Ge Hong 葛洪 (283–343), the well-known compiler of books on the quest for transcendence. The putative author of the Lingbao scriptures was Ge Chaofu 葛巢甫, a grand-nephew of Ge Hong, who may have felt slighted by the low status accorded his ancestors in the *Shangqing* scriptures.[46] The two textual corpora are thus clearly associated with two distinct temporal moments. The significance of the distinctions between these two textual divisions has been the subject of debate.[47] Some have argued that these two textual groups were composed by two distinct lineages, or at different times. As the latter texts cite the former texts, however, it appears that a better explanation is to see the two textual units as a coherent scheme that presents the Celestial Worthy texts as the perfect, primordial scriptures whereas the second group is seen as the elaboration of the texts revealed on earth in the third century.

While Laozi does not have an important role in the transmission narratives of the Perfect Scriptures, he appears in the second group of texts, often along with Zhang Daoling. The teachings voiced by Laozi and Zhang Daoling in these texts, however, celebrate *Lingbao* teachings and repudiate the Celestial Master teachings. For example, the *Questions of Duke Transcendent,* one of the "new" *Lingbao* scriptures, states in the voice of Laozi:

> In studying the *dao*, nothing is prior to *zhai* 齋. Among *zhai,* none surpass the *Lingbao zhai*. Its methods are eminent and marvelous, and should not be revealed in the mundane realm. . . . In the past, when the Perfected of Orthodox Unity [Zhang Ling] studied the *dao* he received the *Lingbao zhai*. After his *dao* was complete, he said this *zhai* was the most eminent. . . . When one first begins to study, one is at the stage of the Small Vehicle. But one who reveres the profound scriptures of the Three Caverns is called a master of the Great Vehicle. First, he saves others, and later saves himself.[48]

46. For discussion, see Stephen Bokenkamp, "Sources of the Ling-pao Scriptures," in *Tantric and Taoist Studies in Honor of R.A. Stein*, ed. Michel Strickmann, 2 vols. (Bruxelles: Institut Belges des Hautes Études Chinoises, 1985), 2:434–86.

47. Raz, *Emergence of Daoism*, 216–19.

48. *Xiangong qingwen* 仙公請問, in *Taishang dongxuan lingbao benxing suyuan jing* DZ 1114.5a6a.

This passage is remarkable for borrowing the Buddhist terms "Small Vehicle" and "Great Vehicle" to refer respectively to Celestial Master and *Lingbao* Daoism. The final line calling for saving others also resonates with the Mahayana doctrines of universal salvation, which inform the *Lingbao* scriptures. The term *zhai* refers to the ritual system developed in the *Lingbao* scriptures, which remains the basis of Daoist ritual to the present day.[49] Zhang Daoling, the first Celestial Master, is here extolling the *Lingbao zhai*. The phrase "Three Caverns" is a key term for understanding the growing sense of identity among the various Daoist lineages active in the fifth century. The *Lingbao* scriptures include a few different listings of the Three Caverns, but in all cases the phrase refers to a tripartite collection of texts composed of *Lingbao* and *Shangqing* scriptures, and a third set of texts named Three Sovereigns (*Sanhuang*) consisting of older mantic, exorcistic, divinatory, and technical texts belonging to the local southern tradition. Most important, the Three Caverns did not include the Celestial Master texts. The *Lingbao* scriptures thus presented themselves as the ultimate teaching, displacing both Buddhism and Celestial Master Daoism. The first compilation of Daoist texts that we may call a Daoist canon—the *Catalogue of the Three Caverns*, completed by Lu Xiujing in 471—excluded the Celestial Master texts.[50]

The notion of the Three Caverns developed in the *Lingbao* scriptures was thus a vision of a universal religion, yet uniquely suitable for China. Contemporary adherents of the Celestial Master community were of course unhappy with these developments and soon responded with new texts and canonic formulations. It is within this context that the term *daojiao* was first introduced in Celestial Master texts to distinguish their own tradition from *Lingbao*, or Three Caverns, Daoism. By the end of the fifth century, however, as more texts composed by adherents from both the Celestial Master tradition and the Three Caverns continued to integrate the various Daoist traditions, the term *daojiao* (or *daojia*) came to be applied to the tradition as a whole, especially when opposed to Buddhism (*fojiao*). Nevertheless, different Daoist lineages perceived the history and

---

49. Lü Pengzhi, "Daoist Rituals," in *Early Chinese Religion: Part 2, The Period of Division (220–589)*, ed. John Lagerwey and Lü Pengzhi (Leiden: Brill, 2010), 1245–349.

50. This catalogue is not extant, except in later fragmentary citations. For Lu's catalogues, see Stephen Bokenkamp, "Buddhism, Lu Xiujing, and the First Daoist Canon," in *Culture and Power in the Reconstitution of the Chinese Realm, 200–600*, ed. Scott Pearce, Audrey Spiro, and Patricia Ebrey (Cambridge, MA: Harvard University Press, 2001), 181–99.

contours of Daoism in different ways. It is within this continuing context of internal contestation that we should place the full passage of the essay "Origins of Daoism" with which we began:

> In seeking the source of Daoist scriptures and declarations, we find they arose during the era of the three Primordials. In accord with their source, they sent down their traces, which formed the five virtues. Combining three and five, thus were formed the eight nodes. The graphs of the eight nodes were formed out of marvelous *qi*. . . . As for the currently circulating *Lingbao* scriptures, they were transmitted by the Celestial Perfected Luminary Person to Xuanyuan, the Yellow Thearch, on Mount E'mei. The Celestial Perfected Luminary Person also transmitted them to Di Ku at the tower of Mude. Yu of Xia caused their descent to Mount Zhong. King Helü stealthily viewed them at Juqu. Later, the likes of Ge Xiaoxian and the disciples of Zheng Siyuan transmitted it from master to disciple in an unbroken line. As for Laozi's *Daode jing*, it is a supplement to the texts of the great vehicle. It is a scripture of the four auxiliaries (*fu* 輔) and is not included in the teachings of the Three Caverns. The learning of contemporaries is mostly shallow. They only recite the Daode and do not know about the Perfected Scriptures, so they say Daoism arose from Zhuang Zhou and began with "Below the Pillar" (Laozi). . . . It is clear from the above that the scriptures of the Daoists are not limited to the Five-thousand (graphs, i.e., *Daode jing*) alone.[51]

This passage is clearly based on *Lingbao* cosmology, which perceived the emanation of the cosmos as a series of transformations of primordial talismanic scripts. This cosmology emphasized that the most eminent deity, the Celestial Worthy of Primordial Commencement, and the *Lingbao* scriptures appeared within the primordial *dao* prior to the manifested world. This time before time is here referred to as the Three Primordials, who are also identified as incomprehensibly ancient deities, each of whom transmitted the scriptures of one of the Three Caverns. Significantly, this passage uses the term "great vehicle" to label the texts of the Three Caverns, adopting the Chinese translation term for Mahayana as a category of

51. *Yunji qiqian* DZ 1032: 3.2b-4a.

superior texts, clearly contrasting them to the texts labeled "auxiliaries." The four auxiliaries are a canonic category introduced in the sixth century to include the texts of the Celestial Master tradition (*Zhengyi*), as well as the Great Peace (*Taiping*), alchemical texts (*Taiqing*), and *Daode jing* and its commentaries (*Taixuan*).

The transmission narrative in this text shifts from the primordial emanation of the Perfect Scriptures to the transmission of the *Lingbao* scriptures, which represent traces in the human realm of these Perfect Scriptures, in human history. The transmission begins with mythic sage rulers, the Yellow Thearch, Di Ku, and Yu in the ancient past. These mythic rulers secreted the scriptures, which were recovered and transmitted by the Transcendent Duke Ge (Ge Xiaoxian) and Zheng Siyuan. As these were the teachers of Ge Hong, the passage hints at the correct lineage of transmission. Finally, however, we are told that the lesser texts of the four auxiliary collections are all part of the expanded, integrated self-identification of Daoism.

## *Conclusion*

Our survey of the early history of Daoism shows that the category Daoism is extremely problematic. Whether we refer to the early texts of the *Daode jing* and *Zhuangzi* from the third century BCE or to the religion that emerged in a complex process beginning in the second century CE, we are faced with difficult questions of defining the terms of the category. Moreover, we find that Laozi, while a critical figure in all the various permutations of the category Daoism, cannot be considered a founder of the tradition. Permutations of the image of Laozi and changes in the category of Daoism are related but do not necessarily form a single historical process.

First, there is no community or specific social context that we can firmly associate with the *Daode jing*. Recent manuscript discoveries of the *Daode jing* have not only revealed a complex process of redaction for the text but have also raised further doubts about the very existence of Laozi as a historical figure. Second, from the earliest biographical notices of Laozi in the early Han it is evident that he was already viewed as an extraordinary figure, beyond the reach of ordinary men, and perhaps not actually a human at all. The vision of Laozi as identical to the *dao* was central to several of the Daoist movements that appear in the late Han, the

Celestial Master community in particular. Laozi was for them an early manifestation of the *dao*, who bestowed the *Daode jing* on humanity. The revelations upon which the Celestial Master based his communal organization and practice were transmitted from a more recent manifestation—that of Lord Lao who, although a development in the imagination of Laozi, was clearly perceived as a distinct figure. Later Daoist lineages and groups held diverse views of Laozi, Lord Lao, and various other reformulations of this elusive figure. Third, the development of the Daoist tradition consisted of several revelations—and probably many more of which we are no longer aware. Should we label any of the revelators, creators, or originators of these various lineages and groups the founder of Daoism?

The position of Laozi in the Daoist tradition is particularly ambiguous. At various times he was considered a humble philosopher of the *dao*, a successful adept of esoteric practice who attained the *dao*, an emanation of the *dao*, and a supreme deity who transmits teachings to the world. In the most developed narratives he is all of these things at once. By tracing debates about the identity of Laozi and his place within specific subtraditions we can see how different Daoist lineages distinguished and defined themselves in relationship to other lineages, and the emerging tradition as a whole. Moreover, in the religious landscape of traditional China where genealogical discourse was central to individual and social identity, debates about founders were critical both to creating identity and claiming status. As the mythical author of the ancient classic about the *dao* yet devoid of historicity, Laozi could thus be transformed and accepted as the embodiment of the *dao*.

## *For Further Reading*

Bokenkamp, Stephen R. *Early Daoist Scriptures*. Berkeley: University of California Press, 1997. Provides annotated translations and accessible introductions to six fundamental texts of early medieval Daoism.

Csikszentmihalyi, Mark, and Philip J. Ivanhoe, eds. *Religious and Philosophical Aspects of Laozi*. Albany: State University of New York Press, 1999. A collection of essays examining various key aspects of the Laozi literature.

Espesset, Grégoire. "Latter Han Religious Movements and the Early Daoist Church." In *Early Chinese Religion, Part One: Shang through Han (1250 BC–220 AD)*, edited by John Lagerwey and Marc Kalinowski, 1061–102. Leiden: Brill, 2010. A detailed essay on the religious history of the second century and the emergence of the early Daoist movements.

Kleeman, Terry. "Community and Daily Life in the Early Daoist Church." In *Early Chinese Religion, Part 2: The Period of Division (220–589)*, edited by John Lagerwey and Lü Pengzhi, 395–436. Leiden: Brill, 2010. A study of the early community of the Celestial Master, with close attention to ritual and social life.

Kohn, Livia. *God of the Dao: Lord Lao in History and Myth*. Ann Arbor: Center for Chinese Studies, University of Michigan, 1998. A study of the developing mythology of Laozi spanning the period from the Han to the thirteenth century.

Raz, Gil. *The Emergence of Daoism: Creation of Tradition*. London: Routledge, 2012. A study of the emergence of the Daoist communal religion between the second and sixth centuries.

Robinet, Isabelle. *Taoism: Growth of a Religion*. Translated by Phyllis Brooks. Stanford, CA: Stanford University Press, 1997. A history of Daoism from the classical era of Laozi and Zhuangzi to the fourteenth century.

Seidel, Anna. "Taoism: The Unofficial High Religion of China." *Taoist Resources* 7.2 (1997): 39–72. A brief but thorough analysis of the place of Daoism in Chinese social history.

# 5

# *Jesus, Paul, and the Birth of Christianity*

*Patrick Gray*

THE EARLIEST AVAILABLE sources indicate that followers of Jesus referred to themselves as "the saints" (Rom. 15:25; 1 Cor. 6:1–2; 14:33; Phil. 1:1) or "the Way" (Acts 9:2; 19:9, 23; 24:22). According to the author of the Acts of the Apostles, the label that becomes standard for the next two millennia originates in Antioch, where "the disciples were for the first time called Christians" (11:26). It may well be that outsiders coined the term and applied it pejoratively to members of the movement who, in turn, embraced it, as happened much later with other groups such as Methodists, Mormons, Pagans, Quakers, and Shakers. Whatever its genesis, the name "Christian" accurately reflects the fundamental link between the figure of Jesus Christ and the religion of which he is traditionally regarded as the founder.[1] The earliest non-Christian sources to mention Christianity draw this connection as well (e.g., Tacitus, *Annales* 15.44; Pliny, *Epistle* 10.96; Josephus, *Antiquities* 18.64).

Diversity within Christianity, as in most religions, is more palpable to insiders than to outsiders. Notwithstanding the differences to be found among the hundreds of millions of adherents over many centuries, one

1. "Christ" was not Jesus' family name. It is a title, from the Greek translation (*christos*) of the Hebrew title *messiah*, "the anointed one." Not long after his death, "Christ" begins to function as a name, either in combination with "Jesus" or by itself (e.g., Matt. 1:17; Mark 9:41; Acts 2:38; 8:12; 1 Cor. 1:2; 6:11; 1 Pet. 4:14). Unless otherwise noted, quotations from the New Testament are taken from the NRSV translation.

may safely venture the following generalization: a special regard for Jesus Christ is the tie that binds those who identify themselves as Christian. "Special regard" can, of course, denote a wide range of responses. Was Jesus God incarnate? Was he God's "only son" though not co-equal with God? Was he the one chosen by God to redeem the world by his death, after which he rose from the grave? Was he a perfect human being? Was he a great prophet, if not something more than a prophet? Was he a pre-eminent teacher of moral principles? Did he intend to start a new religion? Debate about the life and legacy of Jesus touches on far too many questions to be answered in a brief survey. To paraphrase one of his earliest admirers, "the world itself could not contain the books that would be written" in any effort to do justice to the subject (John 21:25). As it turns out, the task of articulating and adjudicating the various claims about Jesus as a founder cannot be neatly separated from broader historical, theological, and ideological questions that are raised in the earliest stages of Christian history but take on increased urgency during the Enlightenment. The aim of this chapter is to highlight what debates about Jesus suggest about the character of Christianity—in particular, its status as a "religion of the book" and shifting attitudes about the singularity of Jesus as a figure in history—and how these debates reflect as well as shape the cultural contexts in which they take place.

## *Jesus: Proclaimer and Proclaimed*

A preliminary question about Jesus's status as founder is one posed regularly with respect to figures such as Moses, Zoroaster, and Laozi: Did he exist, or does he belong exclusively to the realm of myth and legend? Under no customary definition of the term can Jesus be considered the founder of Christianity if he never lived. With the rise of the comparative study of myth and religion and the critical approaches to the Bible that emerge in the early modern period, the notion that Jesus never lived first enjoys currency in the nineteenth century.[2] Christian and non-Christian scholars alike now almost universally reject the "Christ myth" hypothesis.

---

2. Robert Van Voorst, *Jesus Outside the New Testament: An Introduction to the Ancient Evidence* (Grand Rapids, MI: Eerdmans, 2000), 6–16. The theory had its most prominent advocate in Bruno Bauer (1809–1892), a student of Hegel and teacher of Marx; cf. Shirley Jackson Case, *The Historicity of Jesus* (Chicago: University of Chicago Press, 1912), 35–40.

That Jesus did in fact walk the earth in the first century is no longer seriously doubted even by those who believe that very little about his life or death can be known with any certainty.[3]

While Jesus's historicity is a settled question, it is worth noting that there are understandings of the Christian faith for which his existence is, theoretically speaking, relatively inconsequential. Many Enlightenment thinkers admire Jesus for the service he provided humanity in exposing the errors of superstition, providing a rational expression of universal ethical principles, and setting an impeccable moral example for all to follow. Had Jesus never lived, however, the duty of the individual to lead a moral life would be no different. If Christianity is essentially a reiteration of timeless moral truths—a claim made explicit in Matthew Tindal's 1730 Deist manifesto *Christianity as Old as Creation: or the Gospel a Republication of the Religion of Nature*—then it makes little chronological sense to regard Jesus as its founder, however effective and articulate he may have been as a proponent of this religion. Liberal Protestant theologians in the nineteenth and early twentieth century likewise emphasize not anything special about who Jesus was or what his death may have accomplished but, rather, what he taught. Adolf von Harnack summarizes this body of teaching in his aptly titled *What Is Christianity?* Simply put, its essence consists of "the fatherhood of God, the brotherhood of man, and the infinite value of the human soul." Conspicuously absent is anything specific about Jesus, who demanded "no other belief in his person and no other attachments to it than is contained in the keeping of his commandments."[4]

---

3. Although it remains a fringe phenomenon, familiarity with the Christ myth theory has become much more widespread among the general public with the advent of the Internet.

4. A. von Harnack, *What Is Christianity?*, trans. T. B. Saunders, 2nd rev. ed. (New York: G. P. Putnam's Sons, 1908), 65. Harnack's father took issue with his famous son's presentation of the faith: "To name only the all-decisive main issue: whoever regards the fact of the resurrection as you do is in my eyes no longer a Christian theologian" (quoted in Agnes von Zahn-Harnack's biography, *Adolf von Harnack* [Berlin: de Gruyter, 1936], 143). A joke about the German-American theologian Paul Tillich pokes fun at this tendency to deemphasize the singular importance of Jesus for the life of faith. When archaeologists find the bones of Jesus in Jerusalem, a discovery that threatens to destroy the foundational belief in the resurrection, the pope calls Tillich for advice on how to deal with the inevitable crisis. After a long pause, Tillich responds, "So there really was a Jesus after all . . ." (cf. Michael Goulder, "Jesus, the Man of Universal Destiny," in *The Myth of God Incarnate*, ed. John Hick [Philadelphia: Westminster, 1977], 48).

Jesus is a great teacher of morality in traditional forms of Christianity, but his significance is a function of much more than his status as a teacher. He is the Lord, the only Son of God. In the words of the Nicene Creed,

> *Through him all things were made.*
> *For us and for our salvation*
> *he came down from heaven:*
> *by the power of the Holy Spirit*
> *he became incarnate from the Virgin Mary,*
> *and was made man.*
> *For our sake he was crucified under Pontius Pilate;*
> *he suffered death and was buried.*
> *On the third day he rose again*
> *in accordance with the Scriptures;*
> *he ascended into heaven*
> *and is seated at the right hand of the Father.*
> *He will come again in glory to judge the living and the dead,*
> *and his kingdom will have no end.*

Jesus plays many roles in this classic formulation of Christian belief. That of "founder" is not among them, nor is it mentioned in other creedal statements such as the Definition of Chalcedon (451), the Scots Confession (1560), the Anglican Thirty-Nine Articles of Religion (1563), the Second Helvetic Confession (1566), and the Westminster Confession of Faith (1646). Yet most Christians of most times and places would likely see nothing self-evidently problematic in regarding him as such.

The concept of a "founding" implies the beginning of something new and distinctive. Working backward from the present, today it is perfectly unremarkable to regard Judaism and Christianity as separate religions. Also uncontroversial is the observation that Christianity begins in the first century as a sect within Judaism. Jesus was Jewish, his earliest followers were all Jewish, and the system of beliefs that comes to be labeled Christianity is expressed primarily in categories derived from Jewish tradition. At some point in between, then, these two roads diverge. Where, when, and why they diverge; how sharply they diverge; whether the decision to part ways is mutual; what consequences follow from this parting—these questions are more complicated, and the answers inform any discussion of the sense(s) in which Christians, past and present, regard Jesus as the founder of Christianity.

Intentionally or not, Jesus acts as the catalyst for its founding. This much is clear from the letters of Paul. It is also clear from the canonical gospels, which were probably written a few decades after Paul is writing in the middle of the first century. Mark's Gospel, believed to be the first narrative account of Jesus's ministry, begins in a way that underscores the ambiguity of Jesus's role in the birth of Christianity. It opens, infelicitously, with a sentence fragment: "The beginning of the gospel of Jesus Christ, the Son of God" (1:1). "Gospel" (Greek: *euangellion*) means "good news" or an auspicious announcement. Grammatically, "the gospel of Jesus Christ" can mean either "the good news brought by Jesus Christ" or "the good news about Jesus Christ," but the author does not make clear which sense he intends to convey.[5] During his lifetime, Jesus proclaims good news that has to do with the arrival of the kingdom of God (Matt. 6:33; Mark 1:15; Luke 8:1; John 3:5). After his death, the proclaimer becomes the proclaimed as Jesus's followers spread the good news that he has been raised from the dead and that those who have faith in him can gain salvation (Matt. 28:18–20; John 20:31; Heb. 5:8–9).[6]

Some observers believe that this shift—with emphasis placed on Jesus himself rather than on God alone—constitutes a profound distortion of the message of the historical Jesus. Whether such a radical shift in fact takes place remains a contested question. Debates about the reliability of the sources, together with Jesus's occasional evasiveness, make it difficult to resolve all the questions about just who Jesus thought he was (see below). Whatever uncertainty may exist, the issue is a pivotal one. Bold claims about Jesus distinguish early Christianity from other sects within Judaism. Try as they might to highlight the continuity with the divine plan as revealed in the scriptures of Israel, his followers do not downplay the novelty of what they claim takes place in the person of Jesus. The accompanying disagreements ultimately prove too large to overcome, and the effective result is the birth of a new religion. Is this what Jesus anticipated, perhaps even desired? Or would he cry out in Prufrockian despair, "That is not what I meant at all"? If the latter, can he be considered the "accidental" founder of Christianity?

---

5. Only at a slightly later stage does "gospel" designate a literary genre with Jesus as its focus; see David E. Aune, *The New Testament in Its Literary Environment* (Philadelphia: Westminster, 1987), 17–19.

6. The phrase "the proclaimer became the proclaimed" originates with Rudolf Bultmann, *Theology of the New Testament*, trans. K. Grobel, 2 vols. (New York: Scribners, 1951–55), 1:33.

## *Canon, History, and Authority*

Jesus's intentions remain unclear because nothing he may have written has survived. Given the popularity of pseudonymous literature in Christian antiquity, it is surprising that only a single document, the Letter of Christ to Abgar mentioned by Eusebius (*Historia ecclesiastica* 1.13), is even alleged to be from the hand of Jesus. He is by no means unique among religious founders in this respect, though it is perhaps surprising given Christianity's status, along with Judaism and Islam, as a "religion of the book." In its formative stage, however, Christianity is not first founded on the New Testament writings since the movement that is later recognized as Christianity predates the New Testament and is described in its pages. To be sure, subsequent centuries of Christian history and thought are based in large part on interpretations of the New Testament, but to the extent that Christianity was founded on any book, it was on a particular way of reading the Hebrew Bible.[7] The early church adopts Jewish scripture as its own and rechristens it the Old Testament, a term first applied by Melito of Sardis in the mid-second century. Seminal interpretations of the Old Testament that define Christian teaching appear in the New Testament on the lips of Jesus (as a character in the gospels) and throughout the writings of his followers.[8]

The canon of texts regarded as authoritative by Christians is not the sum total of Jesus's legacy. The social institutions inhabited by those who worship him and the manifold cultural expressions of their belief are closely related to the Bible but cannot be reduced to biblical forms or "content" without remainder. Once a significant component of a founder's legacy assumes the form of a canonical collection of texts, there is no standard script for what happens next. Do the founder's teachings

---

7. On this process in the first century, see Donald Juel, *Messianic Exegesis: Christological Interpretation of the Old Testament in Early Christianity* (Philadelphia: Fortress, 1988); and Margaret M. Mitchell, *Paul, the Corinthians and the Birth of Christian Hermeneutics* (Cambridge: Cambridge University Press, 2010); and on the patristic period, James L. Kugel and Rowan A. Greer, *Early Biblical Interpretation* (Philadelphia: Westminster, 1986), 126–54; and John J. O'Keefe and R. R. Reno, *Sanctified Vision: An Introduction to Early Christian Interpretation of the Bible* (Baltimore: Johns Hopkins University Press, 2005), 24–44.

8. For example, in the Sermon on the Mount (Matt. 5:21–48) Jesus frequently quotes texts from Torah and proceeds to offer an original and authoritative reinterpretation ("You have heard that it was said . . . , but I say unto you"). Paul goes even further, suggesting that Jews who are not "in Christ" are like Moses with the veil over his face upon his descent from Sinai, keeping them from understanding it rightly (2 Cor. 3:12–16).

represent the final word on any moral or theological questions that may arise? May later followers exercise the same interpretive freedom with respect to Jesus's teachings as exercised by Jesus and the New Testament authors with respect to the Old Testament? Jesus himself appears to have issued few explicit instructions on how to manage such affairs.

What happens next is, properly speaking, a historical question. What ought to happen is a normative question belonging to the domain of theology, though historians frequently participate in the debate with as much zeal as do theologians. In practice, the line between description and prescription becomes blurred when the question is framed as a matter of fidelity to the founder's vision. One rarely finds Christians making the case that Jesus's teachings are irrelevant. Yes, it can be difficult to determine whether Jesus actually taught the doctrines attributed to him in the New Testament. Yes, they are occasionally obscure or even impossible to understand. Yes, they are sometimes difficult to put into practice. But it remains the near-universally shared assumption among Christians that Jesus's particular teachings as well as his wishes about the perpetuation of his teachings emphatically matter to the extent that they can be known, and they therefore deserve the most scrupulous attention. For this reason, how one construes fidelity to the founder and how one defines the "essence" or "core" of Christianity are closely correlated.

Concerns that Jesus may have been misinterpreted, misunderstood, or misappropriated have from time to time given rise to discussion of the relative standing of the New Testament canon vis-à-vis the historical realities to which its writings are the earliest witnesses. If the value of the canon rests on its historical reliability, it is asked, should the church adjust its teaching if it finds some other means of discovering or reconstructing that history? This question lies behind much Christian scholarship beginning in the early modern period.

An attempt to address such concerns is the implicit objective of what comes to be known as "the Quest for the Historical Jesus." Most Christians make no distinction between "Jesus" and "the historical Jesus" because they assume the figure one encounters in the gospels more or less corresponds to the flesh-and-blood man who lived and died nearly two thousand years ago. Only when apparent inconsistencies between the various accounts or the seeming incredibility of the claims made about Jesus are pointed out does the possibility of a disjunction occur. All agree that the gospel accounts are incomplete, a fact that does not scandalize the Christian who trusts in the reliability of the Bible. It is simply acknowledged that no biography can possibly give an exhaustive account of the thoughts and deeds of its subject; nor is an exhaustive account the purpose of the gospels.

But what if the authors of the gospels have made crucial omissions, not concerning such trivial matters as Jesus's physical appearance but on questions of greater consequence such as whether he intended to found a new religion? The desire to fill out the portrait of Jesus found in the New Testament as completely and as faithfully as possible is not easily dismissed as idle curiosity. This desire, coupled with the iconoclasm of the Enlightenment, gave birth to "the Quest," which takes its name from the seminal work of Albert Schweitzer.[9]

Schweitzer's aim is to review the various attempts made by European scholars to reconstruct the life of Jesus. He concludes that nearly every attempt is, in essence, an exercise in projection as "each successive epoch of theology found its own thoughts in Jesus," and indeed "each individual created Him in accordance with his own character."[10] Notwithstanding the many impressive results of these scholarly endeavors, Schweitzer's final judgment was that they revealed as much about the scholars as they did about Jesus: "There is no historical task which so reveals a man's true self as the writing of a Life of Jesus."[11] Lacking the resources for a proper biography, many are content with the proclamation of Jesus's first-century devotees for understanding the beginnings of Christianity. Rudolf Bultmann, a contemporary of Schweitzer and one of the leading New Testament scholars of the twentieth century, claims that it is difficult to know anything about Jesus's life or personality "since the early Christian sources show no interest in either."[12] According to Bultmann, moreover, Jesus is a part of the history of Judaism, not of the history of Christianity, which begins only after his death and the rise of the conviction among his followers that he was no longer among the dead.

---

9. Albert Schweitzer, *The Quest of the Historical Jesus: A Critical Study of Its Progress from Reimarus to Wrede*, trans. W. Montgomery (New York: Macmillan, 1968). It first appeared in German in 1906. The phrase "the historical Jesus" had been used at least twenty years earlier by British poet and Egyptologist Gerald Massey in his lectures on "The Historical Jesus and the Mythical Christ."

10. Schweitzer, *The Quest of the Historical Jesus*, 4.

11. Schweitzer, *The Quest of the Historical Jesus*, 4.

12. R. Bultmann, *Jesus and the Word*, trans. L. P. Smith and E. H. Lantero (New York: Charles Scribner's Sons, 1958), 8.

Not everyone agrees with Bultmann's characterization of the attitude of the early church nor with his assessment of Jesus's role in the founding of Christianity. Joachim Jeremias, for example, notes, "To anyone who is not aware of the controversy, the question whether the historical Jesus and his message have any significance for the Christian faith must sound absurd. No one in the ancient church, no one in the church of the Reformation period and of the two succeeding centuries thought of asking such a question."[13] This view emphasizes the fundamental continuity one sees in moving from Jesus to the birth of Christianity and later manifestations of the faith.

Others are less inclined to privilege the canonical gospels as a historically reliable source for Jesus's teachings or as a theologically normative guide for the Christian faith. Although it is unlikely that any of them were written as early as the canonical gospels, the "rediscovery" of several other gospels from the first four centuries—not all of them were ever technically "lost"—has generated considerable enthusiasm in some Christian circles. These include such documents as the *Gospel of Peter*, the *Gospel of Philip*, the *Secret Gospel of Mark*, the *Gospel of Mary*, the *Gospel of the Egyptians*, the *Gospel of the Nazareans*, and the Coptic *Gospel of Thomas*.[14] Discovered in Egypt in 1945, the *Gospel of Thomas* contains 114 randomly arranged aphorisms attributed to Jesus, more than half of which closely parallel sayings found also in the canonical gospels. It differs from the canonical gospels in that it does not take the form of a narrative and does not tell the story of Jesus's death and resurrection. Its appeal for many readers has to do with its purported value as evidence of an early form of Christianity for which Jesus's significance has little to do with his death and resurrection or identification of himself as God's son.[15] In this view, the form of Christianity closest to the founder is to be found in a "Jesus movement" that emphasized the socially subversive customs and especially the countercultural teachings of the earthly Jesus and regarded the death and resurrection as, at best, inconsequential. The Jesus of the *Gospel*

13. J. Jeremias, "The Present Position in the Controversy concerning the Problem of the Historical Jesus," *Expository Times* 69 (1957–58): 333.

14. English translations are available in Bart D. Ehrman, *Lost Scriptures: Books that Did Not Make It into the New Testament* (Oxford: Oxford University Press, 2003).

15. It is included alongside Matthew, Mark, Luke, and John in Robert W. Funk et al., *The Five Gospels: The Search for the Authentic Words of Jesus* (San Francisco: HarperCollins, 1993).

*of Thomas* "performs no physical miracles, reveals no fulfillment of prophecy, announces no apocalyptic kingdom about to disrupt the world order, and dies for no one's sins."[16]

Had this image of Jesus become normative, the subsequent development of Christianity would have traced a very different trajectory. Implicit in this as well as in the more traditional portrait of Jesus is the same notion that any claim to represent authentic Christian teaching and practice depends on fidelity to Jesus as founder. Proponents of traditional and non-traditional understandings of Jesus diverge, of course, in their beliefs about what he truly taught and practiced. They also propose different strategies to compensate for the inherent limitations of the canon in transmitting his legacy. One seeks to go around or behind the canon to reconstruct history "as it really happened" to serve as an alternative standard. The other is to treat scripture and church tradition as complementary and mutually illuminating rather than as independent or competing sources of authority, much as the Qur'an and the hadith function together in Islam. The complementary view aligns more closely with Orthodox and Catholic ways of framing the issue than with the classic Protestant position that "scripture alone" (*Sola scriptura*) is sufficient for understanding the significance of Jesus. Yet it long predates the Catholic-Protestant division that takes place at the Reformation, as second-century Christian writers like Irenaeus and Tertullian invoke the principle of apostolic succession, holding that the bishops ensure the reliability of the church's teachings because their lineage reaches in an uninterrupted line back to the apostles who, in turn, walked with Jesus. After the Reformation, furthermore, many Protestants recognize a legitimate role for extra-scriptural sources in confirming the truth of and about Jesus Christ and in providing the necessary context for understanding it. One quasi-formal acknowledgment of this principle is found in the so-called Wesleyan

---

16. Marvin Meyer, *The Gospel of Thomas: The Hidden Sayings of Jesus* (San Francisco: HarperCollins, 1992), 10. In his essay accompanying Meyer's translation, Harold Bloom puts it more pointedly: "Unlike the canonical gospels, that of Judas Thomas the Twin spares us the crucifixion, makes the resurrection unnecessary, and does not present us with a God named Jesus. No dogmas could be founded upon this sequence . . . of apothegms" (111). To deduce from the surviving form of *Thomas* or from the hypothesized collection of Jesus's sayings usually designated by scholars as "Q" (from the German *Quelle*, "source") that there were first-century Christian communities for whom Jesus's death and resurrection did not matter, however, is somewhat suspect. Such a conclusion assumes not only that these documents are reflective of the convictions of specific communities, but also that these communities never read any other writings about Jesus or believed anything about Jesus not explicitly included in *Thomas*.

Quadrilateral. Whereas scripture is primary, the other three "legs"—tradition, experience, and reason—also furnish critical support.

Catholics, Protestants, and the Orthodox can all degree that the shape of Christian faith and life is not exactly the same as in the first century even if Jesus is rightly regarded as the founder. John Henry Newman, drawing on the analogy of the emergence in adulthood of inherent traits not apparent during childhood, argues that change of some sort is to be expected in the history of a complex religious system built on divine revelation.[17] Disagreements arise when specific questions are considered on which Jesus makes no explicit pronouncements (because he never envisioned a given controversy) or where later church teaching or practice appears to differ from that of Jesus. When do later doctrines and customs in such areas as the trinity, the observance of special holy days or spiritual disciplines, the status of women, or veneration of Mary and the saints constitute illegitimate departures from or corruptions of the founder's vision, and when do they represent authentic development of elements already present in seed form but in no way visible at the founding? The former, according to Newman, are to be rejected while the latter are to be embraced. Would applying to Jesus the title of "founder" of a new religion be an instance of the former or the latter?

## *Jesus versus Paul?*

Newman does not directly address it, but this question attracts considerable attention when he is writing in the nineteenth century. "Development" often takes place gradually, organically, and impersonally, but sometimes it is anything but accidental or incidental, fostered instead by an active agent. The agent of development upon whom a wide range of observers have focused is the Apostle Paul. Although not a follower during Jesus's lifetime, Paul becomes one of the most prominent figures in the history of Christianity, writing many of the works that become part of the New Testament. The question that has occupied many thinkers from one end of the theological spectrum to the other for the last two centuries can

17. John Henry Newman, *An Essay on the Development of Christian Doctrine* (London: W. Blanchard, 1845), 113: "From the history of all sects and parties in religion, and from the analogy and example of Scripture, we may fairly conclude that Christian doctrine admits of formal, legitimate, and true developments . . . contemplated by its Divine Author."

be put very succinctly: Who founded Christianity, Jesus or Paul? The answer to the question had long been thought obvious: Who else but Christ could have founded Christianity? With the Enlightenment, an increasing number of historians and theologians credit Paul with a formative role in the course of Christian history even more profound than that of Jesus.

More often than not, Paul's contributions appear as unfortunate detours from the way, the truth, and the life. In a letter written a few years before his death, for example, Thomas Jefferson refers to Paul as the "first corrupter of the doctrines of Jesus." Fellow revolutionary Thomas Paine calls him "that manufacturer of quibbles" whose writings have inspired a religion "very contradictory to the character of the person whose name it bears." Mahatma Gandhi laments the "great distinction between the Sermon on the Mount and the letters of Paul." H. G. Wells bemoans the way Paul "substituted another doctrine for . . . the plain and profoundly revolutionary teachings of Jesus." Similarly blunt are the statements of James Baldwin ("The real architect of the Christian church was . . . the mercilessly fanatical and self-righteous Paul"), Carl Jung ("It is frankly disappointing to see how Paul hardly ever allows the real Jesus of Nazareth to get a word in"), and George Bernard Shaw ("No sooner had Jesus knocked over the dragon of superstition than Paul boldly sat it on its legs again. . . . He does nothing that Jesus would have done, and says nothing that Jesus would have said").[18] Paul's fiercest critic is perhaps Friedrich Nietzsche, for whom he embodies "the opposite type to that of the life of the 'bringer of glad tidings': the genius in . . . the inexorable logic of hatred," without whom there would be no "Christianity."[19]

The fact that this argument about Paul's legacy touches on subjects studied by specialists clearly has not prevented it from stirring the passions of the general public.[20] Ideological adversaries appear to agree that

---

18. For similar assessments, see Malcolm Muggeridge and Alex Vidler, *Paul, Envoy Extraordinary* (New York: Harper, 1972), 11–16.

19. Friedrich Nietzsche, *The Antichrist*, §42 (cf. *The Portable Nietzsche*, trans. W. Kaufmann [New York: Viking, 1954], 617).

20. For discussion of the historical and literary dimensions of the ancient evidence, see A. J. M. Wedderburn, ed., *Paul and Jesus: Collected Essays* (*Journal for the Study of the New Testament Supplements* 37; Sheffield: JSOT Press, 1989); N. T. Wright, *What Saint Paul Really Said: Was Paul of Tarsus the Real Founder of Christianity?* (Grand Rapids, MI: Eerdmans, 1997); Donald Harman Akenson, *Saint Saul: A Skeleton Key to the Historical Jesus* (New York: Oxford University Press, 2000); and Gerd Lüdemann, *Paul: The Founder of Christianity* (Amherst, NY: Prometheus Books, 2002).

the "Jesus versus Paul" dilemma is not simply a matter of who deserves the title "founder of Christianity." If Paul can rightly be called the founder, according to J. Gresham Machen, a staunch opponent of "Modernist" theology in the Fundamentalist controversies of the 1920s, then Christianity faces an unparalleled crisis:

> For—let us not deceive ourselves—if Paul is independent of Jesus, he can no longer be a teacher of the Church. Christianity is founded upon Christ and only Christ. Paulinism has never been accepted upon any other supposition than that it reproduces the mind of Christ. If that supposition is incorrect—if Paulinism is derived not from Jesus Christ, but from other sources—then it must be uprooted from the life of the Church. But that is more than reform—it is revolution. Compared with that upheaval, the reformation of the sixteenth century is as nothing.[21]

Others agree on the underlying principle, if not with Machen's favorable assessment of Paul. Outspoken Episcopal bishop John Shelby Spong asserts that "Paul's words are not the Words of God. They are the words of Paul—a vast difference," while English philosopher Jeremy Bentham goes so far as to remark, at the end of a tome entitled *Not Paul, but Jesus*, that if Christians require an Antichrist, "they need not go far to look for one."[22]

Christianity stands or falls with Paul under the terms of this tacit consensus. Unnoticed by both sides is the way in which this manner of framing the issue implicitly affirms the "Great Man" theory. Thomas Carlyle's aphorism that "the history of the world is but the biography of great men" concisely expresses this approach the study of history. Proponents of "New History" and "People's History" view this approach as elitist and oversimplified.[23] Whatever the merits of these newer schools of historiography, it is curious to find scholars who typically reject the Great Man theory making an apparent exception in the case of Paul.

---

21. J. Gresham Machen, "Jesus and Paul," in *Biblical and Theological Studies* (New York: Charles Scribner's Sons, 1912), 548.

22. J. S. Spong, *Rescuing the Bible from Fundamentalism* (San Francisco: HarperCollins, 1991), 104; J. Bentham, *Not Paul, but Jesus* (London: John Hunt, 1823), 372.

23. Cf. Peter Burke, ed., *New Perspectives on Historical Writing* (University Park: Pennsylvania State University Press, 1992); and Richard A. Horsley, "Unearthing a People's History," in *Christian Origins: A People's History of Christianity*, Vol. 1 (Minneapolis: Fortress, 2005), 1–20.

Is this an accurate evaluation of Paul's place in history? Does it overestimate his historical significance or overlook other viable candidates for the role of founder? Insofar as Christianity is defined by special beliefs about the identity of Jesus, for example, John the Baptist has a strong claim to the title due to his early recognition—according to Luke 1:41, *in utero*, even!—and proclamation of Jesus as the Son of God. Or Peter, who according to the New Testament not only hails Jesus as the Messiah in response to his question "But who do you say that I am?" but also becomes the "rock" on which the church is built, delivers the Pentecost sermon that results in the conversion of three thousand Jews, and first shares the Christian gospel with a non-Jew (Matt. 16:12–20; Acts 2:14–47; 10:1–11:18).[24] Or Mary Magdalene, who appears to be the earliest historical source for the belief in Jesus's resurrection, giving rise to the "threatening thought . . . that Mary Magdalene can be considered a—or the—founder of Christianity."[25]

The numerous historical and theological issues involved may make it impossible to settle this perennial debate once and for all. Quite apart from any definitive answers, the question itself merits attention for what it reveals about the implicit assumptions that participants in this debate bring to the table. Four particular features of this debate about the relationship of Paul and Jesus in the founding of Christianity are worth noting:

1. The Jesus-Paul debate is to some degree a product of the Enlightenment. Its emergence is part of a larger preoccupation with historical processes of development and change, of which the evolutionary theories of Darwin and the dialectical system of Hegel stand as two prominent examples.[26] It also corresponds to the rising tide of suspicion directed toward received tradition, as one witnesses in the writings of Marx and Nietzsche. Yet the notion that Paul had in some fashion betrayed the movement started by Jesus was not absent from the premodern period. As early as the third century, for example, the

---

24. These considerations lead F. J. Foakes-Jackson to remark that Peter "literally founded the Christian religion" by supplying "the first creed of the Church" (*Peter: Prince of Apostles* [New York: George H. Doran, 1927], 60).

25. Jane Schaberg, *The Resurrection of Mary Magdalene: Legends, Apocrypha, and the Christian Testament* (New York: Continuum, 2002), 303.

26. Wayne A. Meeks and John T. Fitzgerald, eds., *The Writings of St. Paul*, 2nd ed. (New York: W. W. Norton, 2007), 397.

Neoplatonist philosopher Porphyry and a Jewish-Christian sect called the Ebionites anticipate later views when they contend that Paul's signature teachings would have been totally alien to Jesus. Some scholars would also number the canonical Letter of James among those who side with Jesus against Pauline teaching. Paul's defensiveness concerning his own status as an apostle suggests that doubts about his relationship with Jesus go back even further (1 Cor. 9; 2 Cor. 12:11–12; Gal. 1:1). While the Qur'an (e.g., 2:252–53; 3:42–64; 21:91–93) reveres Jesus as a prophet, popular and scholarly literature produced by Muslims from the medieval period forward paints Paul as a false apostle.[27]

2. It is inaccurate to reduce the complex history of the question to a simple story of conflict between traditionalists and skeptics. For example, Nietzsche and his near contemporary Adolf von Harnack both regard Paul as an absolutely pivotal figure and perceive a radical break between him and Jesus. But while Harnack sees Paul as having "liberated" for all humanity the parochial, historically conditioned, preeminently *Jewish* message associated with Jesus, Nietzsche finds fault because he thought Paul had taken the noble, universal message of Jesus and shackled it to the "debased" religion of Judaism.[28] The latter tendency is similar to the one that in the 1930s led German scholars at the Institute for the Study and Eradication of Jewish Influence on German Church Life, and even Adolf Hitler himself, to suggest that Jesus was not Jewish but Aryan.[29] Thus, while numerous writers identify Paul as the founder, they often do so for very different reasons. Many of the participants in this debate are interested, perhaps, less in Paul himself than in larger issues that intersect with his controversial teachings. Comparisons of Jesus and Paul thus frequently function as proxy arguments about Christianity and the cultures shaped by it.
3. The pernicious effects of anti-Semitism have led many scholars to reevaluate Paul and his relationship to Jesus. For many, Paul's comments about the Jews and the law of Moses deserve the blame for centuries of

---

27. See Kate Zebiri, *Muslims and Christians Face to Face* (Oxford: Oneworld, 1997), 67–71.

28. Meeks and Fitzgerald, *The Writings of St. Paul*, 398.

29. Susannah Heschel, *The Aryan Jesus: Christian Theologians and the Bible in Nazi Germany* (Princeton, NJ: Princeton University Press, 2008), 26–66.

hostility that culminate with the Holocaust. Since Paul was a follower of Jesus, however, should Jesus perhaps share the blame? The notion that Jesus the Jew might have been anti-Semitic strikes many people as patently ridiculous, and thus they conclude that Paul must be the true source of the problem.

The "solution" to this problem typically takes one of two forms: (a) Some highlight differences between Jesus and Paul to support the claim that Paul started a new religion, something Jesus never intended: Paul was a self-hating Jew who rejected Torah and presented a caricature of Judaism as a legalistic religion quite unlike what was actually practiced in the first century. (b) Rather than criticize Paul, others criticize traditional understandings of Paul's writings as Augustinian or Lutheran misreadings of the apostle's real message. When Paul is properly understood within the context of his first-century milieu, in this reading, his teachings are well within the Jewish mainstream and thus not so different from those of Jesus.[30]

However well intended, these solutions may on occasion end up distorting the historical sources. Glossing lightly over the harsher statements Jesus makes in the gospels—he describes with great relish, for example, the fate of those who will be cast into the outer darkness where "there shall be weeping and gnashing of teeth" (Matt. 8:12; 13:42; 22:13; 25:30; Luke 13:28)—produces an effective foil that throws Paul into sharper relief, but such a selectively drawn portrait may not be true to life. Determinations about which fragments, interpolations, and even whole letters are authentically Pauline likewise betray certain assumptions—some more plausible than others—about what Paul "must" have meant or what "no first-century Jew" could have believed. But in reality, authors sometimes say things that no one would expect them to say.

4. Comparisons of Jesus and Paul bear striking rhetorical similarities to the oft-heard contrast between "religion" and "spirituality" (as when

30. See, e.g., Pamela M. Eisenbaum, who wants to challenge "the portrait of Paul that has reigned for nearly two millennia" and "to expose the bias embedded in the traditional portrait of Paul and the ways in which it has contributed to gross misrepresentations of Judaism and played no small role in the history of anti-Semitism" (*Paul Was Not a Christian: The Original Message of a Misunderstood Apostle* [San Francisco: HarperCollins, 2009], 3).

someone says, "I'm not religious, but I'm spiritual").[31] Whereas Jesus strove to spread a system of simple but universal ethical truths, it is argued, Paul is responsible for the theological speculation and dogmatic hair-splitting that carried the church away from its roots. James Vernon Bartlet's entry on Paul in the classic *Encyclopedia Britannica Eleventh Edition* (1911) demonstrates that this trope is at least a century old when he quotes an anonymous "modern Jew" who says "Jesus seems to expand and spiritualize Judaism; Paul in some senses turns it upside down." Efforts to rehabilitate Paul or rescue him from the role of villain bear witness to the negative image he conjures in many minds. A. N. Wilson, for example, wants to correct the "preconceived view of Paul as a stiff-necked reactionary who wanted the free-and-easy Jesus-religion to become a church with a set of restrictive rules and regulations" and even suggests that he is better seen as "a prophet of liberty, whose visionary sense of the importance of the inner life anticipates the Romantic poets more than the rule-books of the Inquisition."[32]

Especially when read out of context, differences between Jesus and Paul are easy to find. Did Paul make these putative changes as part of a master plan to hijack the movement, or were any deviations from Jesus unintentional? Because Paul was a Diaspora Jew, lack of familiarity with the ministry of Jesus and misguided zeal—rather than malice—are commonly cited as the cause of any differences. Only rarely does one find Paul playing the rogue, as Hyam Maccoby casts him. Maccoby claims that Jesus was in fact a Pharisee and that Paul, "a compound of sincerity and charlatanry," is lying when he represents himself as a Jew.[33] In the same spirit is a Muslim tradition passed down by Abu al-Muzaffar al-Isfarayini in the eleventh century that paints Paul as an infiltrator who wanted to

---

31. Cf. Robert C. Fuller, *Spiritual, but Not Religious: Understanding Unchurched America* (New York: Oxford University Press, 2001); and C. John Sommerville, *Religion in the National Agenda: What We Mean by Religious, Spiritual, Secular* (Waco: Baylor University Press, 2009).

32. A. N. Wilson, *Paul: The Mind of the Apostle* (New York: W. W. Norton, 1997), 14. Wilson's rhetoric is echoed in Marcus J. Borg and John Dominic Crossan, *The First Paul: Reclaiming the Radical Visionary Behind the Church's Conservative Icon* (San Francisco: HarperCollins, 2008).

33. Hyam Maccoby, *The Mythmaker: Paul and the Invention of Christianity* (New York: Harper & Row, 1986), 17.

corrupt the Christian movement by smuggling alien concepts into its teachings.[34]

In his own letters, Paul emphasizes his continuity with Jesus. Rather than laying a separate foundation, he is building on the foundation that is Jesus Christ, "for no other foundation can anyone lay than that which is laid" (1 Cor. 3:10–11). He is "handing on" traditions received from his predecessors (1 Cor. 11:23–26; 15:1–11). Continuity, however, need not preclude any and all development or adaptation of Jesus's teachings. Before "What would Jesus do?" it appears that Paul's instinct was to ask, "What would Jesus have us do in light of his death and resurrection?" Had Paul been more specific when he advised the Corinthians, "Be imitators of me, as I am of Christ" (1 Cor. 11:1), it might be easier to settle the matter.

## *Conclusion*

Consensus on these questions will likely remain elusive because the competing claims rely on ceteris paribus arguments. In other words, it is impossible to know whether Christianity would have emerged and developed as it did without Jesus or Paul, "all other things being equal," since "all other things" are never quite the same in the ebb and flow of history. Economists study various factors and use regression analysis to help differentiate between causation and correlation, but those who study history and religion have no such instrument at their disposal. Historians can do little more than speculate about the specifics of a world without Jesus or Paul, not to mention other figures who rarely get the credit or the blame for founding Christianity, such as Peter or John the Baptist. Was Jesus unique? Is it conceivable that others could have arrived at similar insights and achieved similar missionary results in Paul's absence?

Considering counterfactual historical claims is not without an intellectual pedigree: Pascal mused that "the whole face of the world would have changed" had Cleopatra's nose been a little shorter. Military historians have wondered whether different weather would have affected the outcome of the Battle of Waterloo or the invasion at Normandy on D-Day. Hypothetical questions of this sort are captivating in part precisely because there can be no closure, but they also serve as salutary reminders of the contingency of history.

---

34. See also the similar remarks of ash-Shahrastānī in the twelfth century (W. Montgomery Watt, *Muslim-Christian Encounters: Perceptions and Misconceptions* [London: Routledge, 1991], 69).

## *For Further Reading*

Beilby, James K., and Paul Rhodes Eddy, eds. *The Historical Jesus: Five Views.* Downers Grove, IL: InterVarsity, 2009. Five scholars—one who argues for an evangelical portrait of Jesus, one who has doubts that he actually existed, and three in between—respond to one another on the question of what can be known about Jesus.

Boyarin, Daniel. *Border Lines: The Partition of Judaeo-Christianity.* Philadelphia: University of Pennsylvania Press, 2004. Boyarin presents a Jewish perspective on the "parting of the ways" between Judaism and Christianity in the first centuries of the common era.

Dodd, C. H. *The Founder of Christianity.* New York: Macmillan, 1970. Dodd provides an overview of Jesus's life and message, explicitly embracing the title "founder."

Eisenbaum, Pamela. *Paul Was Not a Christian: The Original Message of a Misunderstood Apostle.* San Francisco: HarperCollins, 2009. Eisenbaum challenges the traditional understanding of Paul's teachings, espousing what has come to be called "the New Perspective" on the apostle.

Evans, C. S. *The Historical Christ and the Jesus of Faith: The Incarnational Narrative as History.* Oxford: Clarendon, 1996.

Hurtado, Larry W. *How on Earth Did Jesus Become a God? Historical Questions about Earliest Devotion to Jesus.* Grand Rapids, MI: Eerdmans, 2005. Evans and Hurtado both consider the earliest developments that lead to the normative understanding of Jesus's significance and the degree to which later church teachings stand in continuity with this "classic" view or depart from it.

Kähler, Martin. *The So-called Historical Jesus and the Historic Biblical Christ.* Translated by C. E. Braaten. Philadelphia: Fortress, 1964. Originally published as *Der sogenannte historische Jesus und der geschichtliche, biblische Christus* (Leipzig: A. Deichert, 1896), this study appeared a few years before Albert Schweitzer's classic work but highlights the same theological questions raised by Schweitzer's historical survey.

Kirk, J. R. D. *Jesus I Have Loved, but Paul? A Narrative Approach to the Problem of Pauline Christianity.* Grand Rapids, MI: Baker Academic, 2012. Kirk presents a literary and theological approach to mediating the "Jesus versus Paul" debate.

Pelikan, Jaroslav. *Jesus through the Centuries: His Place in the History of Culture.* New Haven, CT: Yale University Press, 1985. Pelikan provides a classic survey of the different personas of Jesus (e.g., "the Cosmic Christ" and "the Monk Who Rules the World") to be found across the last two thousand years.

Wenham, David. *Paul: Follower of Jesus or Founder of Christianity?* Grand Rapids, MI: Eerdmans, 1995. This book is a wide-ranging exegetical discussion of the many questions on which Jesus and Paul are often thought to be at odds.

# 6

# *Muḥammad's Mission and the* Dīn *of Ibrāhīm according to Ibn Isḥāq*

*R. Kevin Jaques*

ALTHOUGH IT IS customary for non-Muslims to regard Muḥammad as the founder of Islam, it is important to note that Muslims do not typically speak of the prophet in these terms. Is this simply a matter of semantics? Or is it more complicated, with other, more fundamental factors involved? Before determining whether one can in any sense refer to Muḥammad as a "founder," it may be necessary to raise an even more basic question: What is "Islam"? Not, "what is Islam as a religious tradition," but what did the term symbolize to early followers of Muḥammad as well as those in the early centuries who lived through dynamic processes and events that caused the term to become reified, concretized, to denote a religious tradition. Such questions have theological as well as linguistic and historical dimensions, and one might attempt to answer them from a variety of directions. This chapter focuses on what can be learned from a particular early Muslim source—the *Sīrat Rasūl Allāh*—that, as the earliest biography of Muḥammad and the basis for virtually all later biographies of the prophet, merits close reading. Early Muslim sources and the vast commentary tradition devoted to Ibn Isḥāq's text that developed over the past millennium do not approach these questions in quite the same way that contemporary students of comparative religion might. But their portrayals of Muḥammad nonetheless bring to the fore critical questions about the self-understanding of people within the tradition as well as its relation to other religious traditions that remain a part of popular and scholarly discourse.

The *Sīrat Rasūl Allāh* (*The Biography of the Messenger of God*) was written by Muḥammad b. Isḥāq b. Yasār (d. 767), better known as Ibn Isḥāq. This work was written a little more than a century following the prophet's death in 632 CE and is based on stories collected from many of those who had "living memories" of Muḥammad and his companions. The text was originally quite large, containing three primary sections: *al-Mubtada'* (The Beginning), which starts with the story of creation and ends with the birth of Muḥammad; *al-Mab'ath* (The Mission), which includes the birth of Muḥammad, his early life, his rise as prophet, the resistance to his call in Mecca, the migration (*hijrah*) to Medina, and ends with the beginning of the so-called Caravan Wars; and *al-Maghāzī* (The Expeditions or The Battle Days), which covers the raids and battles between Muḥammad's community and the Meccan polytheists and their allies, the victorious pilgrimage to Mecca, and ends with Muḥammad's death.

Ibn Isḥāq's original text is no longer extant in its original form, but large parts of the last two sections of the text were redacted, commented on, and edited by 'Abd al-Mālik b. Hishām (d. 828 or 833), known most commonly as Ibn Hishām, whose edition has been preserved and will serve as the primary source of the following analysis.[1] Ibn Hishām removed the earlier sections of the text, those relating to the stories of the pre-Muḥammad prophets found mostly in the Bible, because he appears to have objected to Ibn Isḥāq's liberal use of the so-called *Isrā'īlīyat*, Jewish source material that included commentarial traditions on biblical narratives that he apparently received directly from Jewish interlocutors.[2] Many passages redacted by Ibn Hishām have been reconstructed by Alfred Guillaume from other medieval Arabic texts.[3] In addition to Guillaume, Gordon Newby has reconstructed lost sections of *al-Mubtada'* that begins with Ibn Isḥāq's account of creation and recounts

---

1. 'Abd al-Mālik b. Hishām, *al-Sīrah al-nabawīyah*, 4 vols., ed. Muṣṭafā al-Shaqqā, Ibrāhīm al-Ibyārī, and 'Abd al-Ḥafīẓ al-Shalabī (Cairo: Muṣṭafā al-Bābī al-Ḥalabī, 1936) Unless otherwise indicated, the translations provided in this chapter are mine.

2. See Gordon Newby's introduction to his *The Making of the Last Prophet: A Reconstruction of the Earliest Biography of Muhammad* (Columbia: University of South Carolina Press, 1989).

3. Alfred Guillaume, *The Life of Muhammad: A Translation of Isḥāq's* Sīrat Rasūl Allāh (Oxford: Oxford University Press, 1955). When quoting from passages in Ibn Isḥāq's "original" text I provide the page numbers for Guillaume's translation as well as the Arabic source for the text. For instance, if a passage occurs in the translation on p. 68 and in Ibn Hishām's text on vol. 1, p. 164, I cite it as "G 68/IH 1:164." Passages included by Guillaume but not found in Ibn Hishām, such as al-Azraqī's *Akhbar al-Makkah* (= "Az") or al-Ṭabarī's *Tārīkh al- rusul wa'l-mulūk* (= "Ṭ") are cited in similar fashion.

the stories of Muḥammad's prophetic predecessors.[4] Although it can be difficult to interpret the nuances and symbols that Ibn Isḥāq employs in his fascinating description of Muḥammad's purpose in God's larger sacred drama, Newby and Guillaume offer non-specialists an opportunity to examine early Muslim views of prophecy and of Muḥammad's relationship to the larger "Abrahamic tradition" of the late antique/early medieval Near East.

## *The* Sīrat *as History or Epic*

There has been a rather unfortunate tendency for many readers of Ibn Isḥāq to treat the *Sīrah* as a history of the formation of Islam and the life of Muḥammad. Many scholars assume that his goal was to tell a "historically accurate" account of the way things *actually* unfolded during Muḥammad's life. I am not arguing here that the text cannot be used as a history or that Ibn Isḥāq was attempting to write a fraudulent account of the community's first twenty-three years. But by treating it as a historical source we are using the text in a way that the author would have probably found troubling.[5] *Sīrah* literature in general is better understood as "popular epics" than as historiographies, originally intended to be performed by storytellers to often illiterate audiences and concerned with presenting heroic figures as examples and instruments of God's will.[6] It is thus better to imagine Ibn Isḥāq as a performer than as a historian, one who creates an image of Muḥammad's life through a series of narrative cycles that, in many instances, do not fall into a coherent chronological order. In the case of Ibn Isḥāq's epic of Muḥammad, there is no greater example and instrument of God's will than the prophet himself, whom the author uses to communicate a greater truth about God's intervention *into* history.

Ibn Isḥāq's central concern is to depict Muḥammad as a man, chosen by God to reestablish a lost tradition of ritual worship and slavery to God centered on the pilgrimage (*ḥajj*), which Ibn Isḥāq refers to as the *ḥanīfīyah dīn* Ibrāhīm and not as a "new religion" that came to be known as "Islam." For Ibn Isḥāq, the term *islām* signifies (1) the rejection of aberrant practices introduced to the *dīn*—often incorrectly translated as "religion"; it can be

4. In sections dealing with the reconstructed *al-Mubtada'* I provide citations for the Arabic source as well as the English translation provided by Newby (= "N").

5. On the historical value of Ibn Isḥāq and his *Sīrah, see* Josef Horovitz, *The Earliest Biographies of the Prophet and Their Authors,* ed. Lawrence I. Conrad (Princeton, NJ: Darwin, 2002), 74–75.

6. Sabine Dorpmueller, "Introduction: History and Fiction in Arabic Popular Epic," in *Fictionalizing the Past: Historical Characters in Arabic Popular Epic,* ed. Sabine Dorpmueller (Leuven: Uitgeverij Peeters en Department Oossterse Studies, 2012), 1–2.

interpreted several ways, as discussed later in the chapter—established by Ibrāhīm (Abraham) and his son, Ismāʿīl (Ishmael) when they built the Kaʿbah as the original temple to God; and (2) the escape from *ʿibādat al-awthān* (the servile worship of images, figures, and objects).

The following analysis focuses on what it is that Ibn Isḥāq understood Muḥammad to be creating or "founding" as a prophet in the line of biblical prophets. In other words, did Ibn Isḥāq think that Muḥammad was bringing a new "religion"? What can be said about the tradition that Muḥammad was sent to (re)establish? In examining these questions we rely primarily on the last section of *al-Mubtada'* and the first part of *al-Mabʿath* that is preserved by Ibn Hishām as well as the section of the *Mubtada'* redacted by Ibn Hishām that depicts the story of Ibrāhīm. The choice of these parts of the *Sīrah* may sound curious as they do not describe in detail what Muḥammad did once prophecy begins and he starts to establish a community based on the revelations Ibn Isḥāq sees as coming from God. But Ibn Isḥāq uses these sections of the text to set up the crises that causes God to send Muḥammad as a prophet. It is thus not possible to fully understand the latter parts of *al-Mubtada'* or *al-Mabʿath* without taking the earlier redacted stories of the prophets into account. Ibn Isḥāq's Ibrāhīm lies in the background as the prelude to Muḥammad's mission and sets up the causes requiring Muḥammad's appearance.

## Setting the Table: The Story of Ibrāhīm as the Context for the Mission of Muḥammad

In presenting his tale of the rise of "idolatry" among Muḥammad's ancestors, Ibn Isḥāq states that it began as the "ritual worship of stones" (*ʿibādat al-ḥijārah*)[7] following the original monotheist worship of God at the Kaʿbah in Mecca. He says, however, that when Mecca became overpopulated, and as individuals and clans drifted away, they took stones (*ḥijārah*) from the *ḥaram* (the sacred space around the Kaʿbah that included a significant part of the entire village of Mecca) for the "glorification of the *ḥaram*." Wherever they settled they would erect the stone and circumambulate it as if it were the Kaʿbah. Over time, this led them to ritually worship (*ʿabada*)

7. The terms "idolatry" and "idol" are used in this chapter to indicate the worship of various images by the pre-Muslim Arabs, but they are highly problematic as there appears to be no term denoting "idolatry" in classical Arabic. The term approximating "idolatry," *wathanīyah*, does not arise until the eighteenth century, most likely under the influence of European discussions of idol worship.

> what they esteemed among the stones and which excited their wonder until eventually corrupting and forgetting what they followed, and they exchanged the *dīn* of Ibrāhīm and Ismā'īl for another. So they ritually worshipped (*'abada*) idols (*awthān*) and they turned toward following the errors of the peoples before them.[8]

Strangely, however, Ibn Isḥāq states that while Muḥammad's ancestors turned to the ritual worship of stones and, eventually, of *awthān*, they

> continued to submit themselves according to the covenant (*'ahd*) of Ibrāhīm, such as glorifying the House (*al-bayt*), the circumambulation of it, the major pilgrimage (*ḥajj*), the minor pilgrimage (*'umrah*), the standing at 'Arafah and Muzdalifah, sacrificing the animals, and the *ihlāl* during the major and minor pilgrimage, while adding to it [things that were] not a part of it.[9]

As Ibn Isḥāq presents it here, the introduction of the ritual worship of stones and *awthān*, however, was quickly followed by changes in the *ḥajj* ritual. For Ibn Isḥāq this is a central crisis that necessitates the mission of Muḥammad because changes in the *hajj* ritual, perhaps more than the rise of *awthān* worship, signified the abandonment of the original *dīn* of his ancestors, rooted in the covenant (*'ahd*) of Ibrāhīm, although the significance of this is lost on the reader without examining Ibn Isḥāq's story of Ibrāhīm.

Ibrāhīm has a special status in Muslim sacred history. In the Qur'ān, only Muḥammad, and Mūsā (Moses) are mentioned more often. Insofar as he predated all sectarian divisions and was a "pure monotheist" (*hanīf*) who "submitted to God" (*muslim*) and was not an "idolater," Ibrāhīm was central to Muḥammad's arguments with the Jewish community of Medina. Newby argues that Ibrāhīm is presented by Ibn Isḥāq as the restorer of the worship established by Adam and that Muḥammad, as the reviver of the *dīn* restored by Ibrahīm, should be understood as the "new Adam and Abraham."[10]

---

8. G 35–36/IH 1:79–80.

9. G 36/IH 1:80. Ibn Isḥāq often refers to the Ka'bah as "The House." The *ihlāl* consists of the pilgrim shouting "labbayka Allāhumma labayka" (At your service, O God, at your service).

10. Newby, *The Making of the Last Prophet*, 65, quoting Qur'ān 3:56–68.

Ibn Isḥāq opens his story of Ibrāhīm by stating that "God desired to send (*yuba'ath*) Ibrāhīm . . . as a proof (*ḥujjah*) to his people and a messenger (*rasūl*) to His servants (*'ibād*)."[11] He is "sent" and thus for Ibn Isḥāq, Ibrāhīm functions as God's instrument. He does not set out to found a new religion of his own accord. The term used to describe his mission, *ḥujjah*, implies something more forceful than merely to function as "proof" or "evidence" but to function as an active agent refuting the ritual worship of *awthān*. Furthermore, Ibn Isḥāq does not say that Ibrāhīm was sent as a messenger to Ibrāhīm's community *(qawm)* but to God's servants (*'ibādahi*). This term, *'ibādah*, is perhaps the most important word in understanding Ibn Isḥāq's view of Muḥammad's mission. The related verb *'abada* means "to serve, worship, or adore." It indicates that worship is an action and not simply a state of mind. The noun *'abd* is used throughout the Qur'ān to indicate the status of slavery, especially to God. Its use in names is especially important for Ibn Isḥāq. In his description of the rise of the "ritual worship of idols" (*'ibādat al-awthān*), the conjunction of the names of gods embodied by *awthān* with *'abd*, such as 'Abd al-'Uzzā, marks not just a change in worship but an actual shift in the object of abject submission.[12]

The connection between worship and abject submission is important in appreciating the idea central in Ibn Isḥāq's understanding of the *dīn* that Muḥammad represented: that ritual worship performed properly is an act of abject submission, an expression of the complete status of obedience that the worshipper-slave undertakes. According to Ibn Isḥāq, then, Ibrāhīm's roles as (1) *ḥujjah* against the worship/submission to *awthān* and (2) messenger to God's worshipper-slaves are not the same but, rather, two distinct activities.

Ibn Isḥāq divides his story of Ibrāhīm along the lines of his dual role as *ḥujjah* and *rasūl*. The first part of the story deals with Ibrāhīm's miraculous birth and rapid maturation, his innate monotheism, and his actions among his people to demonstrate the futility of ritually worshipping-submitting themselves to images made of stone and wood. God also performs miracles through Ibrāhīm as proof that ritually worshipping-submitting to the One God (Allāh) is better than *'ibādat al-awthān*.[13] A brief interlude tells how Ibrāhīm leaves his homeland and begins to

11. N 67/Ṭ 1:254.

12. G 36/IH 1:80–81.

13. N 68–70/Ṭ 255–61.

wander the land with his brother Lūṭ (Lot) and his wife Sārah (Sarah) in an effort to find a place to safely ritually worship-serve God. The final stage of the story begins with the appearance of Hājar (Hagar), a slave girl belonging to Sārah whom she gives to Ibrāhīm because Sārah is barren. Ibrāhīm sleeps with Hājar and she gives birth to a male child, Ismā'īl. Once Ismā'īl is born, God orders Ibrāhīm to "Build the House and call (*adhān*) the people (*al-nāss*) to pilgrimage (*al-ḥajj*)."[14] Ibn Isḥāq then provides four slightly different accounts of how Ibrāhīm and Ismā'īl arrive in Mecca and build the House, the "first made for mankind on earth."[15] Once the House is completely rebuilt, Ibrāhīm is shown by Jabra'īl how to perform all of the rituals of the *ḥajj*. God then commands Ibrāhīm to call (*da'ā*) mankind (*al-nāss*) to perform the pilgrimage. In a scene reminiscent of the Exodus story where Moses demurs when God tells him to go to Pharaoh and free the children of Israel,[24] Ibrāhīm complains "O Lord, my voice will not reach." But God reassures him saying, "Announce it and it will reach."[25] So Ibrāhīm, in complete obedience,

> raised his voice up over the place until it went to the tops of the mountains and along their length. The earth, its plains, its mountains, its dry land and sea, its men and *jinn* gathered that day so that they all heard it together. He put his fingers in his ears and turned his face to the south, saying "O mankind, the pilgrimage (*ḥajj*) is ordained in the ancient [House], so respond to your Lord." And they responded from the seven limits and from the east and the west, from the ends of the earth, [saying] "At your service, O God, at your service" (*labbayka Allāhumma labayka*).[26]

Unlike Moses in the Book of Exodus (4:1–17), who demurs when God tells him to go to Pharaoh and free the children of Israel, Ibrāhīm exhibits complete faith. When God reassures him, he immediately goes forth and calls the *ḥajj*, to which the people and the *jinn* respond at once and proclaim their obedience with the *ihlāl*, the shout of the pilgrim "labbayka Allāhumma labayka" (at your service, O God, at your service). It is the expression of servitude that the faithful *'abd* declares as a proclamation of

---

14. N 73/T 270–71, 277.

15. N 74–76. In these accounts, they are led to Mecca by the *Sakīnah*, described by Ibn Isḥāq as a wind and generally understood as "the presence of God," by the angel Jabra'īl (Gabriel), or by both.

servile obedience. The pilgrimage, therefore, becomes worship-submission par excellence, the fullest sign of submission to the One God, which is required for God's *ʿibād*. For Ibn Isḥāq, this is Ibrāhīm's covenant with God: announce the *ḥajj* and they will come.[16]

## The Pilgrimage as the Dīn of Ibrāhīm

Ibn Isḥāq refers frequently to the "*dīn* of Ibrahīm" in his work. Although *dīn* is usually translated as "religion," this term is highly problematic as a description of human experience and activity, especially when applied to pre-modern traditions. Wilfred Cantwell Smith, a leading twentieth-century theorist in the field of comparative religion who has written extensively on Islam, argues that the modern English term "religion" comes from the Latin *religio* and originally referred to ritual acts and not to systems of "faith" (also a problematic term) as it comes to be used after the Enlightenment.[17] Over time the term came to describe a multiplicity of ritual communities in the Greco-Roman world and began to be used as a way to describe "my ritual practice" against the ritual practices of others. It also was used as a way of describing the "bonds" that ritual practice creates between God and the practitioner. The term "faith" was more commonly used to describe a community held together by a set of assumptions about the divine that carried with it exclusive qualities. It is only after the fifteenth century that the term "religion" emerges as a way of describing the relationship between God and man in the way that "faith" had previously been used. During this time, *religio* begins to connote personal piety and, by the seventeenth century, it comes to refer to systems of ideas or "belief" and not to acts, practices, or bonds. This is largely due to the anti-ritual disposition of Protestant traditions that sought to focus more exclusively on "belief" in God or Christ as the litmus test for salvation. "Religion" thus becomes a system of beliefs that can be falsified or proven.[18] Following the Enlightenment "religion" also begins to be used

16. While the Qur'ān refer to a number of covenants between God and God's prophets, neither the Qur'ān nor Ibn Isḥāq makes any mention of the covenant described in the Hebrew Bible involving circumcision and a promise to the elderly Ibrāhīm and Sārah that they will have many descendants (cf. Gen. 17:1–27).

17. Wilfred Cantwell Smith, *The Meaning and End of Religion: A New Approach to the Religious Traditions of Mankind* (New York: New American Library, 1964), 23–24.

18. Smith, *The Meaning and End of Religion*, 28–43.

to describe historical entities that develop over time, which, according to Smith, leads to the search for common "essences" that link all "religions" together under the broader category of "religion" as a common aspect of being human.

Because of a series of historical events that occur in the pre-Islamic Near East, Smith argues that Islam emerges into the world as a fully self-aware religion that causes the term *dīn* to signify a religious community and its plural *adyān* to indicate multiple religious communities in which only one represents "the best of its kind," a process that would not occur in Europe or the rest of the world for almost another millennium.[19] In the Near East, therefore, by the seventh century, *dīn* comes to refer to (1) a religious community in the modern sense, in which members drew distinctions between traditions based on understandings of the relative "truth" of their tradition and those of others; (2) an "abstract pattern of beliefs and practices characterizing a particular tradition or group" that typified the outsider view; (3) a "systematic religion," or a coherent unified structure of belief and practice that held a community together that represented the insider view; and (4) a path or way of conducting oneself.[20]

Smith's account is problematic in certain respects in that he sees the early community as unified in sensing that what they did and thought was different from and superior to those around them and, above all, in the way he describes Islam as a "self-aware" agent. This emphasis in effect essentializes the early tradition, whereas "Islam" is, in reality, simply the product of Muslim activity. Nevertheless, if we take Smith's four definitions of *dīn* in early Islam as a guide, we appear to see aspects of each in Ibn Isḥāq's usage. He uses *dīn* seventy-eight times in the sections of the *al-Mubtada'* and *al-Mab'ath* under examination. In most instances it is used to refer to the *dīn* of a particular group (such as Christians, Jews, and Mazdians) or of certain individuals.[21] Thus, it would seem that Ibn Isḥāq uses *dīn* in a comparative sense, drawing distinctions between groups and individuals. But in instances where he draws a distinction between different *dīns*, he focuses almost exclusively on differences in ritual practice-servitude (*'ibādah*) and not on "belief" or understandings of the nature of God. In fact, Ibn Isḥāq hardly ever uses the terms generally

19. Smith, *The Meaning and End of Religion*, 76.

20. Smith, *The Meaning and End of Religion*, 93–95.

21. E.g., G 6, 17, 20, 95/IH 1:19, 36, 43, 229.

interpreted as "belief" (*āmana*) or "believer" (*mu'min*) in passages that are not direct quotations from the Qur'ān. This is remarkable given that references to *āmana* in its various forms occur in the Qur'ān more than a thousand times. Additionally, given the importance of monotheism in the Qur'ān, it is striking that the explicit coupling of *dīn* and the discussion of God's unity (*tawḥīd*), occurs in only one story, that of 'Abd Allāh b. Thāmir and the Christianization of Najrān—where "submission" (*aslama*) refers to acknowledging the oneness of God and referred to becoming a Christian, not a Muslim.[22]

In virtually every other instance where the term can be linked to an idea or an action, *dīn* is used by Ibn Isḥāq in reference to *'ibādah*.[23] It is likewise evident that when Ibn Isḥāq uses the phrases *dīn Ibrāhīm* and *ḥanīfīyah dīn* Ibrāhīm he specifically refers to *'ibādah*—in this instance, the *ḥajj*. Ibn Isḥāq uses the phrase "*dīn* Ibrāhīm" seven times in the sections of the text under examination. All but one of the references occurs in the context of the corruption of the *ḥajj* ritual by a group known as the *Ḥums* that begins around the time of Muḥammad's birth.[24] The only other reference occurs in the story of Salmān the Persian, who was raised as a Mazdian and upon leaving his home on an errand for his father encounters a group of Christians praying in a church. Like 'Abd Allāh b. Thāmir, Salmān is taken by the beauty of their ritual prayers and he sets off on a quest to learn more about them. Salmān travels to Syria and seeks out the "most excellent of [the] *dīn* who is most knowledgeable."[25] Throughout the account of his travels, *dīn* refers to a way or path that the pious men follow and that path, at least for Salmān, seems to center on ritual, specifically prayer. It is prayer that attracts him to the Christians in the first place and when he describes to his father his attraction to the Christians and tells him that the Christian *dīn* is better than the *dīn* of his father, Salmān is comparing the fire ritual of the Mazdians to the ritual prayer (*ṣalāt*) of the Christians. In these passages, Ibn Isḥāq clearly uses *dīn* in reference to ritual practice. There are no discussions of "belief" or conceptions of God. Given that most uses of the term *dīn* by Ibn Isḥāq refer to

22. G 16/IH 1:35.

23. E.g., the *dīn* of the Mazdians is linked to maintaining the "sacred fire" (G 95/IH 229).

24. See G 87, 99 (twice), 100, 103/IH 1:238, 240 (twice), 264 (twice). See below on the importance of the *Ḥums* in Ibn Isḥāq's understanding of the causes of Muḥammad's mission.

25. G 95/IH 1:229.

servile ritual worship, with the majority referring to the pilgrimage ritual, it is clear that when Ibn Isḥāq refers to the *dīn* of Ibrāhīm he intends the reader to understand it not as "the religion" of Ibrāhīm, but the *ḥajj* as servile ritual worship established by Ibrāhīm through God's direction.

The same is true for *ḥanīfīyah dīn* Ibrāhīm. Generally, the term *hanīf* has been translated as a kind of nondescript monotheism, or in Ibrāhīm's case, as "pure monotheism."[26] But interpretations of the term are often tied to understandings of the term *dīn* as "religion" instead of ritual practice or way of ritual practice. It is therefore always assumed that when the term *ḥanīf* is used it refers to a theological understanding of the nature of God and not to ways of worshipping or serving God. Central to understanding *ḥanīf* is one of the definitions of the term *dīn* passed over by Smith. In classical Arabic, the word *dīn* comes from a root (*d y n*) that connotes obedience, submission, or enslavement. For instance, in a poem Ibn Isḥāq attributes to the latter-day *ḥanīf* Zayd b. ʿAmr b. Nufayl, who breaks with the Quraysh when they institute innovations to the *ḥajj*, Zayd laments, "Am I to worship (*adīn*) one Lord or a thousand? . . . I will not worship (*adīn*) another God besides you."[27] This poem takes place in the context of Zayd's search for a proper way to worship-serve God, which he characterizes as the *ḥanīfīyah dīn Ibrāhīm*. The poem clearly refers to *adīn* as an act of worship, specifically the pilgrimage established by Ibrāhīm.

With this is mind it is evident from the stories of Salmān the Persian and Zayd b. ʿAmr that when Ibn Isḥāq uses the phrase *ḥanīfīyah dīn* Ibrāhīm he does not mean "pure monotheism." In classical Arabic the word *ḥanīf* meant to "incline toward the right state or tendency." It is therefore likely that *hanīfīyah dīn* Ibrāhīm means, in Ibn Isḥāq's usage, "Ibrāhīm's inclination toward servile worship," an admittedly unwieldy phrase, but one that encapsulates the story of Ibrāhīm and the centrality of the *ḥajj* as the ultimate expression of the servile worship of God.

## *The Rise of* ʿIbādat al-Awthān *among the Descendants of Ismāʿīl*

After Ibrāhīm establishes the *ḥajj* as the ultimate act of worship-servitude to God, his descendants, through his son Ismāʿīl (Muḥammad's ancestors),

26. Cf. Newby, *Making of the Last Prophet*, 65.

27. G 100–101/IH 1:241–42.

begin to reintroduce *ʿibādat al-awthān* several generations later. The timeline for this process is extremely confused in Ibn Isḥāq's story. Ibn Isḥāq begins by describing tribal disputes that all revolve around control of the Kaʿbah almost immediately after Ibrāhīm's death. These disputes eventually lead to the capping of the Zamzam well. Ibn Isḥāq refers to this event as occurring in the *jāhilīyah*, generally translated as "time of ignorance."[28] Muslim commentators usually took this term, when it appears in the Qurʾān, to indicate the opposite of *ʿilm* (religious knowledge) and the absence of *islām* in both its symbolic meaning of "submission" and its more reified form signifying the period in which Islam as a religious tradition became established.

Initially, Ibn Isḥāq refers to the *jāhilīyah* in the context of disputes over control of the Kaʿbah that result in the further corruption of the *dīn* of Ibrahim. The *jāhilīyah* is understood as a period of foolish actions or wrong conduct that begins, not with the beginning of the *ʿibādah* of stones or even of *awthān*, but when disputes within the tribe of Ismāʿīl led to the capping of the Zamzam well and the decline of the Kaʿbah as the central site of pilgrimage. In Ibn Isḥāq's depiction of the sacred history of Mecca, the closing of the Zamzam well seems to have prompted or coincided with the migrations of the descendants of Ismāʿīl that led to stone worship. Although the members of the tribe of Ismāʿīl took stones in order to glorify the *ḥaram*, they continued to perform the *ḥajj* according to the covenant of Ibrāhīm; even though they "added to it [things that were] not a part of it" they are not described as "adding deviations" (*ghayyar*) or "innovations" (*bidʿah*).[29]

Some thirteen generations after the capping of the Zamzam Well, the situation changes when ʿAmr b. Luḥayy becomes the first to "deviate" (*ghayyar*) from the *dīn* of Ismāʿīl. It is clear from the text that ʿAmr b. Luḥayy did not begin the practice of *ʿibādat al-ḥijārah*. His crime, for which he is "dragging his intestines in hell," was building temples (*ṭawāghīt*, sing. *ṭāghūt*) and installing idols (*aṣnām*) in them that he gave the names of gods.[30] No longer were the stones or images extensions of the *ḥaram* that the people glorified; now they began to signify the presence of

28. G 47/IH 1:119–20.

29. See G 35 and 87/IH 1:79 and 211 to contrast the degrees of corruption these terms suggest.

30. G 35/IH 1:79.

gods in addition to the One God, making the *'ibād* "unclean people of association" (*najas ahl shirk*).[31] In addition, 'Amr b. Luḥayy extended the *ḥajj* ritual to include circumambulation of these temples while remaining in a state of ritual purity, normally reserved only for the *ḥaram*, as well as other parts of the *ḥajj* ritual established by Ibrāhīm for the Ka'bah alone. Aspects of the *ḥajj* ritual were even extended to the worship-service of household gods, a practice that spread across Arabia.[32]

## *The Tradition of Quṣayy b. Kilāb and its Replacement of the* Dīn *of Ibrāhīm*

Approximately two generations after 'Amr b. Luḥayy, the remaining clans in Mecca began to fight over control of the Ka'bah and the *ḥajj* leading to further deviations from the *dīn* of Ibrāhīm and Ismā'īl. Eventually, Quṣayy b. Kilāb, the most important figure in the pre-Muslim Quraysh tribe, seized control of Mecca and of the pilgrimage rites, establishing himself and his family as the source of authority for the rituals attached to the Ka'bah.[33] From this point until the revival of the *dīn* of Ibrāhīm, the performance of the stages of the *ḥajj* was dictated by the whims of certain clans not according to the traditions established by Ibrāhīm. Quṣayy's standing was so great that he irrevocably replaced Ibrāhīm as the source of authority for the pilgrimage and the rituals attached to the Ka'bah. Although conflicts continued within the Quraysh after Quṣayy's death, his control over the Ka'bah and the pilgrimage, according to Ibn Isḥāq, was passed to Hāshim, his grandson and the eponym of Muḥammad's clan, the *Banū* Hāshim. His son, Shaybah, also known as 'Abd al-Muṭṭalib, inherited these rights as well.[34]

## *The Rediscovery of the Zamzam Well and the Rise of the Cult of Ibrāhīm*

The nature of Ibn Isḥāq's story changes with the beginning of his account of Muḥammad's grandfather, 'Abd al-Muṭṭalib, and the rediscovery of the

31. G 9/IH 1:25.

32. G 38–39/Az 1:73–74.

33. G 52–56/IH 1:130–37.

34. G 59–61/IH 1: 144–50.

Zamzam well. It marks the point at which God, having set out the corruption of the *dīn* of Ibrahīm and his final replacement as a source for authority for the *ḥajj* by Quṣayy, begins to intervene directly in human affairs to create the conditions necessary for Muḥammad's mission.

He opens this cycle of his story by describing how ʿAbd al-Muṭṭalib, while sleeping near the Kaʿbah, was visited by an unseen entity (*āt*$^{an}$) over the course of several nights. On the fourth night, he is told, "Dig Zamzam," but he has no idea what this means. Ibn Isḥāq uses this story to illustrate how far the Quraysh had drifted from the covenant of Ibrāhīm and to demonstrate how little the people, and even someone with as much religious authority as ʿAbd al-Muṭṭalib, remembered about the sacred history of Mecca and the purposes and activities of the *ḥanīfīyah dīn* Ibrāhīm. When ʿAbd al-Muṭṭalib says he has no idea what "Zamzam" means, the entity gives him clues in the form of a poem so that he can understand and find its location. Once he deciphers the clues, ʿAbd al-Muṭṭalib and his son al-Ḥārith, begin to dig until they hit the top of the well.[35]

The rediscovery of the well rouses the Quraysh from their historical stupor. Once they connect Zamzam to the story of Ibrāhīm and Ismāʿīl, members of the tribe begin to assert this relationship as a claim to superiority. When they hear of ʿAbd al-Muṭṭalib's discovery, they say, "This is the well of our father Ismāʿīl, and we have a right to it, so give us a share in it." In Ibn Isḥāq's narrative this remark is the first reference to the patriarch since the time of Quṣayy. A crucial byproduct of the rediscovery of the Zamzam well in this telling is the revival of the importance of the Kaʿbah as a pilgrimage center in Arabia and the centrality of the "cult" of Ibrāhīm to the claims of the Quraysh as its guardians. I use the term "cult" to emphasize Ibn Isḥāq's contention that while claiming to be "the children of Ibrāhīm" and thus the heirs to his authority, the Quraysh do not seek to revive the ancient *dīn* of Ibrāhīm but instead use him to promote their importance and the importance of the Kaʿbah as the chief pilgrimage site in Arabia.

## The Battle of the Elephant and the New Covenant

Through his telling of two events that both occur around the time of Muḥammad's birth, Ibn Isḥāq indicates that the rediscovery of the well caused an increase of pilgrims to Mecca that led directly to its reemergence

35. G 62/IH 1: 151.

as the major center of pilgrimage. The discovery of the well and the conflict over its control also sets in motion a series of events that steers history toward Muḥammad's mission.

The first event, known as the "Year of the Elephant," takes place when Abrahah, an Abyssinian-Christian general, takes control of Yemen and builds a massive church in Sana'ā', intending to make it the central pilgrimage site for the Arabs. Hearing of the plan, a Meccan from the Kinānī tribe travels to Sana'ā' and defiles the church to make it unfit for pilgrimage.[36] Abrahah becomes so enraged that he marches toward Mecca, led by a war elephant, intending to destroy the Ka'bah. When Abrahah attacks the outskirts of Mecca and takes two hundred camels belonging to 'Abd al-Muṭṭalib, the Meccans cannot agree about the best way to respond to the threat posed by the Abyssinians. 'Abd al-Muṭṭalib states that he is more concerned about the return of his camels than defending the Ka'bah because there is no way they can muster a force sufficient to oppose the Abyssinian army:

> This is God's sacred house and the house of his friend Ibrāhīm. . . . So if He protects it from [Abrahah] it is [truly] His house and His holy place and if He allows him in [the *ḥaram*], by God, there is nothing we can do to prevent him from it.[37]

While one might read this statement as fatalism on 'Abd al-Muṭṭalib's part, it functions to demonstrate his Ibrāhīm-like trust in God and, when God inevitably defends the Ka'bah from destruction, this event is depicted as evidence of the sacredness of the Ka'bah in the eyes of the Arabs and at the same time as buttressing the claims of the Quraysh as having a special link to Ibrāhīm that they alone possess.

Abrahah returns the camels to 'Abd al-Muṭṭalib—whose insouciance in the face of the looming destruction of the Ka'bah shocks the Abyssinian—but proceeds with the attack. The next day the Quraysh decide to leave Mecca to God's protection and flee into the mountains. Before abandoning the village, 'Abd al-Muṭṭalib goes to the Ka'bah along with a few of his male kin and prays to God (Allāh) to protect His House, saying,

---

36. G 20–22/IH 1: 44–47, most likely meaning that he defecated in the sanctuary.

37. G 20–22/IH 1: 50.

> O God, indeed the slave (*ʿabd*) defends his saddle, so defend your people. Do not be overcome by their strength tomorrow and [do not allow] their guile to be greater than your guile.[38]

The prayer sets out the relationship between God and His people as being analogous to the slave and his saddle. Just as a slave has nothing but his saddle and would fight to the death to protect it, so to does ʿAbd al-Muṭṭalib implore God to hold nothing back to protect his people. After the prayer, they then go up into the mountains that surround Mecca and take up defensive positions. Abrahah begins his attack on Mecca the following day, but the elephant he had brought with him refuses to attack and flees toward Yemen. The Abyssinian forces follow suit as God intervenes to bring about their destruction; even Abrahah dies a gruesome death in the retreat.

Ibn Isḥāq says that when God sent Muḥammad, "he used to recount to the Quraysh how God preserved and put His blessing on them when the power of the Abyssinians was turned away so that their authority [over the Kaʿbah] would permanently endure." In light of his repeated emphasis on the covenant of Ibrāhīm, Ibn Isḥāq thus indicates that the prayer of ʿAbd al-Muṭṭalib before leaving Mecca should be interpreted as creating another covenant between God and the Quraysh, "so that nothing changed about their condition which they possessed by the will of God for the good, if [only] they would accept it."[39]

This notion was not original to Muḥammad or the Qurʾān but appears to have been current among the Arabs as a whole. Ibn Isḥāq makes this clear when he states that, following the defeat of Abrahah, the Quraysh were "glorified" (*aʿẓama*) by the Arabs, echoing language normally reserved for the veneration *ʿibād* have for God and his House. He quotes poetry written in tribute to the special nature of the Quraysh, who are described as "the people of God" on whose behalf God fought. The last of these poems links the battle directly to the *ḥanīfīyah dīn* Ibrāhīm and the elephant's inability to attack Mecca, concluding, "Every *dīn* on the Day of Resurrection, God, except for the *dīn* of the *ḥanīfīyah,* will destroy."[40] Here

38. G 26/IH 1: 52.

39. G 27–28/IH 1: 56.

40. G 29–30/IH 1: 62.

one finds the clearest expression of the new covenant created by ʿAbd al-Muṭṭalib's prayer before the attack. The Quraysh thus stake their claim as the inheritors of the *ḥanīfīyah dīn* Ibrāhīm, a status made manifest through God's defeat of the Abyssinians.

## *The Ḥums*

The restoration of Mecca as a major pilgrimage site after the rediscovery of the Zamzam well and especially the miraculous defeat of the Abyssinians elevated to new heights the Quraysh's belief in their own special status. The Quraysh "created" a group known as the *Ḥums*, a cult association tying members of several western Arabian tribes to the Meccan shrine. Ibn Isḥāq states that the founders of the *Ḥums* had said,

> We are the sons of Ibrāhīm, the people of the *ḥaram*, the guardians of the House, and inhabitants of Mecca. There is no one among the Arabs [who] have rights like ours and nothing resembling our rank. The Arabs do not acknowledge [others] as they acknowledge us. So we must not glorify a thing from the outside (*ḥill*) like we glorify the *ḥaram*.[41]

As an outgrowth of their arrogance, Ibn Isḥāq states that the Quraysh divided the Arabs into two groups, the *Ḥums* (sing. *aḥims*) and the *Ḥillah*. Ibn Isḥāq says that "they were called '*ḥums*' because they were 'zealous' (*ḥums$^{an}$*) in the intensity of their ritual practice (*dīn*)."[42]

In their zeal to draw distinctions between themselves and the *Ḥillah*, the *Ḥums* gave up any part of the pilgrimage ritual that took place outside the precincts of the *ḥaram* even though they acknowledged that they were aspects of the *ḥajj* and the *dīn* of Ibrāhīm commanded by God. The *Ḥums* still thought that the *Ḥillah* should perform these aspects of the *ḥajj* but that they, as people of the *ḥaram*, should not and, as Ibn Isḥāq sees it, thereby placed their status above the will of God. Ibn Isḥāq goes on to say that the *Ḥums* created new rituals and customs regarding such matters as ritual purity and conduct during pilgrimage for which there was no divine command.[43]

---

41. G 87/IH 1: 211–12.

42. Az 1:116.

43. G 87/IH 1:214.

He follows the story of the *Ḥums* with tales in which Christian monks, Jewish rabbis, and even pagan soothsayers foretell of Muḥammad's coming. The narrative pace quickens with these tales, anticipating the moment of the first revelation. Even the carcass of a sacrificed calf calls out to the Quraysh, saying that "a man will call, saying, 'There is no god but God!'" Most of the references to the *ḥanīfīyah dīn* Ibrāhīm occur in this section. In each case they emphasize the purpose of Muḥammad's mission, that is, to return to the original covenant of Ibrāhīm and reinstitute the *ḥajj* according to the "right inclining ritual practice" of Ibrāhīm. The story of Salmān the Persian is found here. Salmān leaves the *dīn* of his father and goes on a quest to find the true *dīn*. He is finally told by his last teacher that he is living in the time of a prophet from the land of the Arabs who is reviving the *dīn* of Ibrāhīm.[44] When Salmān sets out to find this prophet, he is captured and taken as a slave to Medina. In Medina he meets Muḥammad and becomes a close companion after the prophet helps him buy his freedom. One day Salmān tells a story of seeking out a healer who lived in the wild in Syria on the instructions of his last teacher. In his story, Salmān confronts the man and says, "Tell me about the *ḥanīfīyah dīn* Ibrāhīm." The man responds, "Indeed, you ask about something the people today no longer ask about. Already, you overshadow the time of a prophet [who] is reviving this way among the people of the *ḥaram*. So, go to him, he [will] take you to it." When Muḥammad hears the story, he replies, "If you have been truthful with me, O Salmān, you truly encountered ʿĪsā (Jesus) son of Maryam (Mary)."[45]

Ibn Isḥāq closes his account of the pre-mission portion of his text with the story of four men of Quraysh who separate themselves from the *Ḥums*. They decide to meet in secret and, in a scene reminiscent of Ibrāhīm's testimony to his people regarding their idol worship, say of the *Ḥums*:

> By God, they know [that] our people dismiss everything [right], for already they have followed the wrong way in the *dīn* of their father Ibrāhīm; of the stone they circumambulate, it does not hear, it does not see, it does not harm, nor does it benefit. O people, seek for yourselves a *dīn*, because, by God, you follow nothing.[46]

---

44. G 87/IH 1: 232.

45. G 96–98/IH 1: 232–36.

46. G 99/IH 1: 238.

Here Ibn Isḥāq implies that just as Ibrāhīm's people knew they worshipped powerless images, the Quraysh know what they do is wrong and contrary to the *dīn* of Ibrāhīm. Yet, because they arrogantly think that "there is no one among the Arabs [who] have rights like ours and nothing resembling our rank," the Quraysh reject the *dīn* of Ibrāhīm and now "have no *dīn* at all."[47] In other words, they have completely abandoned all pretenses of worship-service, not just to God, but even to the idols themselves. Instead, for the Quraysh, it is their glorification that matters most.

For Ibn Isḥāq, therefore, the *Ḥums* represents the complete break with the ritual practice of Ibrāhīm and the embodiment of *jāhil*. The *jāhilīyah* is frequently referred to as the "time of ignorance." Yet Ibn Isḥāq does not portray the Quraysh as ignorant of what they are doing but as fully aware, and thus culpable, for their wrong conduct. They may not know how the *dīn* of Ibrāhīm is to be performed in all of its specific aspects since it had been lost slowly over the generations and almost completely forgotten before the rediscovery of the Zamzam well, but they are completely aware that they are violating the fundamentals of the *ḥajj* ritual. In a sense, they have abandoned the worship-service of God and begun worshipping themselves.

To demonstrate the need for Muḥammad's mission, Ibn Isḥāq then introduces four men who decide to break with their kin and seek the *ḥanīfīyah dīn* Ibrāhīm that has now been completely lost, forgotten, or arrogantly ignored. Three of the four, Waraqah b. Nayfal, Ubayd Allāh b. Jaḥsh, and ʿUthmān b. al-Ḥuwayrith become Christians (*tanaṣṣar*). Waraqah, the cousin of Muḥammad's first wife Khadījah, is described as studying the books of the Christians until "he was one of the most knowledgeable among the People of the Book (*ahl al-kitāb*). Ubayd Allāh, according to Ibn Isḥāq,

> Was constantly occupied with his search [for the *dīn* of Ibrāhīm] among the confusion [of different paths of worship-service] until he *aslama* (abandoned his old ways and surrendered). He then migrated with the *muslimīn* (submitters) to Abyssinia with his wife, Umm Ḥabībah bint Abū Sufyān; she was a *muslimah*. So, after he arrived there he became a Christian (*tanaṣṣar*) and withdrew his *islām* (submission) until he died.[48]

---

47. G 87/IH 1: 211–12.

48. G 87/IH 1: 211–12. The term meaning "to become Christian" refers to al-Nāṣirah, or Nazareth, the purported hometown of ʿĪsā (Jesus). Ibn Isḥāq refers to Christians as *al-Naṣrānīyah*, or Nazarenes.

ʿUthmān traveled as far as Byzantium where he became a Christian when he entered the emperor's service.

The focus of this section of Ibn Isḥāq's story, however, is on Zayd b. ʿAmr. Zayd serves a function analogous to that of John the Baptist in the New Testament in that he goes before Muḥammad proclaiming the *dīn* of Ibrāhīm to his people. According to Ibn Isḥāq,

> He resisted and did not enter Judaism or Christianity and withdrew from the *dīn* of his people. He withdrew from the idols, from eating carrion, blood, and sacrifices that were slaughtered to the idols. He forbade the killing of infant girls. He said, "I worship-serve (*aʿbad*) the Lord of Ibrāhīm." He showed open hostility toward his people for the defects of what they followed.[49]

Ibn Isḥāq says that Zayd had decided to leave Mecca to search for the *ḥanīfīyah dīn* Ibrāhīm but his wife held him back. He preached to the people and proclaimed the *dīn* of Ibrāhīm whenever he entered the *ḥaram*. But he began to be harassed by the Quraysh and was forced to flee up to Mount Ḥirāʾ, where Muḥammad would receive his first revelation. He cried to God in his despair that he was not a *Ḥillah*, but a Meccan whose house was in the center of the *ḥaram*, yet he could no longer enter the *ḥaram*.[50]

Zayd finally decides to leave Mecca and seek the *dīn* of Ibrāhīm in other parts of the Near East. After many travels he meets a monk in Syria who tells him, "Indeed, you seek a *dīn* to which no one can take you today." The monk continues, "Already you are in the shadow of a time [when] a prophet is being sent to your land which you just left. He is being sent with the *dīn* of Ibrāhīm *al-ḥanīfīyah*, so follow him, for indeed he is being sent now, this is the time."[51] Zayd sets out immediately for Mecca but is killed before he returns. Muḥammad later says that on the Day of Judgment Zayd "will be resurrected alone of the community."[52]

For Ibn Isḥāq, the extremes of the *Ḥums* were so great that they represented the final break with the *dīn* of Ibrāhīm and necessitated the

49. G 87/IH 1: 239–40.

50. G 100–103/IH 1: 240–47.

51. G 103/IH 1: 247.

52. G 100/IH 1: 240.

mission of Muḥammad. He makes this clear when he says that the practices of the *Ḥums* lasted until God sent Muḥammad:

> So He revealed to him, when He rendered His *dīn* free from defects and made plain for him the customs of the *ḥajj*. . . . Thus God removed the restriction of the *Ḥums* and the innovations of the Quraysh from the people when God sent the messenger with submission (*islām*).[53]

## *Conclusion*

For Ibn Isḥāq the problem that necessitated the mission of Muḥammad was the complete corruption of the *ḥanīfīyah dīn* Ibrāhīm that is represented as the complete and abject submission to God as embodied in the proper performance of the *ḥajj* after the manner of Ibrāhīm. Throughout the sections of the text examined in this chapter, Ibn Isḥāq focuses on actions that demonstrate abject submission to God and rarely mentions ideas or "beliefs" about the nature of God, His unity (*tawḥīd*), or a multiplicity of associates for God (*shirk*). While *'ibādat al-awthān* implies *shirk* in some sense, the fact that Ibn Isḥāq emphasizes changes in actions over changes in ideas indicates that what mattered most to Ibn Isḥāq was the external expression of belief through one's actions as signifiers of one's submission or obedience to God.[54]

The focus on external actions—especially on the correct performance of the *ḥajj*—as signifying true submission to God also says a great deal about Ibn Isḥāq's understanding of Muḥammad's purpose and what it was that he "founded," if anything. On one level, it is clear that Ibn Isḥāq understood Muḥammad to be reviving the lost *ḥanīfīyah dīn* of Ibrāhīm by returning to the practices of the *ḥajj* as they were given to Ibrāhīm by Jabra'īl.

But what about "Islam?" Ibn Isḥāq refers to Muḥammad's followers as *muslimūn* (sing., *muslim*) and what they participate in as *islām*. What, exactly, does he mean? Wilfred Cantwell Smith maintains that Islam came

53. G 88/IH 1:215–16.

54. The fact that Muslims focused primarily on actions over theological conceptions as a means of defining inclusion in the community argues against certain aspects of Fred Donner's thesis that the early community defined itself as a "community of believers" (*Muhammad and the Believers: At the Origins of Islam* [Cambridge, MA: Harvard University Press, 2010]).

into the world as a "self-aware" religion, meaning that Muslims understood Islam to be a religion distinct from, and somehow better than, other religions. Yet the term *dīn,* commonly taken to mean "religion," usually means "to obediently follow a path or method of ritual practice," of which there are many. Ibn Isḥāq does not present a single *dīn* as preferable to all others, as is evident in the stories of Salmān the Persian, ʿAbd Allāh b. Thāmir, and even in references to Waraqah b. Nawfal, who after breaking with the *Ḥums* and becoming a Christian, later becomes an advisor to Muḥammad and even declares him a prophet but, surprisingly, never becomes a follower.[55] Clearly, then, Ibn Isḥāq does not interpret *islām* to refer to an exclusive set of rituals and theological conceptions that represents the only correct "religion."

For Ibn Isḥāq, Islam seems to represent at least two things: (1) a status of submission to God that is expressed through physical acts of ritual, *and* (2) a period of time or state of being that he juxtaposes frequently with the *jāhilīyah* and the period of the *Ḥums.* Ibn Isḥāq describes ʿAbd Allāh b. Thāmir's "conversion" with the verb *aslama* when he becomes a Christian. Clearly, he does not mean here that ʿAbd Allāh became a "Muslim" but that he "rejects or abandons his practice of *ʿibādah al-awthān* and submits to a new *ʿibādah,*" in his case, ritual prayer offered to the One God.[56] Ibn Isḥāq uses the term *aslama* to indicate the abandonment of *ʿibādat al-awthān* and submission to God as expressed by the correct performance of *ʿibādah,* almost always referring to the *ḥajj.* In other words, *aslama* is only used in reference to people who had been "idol worshippers" before becoming "practicing" worshipper-slaves to the One God, whether it is a man who had been a soothsayer and then becomes a follower of Muḥammad or, as in the case of ʿAbd Allāh b. Thāmir, one who becomes a Christian.[57]

When Ibn Isḥāq uses *islām* as a noun, it is never to describe something Muḥammad creates but something to which he "calls" people (*daʿāna ilā al-islām*), just as he is said to have "called" people to God (*daʿāna ilā Allah*),

55. G 99, 107, 144/IH 1:238, 254, 340.

56. G 16–17/IH 1: 35–36.

57. G 92/IH 1:223. The key to the idea of "*aslama*" is to be found in the single exception to the rule, which occurs in the story of an attack on the Jewish tribe of the Banū Qurayẓah (G 461/ibid., IH 3:244–45). Some of the tribe "abandon" their forts and their tribe and "surrender" to Muḥammad's forces and become his followers (G 94/IH 1:227).

or he is described as being sent with *islām*.[58] In most instances *islām* is described as something that "arrives" or "occurs," as an event in time, not as a "religion" as described by Smith.[59] In references to Christianity (throughout the text it is *Naṣrānīyah*, literally, "Nazarenes"), the noun is sometimes made into a verb meaning "he became Christian" (*tanaṣṣar*); there is no equivalent in classical Arabic for "he became Muslim" (*tasallam*) until the fifth Islamic century, long after the time of Ibn Isḥāq.

From Ibn Isḥāq's point of view, it would thus be incorrect to describe Muḥammad as the "founder" of Islam. He is best understood as the "messenger of *islām*" bringing the message of submission to the One God, as the reviver of the *ḥanīfīyah dīn* Ibrāhīm, and, therefore, as the prophet sent to reestablish the community of worshipper-slaves among the descendants of Ismāʿīl whose primary expression of abject submission is the correct performance of the *ḥajj* as established by Ibrāhīm.

The foregoing examination of only one portion of the entire *Sīrat Rasūl Allāh* makes clear that determining precisely what Ibn Isḥāq understands "Islam" to be is extraordinarily complicated. And his is just one of many voices in the early period. To be sure, as the author of the earliest surviving biography of the prophet, his is a voice that cannot be ignored if one's aim is to understand what Muḥammad accomplished, what his followers think he was trying to accomplish, and how Islam through the centuries relates to and yet differentiates itself from other religious traditions, especially those—Judaism and Christianity—that regard Abraham as a pivotal figure. More broadly, thinking with an author like Ibn Isḥāq about the propriety of applying the title "founder" to Muḥammad provides an opportunity to reconsider the question of what, precisely, constitutes a "religion" and what is at stake in the answer to that question, both for those inside the tradition and for those looking on from the outside.

## *For Further Reading*

Benton, Michael. "Visualizing Narrative: Bridging the 'Aesthetic Gap.'" *Journal of Aesthetic Education* 33. 2 (Summer 1999): 33–49. Demonstrating that for many Muslims, the *Truth* of Muḥammad is greater than the mundane details of his

---

58. G 88, 93/IH 1: 216, 225.

59. G 21–22, 39, 47, 52, 56, 57, 78, 83, 94/IH 1:45–46, 90, 119, 131, 137, 140, 189, 202, 226/ Az 1:127.

life, what one might think of as small "t" truth. Benton describes a process whereby authors transform the basic "facts" into "biomythographies," as Ibn Isḥāq does in providing a deeper understanding of Muḥammad as an instrument of God's will.

Donner, Fred. *Narratives of Islamic Origins* (Princeton, NJ: Princeton University Press, 1997). Provides a controversial retelling of the history of the early community and their understanding of the relationship of Islam to Judaism and Christianity.

Guillaume, Alfred. *The Life of Muhammad: A Translation of Isḥāq's* Sīrat Rasūl Allāh. Oxford: Oxford University Press, 1955. The only translation to date of this important text. The author reconstructs the redacted sections of Ibn Isḥāq's text excluding the sections dealing with the stories of pre-Muḥammad prophets.

Hughes Aaron W. *Abrahamic Religions: On the Uses and Abuses of History*. Oxford: Oxford University Press, 2012. Offers a critical assessment of the function of Abraham in Judaism, Christianity, and Islam.

Motzki, Harald, ed. *The Biography of Muḥammad: The Issue of Sources*. Leiden: Brill, 2000. An excellent resource on debates about the historicity of early prophetic biographies.

Newby, Gordon. *The Making of the Last Prophet: A Reconstruction of the Earliest Biography of Muhammad*. Columbia: University of South Carolina Press, 1989. Translation and reconstruction of the first section of the lost stories of the pre-Muḥammad prophets.

Rippen, Andrew. "The Function of '*Asbāb al-nuzūl*' in Qur'ānic Exegesis." *Bulletin of the School of Oriental and African Studies* 51.1 (1988): 1–20. Explores the concept of *asbāb al-nuzūl*, "occasions of revelation," which is based on the idea that God intervenes in history in times of grave crisis. The *asbāb al-nuzūl* literature is extensive in medieval Muslim discourse because knowing the "cause" of an instance of revelation is central to understanding the meaning of the Qur'ān and *sunnah* (prophetic example). Rippen provides an overview of this concept and its applications in the various branches of Muslim thought.

Tottoli, Roberto. "The Origin and Use of the Term *Isrā'īliyyāt* in Muslim Literature." *Arabica* 46 (1999): 193–210. Discusses Ibn Isḥāq's extensive use of Jewish lore in his "making" of the image of Muḥammad as a prophet in the line of those listed in the Bible.

# 7

# *Hinduism and the Question of Founders*

*Måns Broo*

THE CONCEPT OF "World Religions" is a contested one today, and for several compelling reasons.[1] Many scholars believe that this category fails to do justice to the complicated reality of human religious experience. Hinduism is arguably the one religion most difficult to fit into this mold—indeed, there are scholars who deny the very existence of any one definable Hinduism, arguing that the whole concept is all too essentializing to meaningfully capture the varieties of lived religion in South Asia and beyond.[2] After all, what we call Hinduism, as Gavin Flood points out, has no unified doctrine or system of belief set down in a creed or declaration of faith, no single system of soteriology, and no centralized authority or bureaucracy.[3] One explanation for this variety is that Hinduism has no recognized founder.

This basic fact would seem to make a chapter on Hinduism a poor fit for the present volume, with its focus on debates about the founders of major religious traditions. Nevertheless, I argue in this chapter that *not*

1. Jacqueline Suthren Hirst and John Zavos, *Religious Traditions in Modern South Asia* (London: Routledge, 2011), 16–21.

2. Robert Frykenberg, "The Emergence of Modern 'Hinduism' as a Concept and as an Institution: A Reappraisal with Special Reference to South India," in *Hinduism Reconsidered*, ed. G. D. Sontheimer and H. Kulke (New Delhi: Manohar, 1989), 26.

3. Gavin Flood, *An Introduction to Hinduism* (Cambridge: Cambridge University Press, 1996), 6.

*having a founder* emphatically matters in Hinduism and that this "absence" can also perform a positive function. Furthermore, much of lived Hinduism occurs within sects or, more accurately, *sampradāyas*, "[groups] with special concepts, forms of worship, and adherence to exclusive leadership exercised by an outstanding religious personality or his physical or spiritual descendant."[4] The *sampradāyas* have their own founders, and whether they are living beings, mythological characters, or something in between, these founders matter very much to their followers. In both of these senses—that is, the lack of a founder of Hinduism per se and the ubiquity of founding figures in the *sampradāyas*—the question of founders is thus a critical and complex one in Hinduism as well.

## *The Supra-Divinity of Not Having a Founder*

While the term "Hinduism" is a relatively modern one, it does not follow that theologians and philosophers in pre-modern India did not engage in defining, delimiting, and defending various kinds of perceived orthodoxy associated with Hindu tradition.[5] In the face of attacks by Buddhists, Jains, and other groups, the various schools (*darśanas*) that conceived of themselves as orthodox (*āstika*), that is, as submitting to the authority of the Veda, mounted a vigorous defense of the Vedic revelation, regardless of the degree to which their submission to Vedic authority really mattered in their doctrines.

In defending the Veda, the Mīmāṃsā school formulated an interesting doctrine with important implications for the question of "founders." The epistemology of Mīmāṃsā is based on the doctrine of the self-validity of knowledge (*svataḥ-prāmāṇya*).[6] All knowledge (except for memory, which is held to be dependent on previous experience) is valid in itself, for it certifies its own truth. It does not rest on any other conditions or knowledge for its validity, for otherwise we would end up in an infinite regress. Whenever individuals act according to their knowledge, they do so convinced

4. Joachim Wach, *Sociology of Religion* (Chicago: Phoenix Books, 1967), 128.

5. David Lorenzen, *Who Invented Hinduism? Essays on Religion in History* (New Delhi: Yoda Press, 2006), 3–36; Brian K. Pennington, *Was Hinduism Invented? Britons, Indians, and the Colonial Construction of Religion* (Oxford: Oxford University Press, 2005), 3–7.

6. See, e.g., Surendranath Dasgupta, *A History of Indian Philosophy*, vol. 1 (Delhi: Motilal Banarsidass, 2006 [1922]), 373–75; and Mysore Hiriyanna, *An Outline of Indian Philosophy* (Delhi: Motilal Banarsidass, 2007 [1932]), 308–10.

that their knowledge is indeed correct. All knowledge is thus deemed valid at the moment of its emergence. This knowledge, of course, may later be proven false, in which case the cause is to be found in some extraneous circumstance that interferes with ordinary circumstances. A favorite Indian example is that of Devadatta thinking that he is seeing a piece of silver glimmering on the beach, but noticing on closer inspection that it really was only a shell. This false "knowledge" of silver was thus later invalidated, and the reason was found to be in the cause or source of that knowledge, that is, in Devadatta's imperfect eyesight. What invalidates that first "knowledge" of silver, again, is subsequent experience.

The main aim of Mīmāṃsā epistemology is to affirm the authority of the Veda, in which no fault can be found. Why can there be no faults in the Veda? First, while verbal testimony in general is dependent on both the moral and the sensory trustworthiness of the speaker, such faults cannot be found in the Veda—quite simply because according to Mīmāṃsā, the Veda has no speaker. It is not created by humans, but neither does it have a divine origin. As a particular combination of eternal words, it is self-existent and without any author (*apauruṣeya*). Nor can the Veda be invalidated by subsequent experience because, according to the Mīmāṃsā interpretation, the Veda deals only with empirically unverifiable otherworldly subjects. Neither does the Veda contain internal discrepancies, once the proper Mīmāṃsā exegesis is applied. This exegesis, then, constitutes the main task of the classical Mīmāṃsā thinkers.

But how can the Mīmāṃsā scholars (and here they were followed by all the Vedānta schools) claim that the Veda has no author? They refer to tradition: while all other texts, even ancient ones, are assigned to some particular person, tradition knows of no author of the Veda. Neither does the Veda itself claim an author, though it does recognize the "seer" (*ṛṣi*) of particular hymns. But these are just the non-specific titles of the persons who first received the eternal Veda in the present time period. As with other historical persons or occurrences specified in the Veda, there is no claim that the Veda records history. Rather, history follows the eternal blueprint of the Veda. Furthermore, the perfect nature of the Veda is reflected in the way the text has been scrupulously passed down intact from generation to generation.

What the Mīmāṃsā philosophers do, then, is to make a virtue of the Veda's lack of authorship. Authorship implies either a faulty human or a possibly capricious god; a text without either is not only superhuman, it is super-divine.

## *Dispensing with Problematic Myths*

The Mīmāṃsā doctrine of the eternal, authorless Veda has another important corollary relevant to the present task: it relegates mythology to a secondary level of importance. According to Mīmāṃsā, the Veda deals only with otherworldly topics. Even within these topics, the only things that really matter are the injunctions and prohibitions of the text ("do this, do not do that"). All the rest—notwithstanding all the efforts of ingenious Mīmāṃsā exegesis that constitutes the majority of the Vedic corpus—is regarded as figurative language (*arthavāda*) intended solely to encourage or discourage people from performing certain actions. The ancient Mīmāṃsā commentator Śabara gives the example of "the trees sat down for a sacrificial session," a statement so evidently in conflict with everyday experience of arboreal capability as to beg for a non-literal reading (namely, that the particular sacrificial act in view is so powerful that even the trees participate in it, if they only could).[7]

However, Mīmāṃsā goes a step further when it denies the validity of Vedic mythology altogether. After all, why would an eternal text deal with actions within time, even divine actions? In fact, on one occasion Śabara seems to agree with the proposition that the Vedic gods may be no more than words.[8] While Kumārila Bhaṭṭa (seventh century CE) and other later Mīmāṃsā philosophers do soften such statements, they retain the right to see mythology in a figurative sense.

Johannes Bronkhorst argues that one of the reasons for this unique interpretative strategy, unprecedented in Indian philosophy, could have been to defend the Veda against Buddhist critique.[9] The Buddhists certainly were not reluctant to attack what they perceived as silly and even immoral myths in the Vedas. By adopting Mīmāṃsā, these Brahmins were able to retain and even strengthen the authority of the Veda, while at the same time discarding myths that they perhaps did not believe in themselves—because, they could argue, once one really knows the Veda (as we do), it is apparent that the myths were simply not meant to be believed.

---

7. Quoted in Johannes Bronkhorst, "The Origin of Mīmāṃsā as a School of Thought: A Hypothesis," in *Vidyārṇavavandana: Essays in Honour of Asko Parpola*, ed. K. Karttunen and P. Koskikallio (Helsinki: Finnish Oriental Society, 2001), 85.

8. Bronkhorst, "The Origin of Mīmāṃsā as a School of Thought," 86.

9. Bronkhorst, "The Origin of Mīmāṃsā as a School of Thought," 83–103.

## *Tapping into the "Spiritual" Discourse*

Mīmāṃsā has never been nor has it even aspired to become a popular tradition. Nevertheless, the Mīmāṃsā idea of the eternity of the Vedic word is of interest for the way it relates to the question of the origin of Hinduism itself and provides modern Hindus a point of entry into the popular "spiritual" discourse of today. Consider the following description from the website of Kauai's Hindu Monastery, an international Śaiva organization founded in 1970 by Hindu convert Satguru Sivaya Subramuniyaswami (1927–2001):

> Hinduism, the world's oldest religion, has no beginning—it precedes recorded history. It has no human founder. It is a mystical religion, leading the devotee to personally experience the Truth within, finally reaching the pinnacle of consciousness where man and God are one.[10]

While not literally holding that Hinduism is eternal, this website—as do countless others—claims that Hinduism is the oldest religion in the world. Having said that Hinduism has no origin in recorded history and no human founder, the author then effortlessly moves on to claim a "mystical" status for Hinduism, here implicitly tapping into the "spiritual" culture of late modernity associated with living experience, inner discourse, individualism, and freedom in contrast with "religion," systems, dogma, hierarchies, and authorities.[11] How does this work? Having no founder, Hinduism also has no clear source of authority or hierarchy. Rather, Hinduism leads "the devotee to personally experience the Truth within." In this way, the discourse emphasizing the antiquity of the religion can at the same time assert that it is the most modern and up-to-date religion.

While it has no beginning, somewhat paradoxically Hinduism is here said to be the "world's oldest religion." Despite the oft-claimed lack of historical interest within Indian culture, antiquity has almost always been

10. "Nine Beliefs of Hinduism," n.p. (accessed 2 February 2013), www.himalayanacademy.com/basics/nineb.

11. Steven Sutcliffe, *Children of the New Age: A History of Spiritual Practices* (London: Routledge, 2003), 214–23.

seen as a mark of authenticity.[12] Within classical Hindu cosmography, being ancient means being a remnant of a better, purer time, before the onslaught of the present age of Kali, an age of discord and dissent. In a contemporary context, being ancient is perhaps better understood as a sign of having withstood the test of time.

## *Everlasting, Universal Values*

The Mīmāṃsā doctrine of the eternity of the Veda is mirrored in many contemporary presentations of Hinduism. Mata Amritanandamayi Devi (b. 1953), better known as Amma or the hugging woman saint, is perhaps the best-known Hindu teacher in the world today. In a short tract in question-and-answer format called *The Eternal Truth*, she gives the following description of Hinduism:

> The great souls living in different countries during different epochs gave their disciples instructions on how to attain God (or the Ultimate Truth). These instructions later became different religions. But that which in India became Sanatana Dharma consists of the everlasting principles, values, and ethical teachings that were revealed to a large number of Self-realized souls as their own experience. Later it came to be known as Hinduism. It is all-encompassing.[13]

Here we see an admirably clear example of the universalizing discourse of modern Hinduism. According to Amma, other religions stem from the instructions of historical persons in different times and places. Yes, these persons are "great souls," but they are temporally and spatially bound. Hinduism, originally known as Sanatana Dharma, "the eternal law" or "the perennial principle," on the other hand, is made up of everlasting principles not created by any one individual but "revealed" to a

12. Måns Broo, *As Good as God: The Guru in Gauḍīya Vaiṣṇavism* (Åbo: Åbo Akademi University Press, 2003), 219–25. See, however, the comments of Roy W. Perret on the characterization of Indian culture as disinterested in history ("History, Time, and Knowledge in Ancient India," *History and Theory* 38/3 [1999]: 307–21).

13. Sri Amritanandamayi Devi, *The Eternal Truth* (Amritapuri: Mata Amritanandamayi Mission Trust, 2010), 10–11.

large number of "self-realized" souls.[14] Amma further says that these persons received this revelation not as some dogma or mere faith but as "their own experience," which resonates with the discourse emphasizing personal experience that is so central to the spiritual culture of late modernity. In contrast to the other, limited religions, Hinduism is therefore all-encompassing.

The question of founders is central to this discourse. It is precisely the fact that they have single, historical founders that make other religions time-bound and limited. They are no doubt important and worthy of respect and praise—Amma speaks elsewhere of her Christian and Muslim "children"[15]—but they are nevertheless limited. Without a single, historically and geographically fixed founder, Hinduism is freed from the constraints of time and place. Particularly when coupled with the monism of a (neo-)Advaita Vedantic worldview, this freedom creates a powerfully universalizing, inclusive Hinduism that lends itself very well to a presentation intended to cross geographical and sectarian boundaries. This inclusivity is well illustrated by the rest of *The Eternal Truth*, where Amma goes on to explain many of the beliefs and practices of popular Hinduism (worship of images, prayer, devotional singing, and the like) from a universalist perspective, in reply to questions from (one supposes) Western followers.

## *Founders in an Eternal Religion*

We have so far seen how ancient and contemporary Hindus make creative use of the absence of a historical founder of Hinduism. Nevertheless, while being presented as an eternal, unchanging truth, Hinduism in both its popular and more scholarly forms is characterized by a multitude of founding fathers and mothers. Sivaya Subhramuniyaswami and Amma are, after all, founders of Hindu religious organizations, though Amma would perhaps avoid "limiting" herself and her teachings to a category labeled "Hinduism."

But if Hinduism is described as an eternal, unchanging truth, of what use are founders? Would not the smallest change or departure be

---

14. For the history of the term Sanatana Dharma, see Wilhelm Halbfass, *India and Europe: An Essay in Understanding* (Albany: State University of New York Press, 1988), 310–48.

15. Devi, *The Eternal Truth*, 88–89.

interpreted as a corruption of the perfect standard? Perhaps.[16] But even a tradition deemed perfect needs custodians to protect and preserve it. And since Hinduism has no single founder, it has no single center of authority or bureaucracy. This religious vacuum provides the context for the emergence of the guru or *ācārya*, the spiritual preceptor.[17]

Hindu texts give elaborate descriptions of the qualities of the guru, often translated as "spiritual master."[18] Often such descriptions combine qualities that appear to be radically discordant. According to the mediaeval Tantric text *Mantra-muktāvalī* (ca. 1530),

> Who is of pure descent, clean, devoted to appropriate conduct, a householder, free from anger; who knows the Veda and all the sciences, is faithful and non-envious; who speaks nicely and is of nice appearance; who is pure, beautifully clothed and young; who is pleased by the happiness of all living beings; who is wise, humble, self-sufficient, gentle and thoughtful; who has good qualities and is determined and knowledgeable in worship; who is affectionate to his disciples, equal when confronted by praise or criticism; who is devoted to sacrifices and mantras; who is expert in logic and debate, pure of heart and an ocean of compassion—a guru with qualities such as these is a sea of venerability [guru-ness].[19]

The qualities here represent a curious mix of the perfect teacher, the saint, and the debonair gentleman: not only should the guru be learned, wise, and well spoken; he should also be affectionate to his disciples and undisturbed in the face of either praise or slander, as well as young, well dressed, and handsome! Such lists should obviously not be taken too literally. They

16. While doing fieldwork for my own study of the guru institution of Caitanya or Gauḍīya Vaiṣṇavism, a strand of devotional Hinduism primarily found in Bengal, I heard one guru referred to as "deviant" for allowing his disciples to occasionally wear turbans (Broo, *As Good as God*, 227–28).

17. For a brief but useful bibliography on the subject of the guru, see Antonio Rigopoulos, ed., *Guru, The Spiritual Master in Eastern and Western Traditions: Authority and Charisma* (Venice: Venetian Academy of Indian Studies Series, 2007), 178–79.

18. Cf. Marie-Thérèse Charpentier, *Indian Female Gurus in Contemporary Hinduism: A Study of Central Aspects and Expressions of Their Religious Leadership* (Åbo: Åbo Akademi University Press, 2010).

19. Quoted in Gopāla Bhaṭṭa Gosvāmī, *Śrī Hari-bhakti-vilāsa*, ed. Haridāsa Śāstrī, vol. 1 (Vṛndāvana: Gaura-Gadādhara, 1986), 38–41.

are relevant for discerning the ideals of guruhood entertained by Hindu authors (and also, perhaps, in discovering the kinds of excellences devoted followers will assign to their gurus), but they say little about what qualities are required of a person who wishes to become a guru. In practical terms, the guru is defined by having disciples who consider him or her a guru.[20] In more general terms, it may be useful to consider why some persons attract followers in the first place.

## *Max Weber and Charisma*

Max Weber's classic concept of charisma ("a certain quality of individual personality by virtue of which he is set apart from ordinary men and treated as endowed with supernatural, superhuman, or at least specifically exceptional powers or qualities") is useful in understanding the mechanics involved in becoming a guru.[21] In contrast to the supposed eternity of the Veda or the "Sanatana Dharma" of Hindu tradition, charisma is a quality bound by time. It is a power that creates extraordinary authority, often surpassing that of tradition or a scriptural canon. It can launch new religious ideas into wider circulation and gain them a following that may survive the charismatic figure.

Following Weber, some scholars see charisma as a revolutionary, almost frightening type of absolute authority, while others have held that being charismatically endowed does not in itself determine the degree of power or authority that the person exerts on others.[22] The second understanding seems to match the Indian context better, where charismatic renewal is often not at all as revolutionary or disruptive as Weber imagines it to be. Weber further describes different types of charismatics, categorized according to the type of charisma they possess. At one end of the spectrum is the magician, whose charisma is purely *personal* as it depends solely on his or her own qualities. At the other end is the priest,

20. For studies of women gurus, see, e.g., Karen Pechilis, ed., *The Graceful Guru: Hindu Female Gurus in India and the United States* (New York: Oxford University Press, 2004); and Charpentier, *Indian Female Gurus in Contemporary Hinduism.*

21. Max Weber, *The Theory of Social and Economic Organization* (New York: Free Press, 1964), 358.

22. For the former view, see C. Lindholm, *Charisma* (Cambridge: Basil Blackwell, 1990); for the latter, see Kimmo Ketola, *An Indian Guru and His Western Disciples: Representation and Communication of Charisma in the Hare Krishna Movement* (Ph.D. dissertation, Helsinki University, 2002), 31.

whose charisma—somewhat paradoxically considering Weber's general definition of the term—does not depend on personal qualities but rather on the qualities of the institution to which he or she belongs. In other words, such a charisma is *institutional*, or a charisma of office. While the magician is self-employed and his practice occasional, the priests form a specialized social group in the service of a cultic enterprise. In contrast with the magician, the priest's occupation is regularly organized and permanent.[23]

Between these extremes stands the prophet. Like the magician, the prophet embodies personal charisma, but the revelatory knowledge that he or she claims to possess concerns specific doctrines and commandments of an older tradition. Whereas the magician functions independently, the prophet works on the fringe of a cultic enterprise. In practice, the establishment of a prophet's charisma is similar to that of a magician, that is, through special ecstatic abilities or magical feats.[24]

As separate charismatic personages, Weber also mentions the sacred legislator, the teacher of ethics, and the mystagogue. The sacred legislator is someone who has been assigned the responsibility of codifying or reconstituting a law, while the teacher of ethics is someone who gathers disciples and counsels individuals on personal matters. The mystagogue, finally, is a religious specialist who performs sacraments or power-filled actions meant to bring salvation. Like prophets, they are part of a larger community, but teaching an ethical doctrine usually is only a subordinate role for them. Like priests, they may also make a living out of the practice. Weber locates the Hindu guru within both of these two last categories.[25]

Weber's typology of charismatic personages has been criticized from many angles.[26] Despite his explicit attempt to make it fit an Indian situation, the typology does not work very well for the guru, who can fit several of the ideals he mentions. Weber's own Protestant background may have contributed to his downplaying the role of the priestly charisma of office, while lending too much importance to the disruptive element of personal charisma.[27] The concepts of individual and institutional

23. Weber, *Theory of Social and Economic Organization*, 28–30.

24. Weber, *Theory of Social and Economic Organization*, 46–48.

25. Weber, *Theory of Social and Economic Organization*, 49–55.

26. See, e.g., Ketola, *An Indian Guru and His Western Disciples*, 26–27.

27. George L. Scheper, "Charisma," *ER*[2] 3:1544.

charisma, however, are useful for understanding different types of gurus. Weber's typology of charismatics is also useful in an indirect way since it reveals how Western concepts may limit our understanding of a non-Western phenomenon.

## *Types of Hindu Gurus*

Ralph Marc Steinmann's short history of the Hindu guru-disciple relationship is divided into five roughly chronological stages.[28] The first stage Steinmann calls the Vedic foundation and the classical brāhmaṇic forms (ca. 1200–800 BCE). Here the guru—in the Veda called *ācārya,* the one who knows and teaches proper behavior—is generally a Brahmin householder, whose task is to is to teach young male pupils (*brahmacārins*) one or several Vedic texts, as well as related subjects such as grammar, pronunciation, and the like. After staying in the (ideally) semi-rural household of the teacher (*āśrama*) and mastering the subjects taught (some authorities prescribe a course of study lasting as long as twenty-four years), the student returns as a full-fledged member of society. Although the relationship includes ceremonies of "rebirth" (into Vedic study) and "graduation," Steinmann argues that it is mainly characterized by a transmission of knowledge. The main function of the Vedic system of education was to keep the orally transmitted Veda alive by inscribing it onto the minds of the pupils. In such a situation, there is little scope for innovation or individual charisma—in fact, Weber sees the whole Brahminical institution as one of his prime examples of institutional charisma.

Steinmann's second stage is the Upaniṣadic period (ca. 800–400 BCE). Here the ritualism of the Veda is seen as worldly, temporary, and thus illusory. To know the words of the Veda by heart is no longer sufficient; one needs to possess realized, mystical knowledge of the fundamental nature of the self (*ātman*) and the divine "ground of all being" (*brahman*). The ideal human life shifts from the Brahmin householder to the ascetic virtuoso, who has given up all worldly responsibilities and entanglements. This means that it is harder to judge who is a "true guru"

28. Ralph Marc Steinmann, *Guru-sisya-sambandha: Das Meister-Schüler-Verhältnis im traditionellen under modernen Hinduismus* (Stuttgart: Steiner, 1986), 278–81. One must bear in mind that in the Indian situation, however, nothing is ever completely supplanted and, as a consequence, the different stages described by Steinmann will overlap to some degree. Even today, for example, it is still possible to find children learning the Veda by heart; see, e.g., Peter Brent, *Godmen of India* (London: Penguin, 1972), 32–51.

(*sadguru*), since such a determination is not quantifiable as is knowledge of the Veda. At the same time, the subtle nature of the perilous path and the esoteric, mystical quality of the metaphysical knowledge endowed the Upaniṣadic guru with much greater authority, in terms of both comprehensiveness and intensiveness of power.[29] Here one finds a broader scope for personal charisma: in fact, it is common to see the Buddha and Vardhamāna Mahavīra as charismatic gurus of this type who ended up founding their own religions by refusing to pay even lip service to the authority of the Veda.[30]

The third stage is the Bhakti tradition (ca. 400 BCE–1500 CE). Instead of striving to transcend the world, the objective here is to draw down the mercy (*prasāda*) of a personal divinity. This is done by taking refuge in this divine being as well as through the practices of bhakti. A guru is also necessary, a person who has already attained this divine mercy and who can therefore act as an intermediary between the individual practitioner and the transcendent divine, or at least as an ideal devotee. Steinmann distinguishes two conceptions of the guru here: during the epic period (400 BCE–400 CE), the guru is adored like a god, but in the Purāṇic and medieval periods (400–1500 CE) he or she is completely identified with one's personal deity (*iṣṭadevatā*). The main qualification of the guru here is ecstatic devotion, a qualification that may override birth in a low caste, illiteracy, or other factors that would disqualify a guru of the earlier types, so that personal charisma again seems to be paramount.

Steinmann's fourth stage is the Jñāna-tradition, preeminently exemplified by Śaṅkara (ninth century CE). This stage features an affinity for the worldview of the Upaniṣads, with an added emphasis on renunciation of the world both for guru and disciple. Also, instead of the sylvan āśrama of earlier times, Śaṅkara founded urban monastic communities (*maṭhas*), probably inspired by Buddhist examples. The ideal guru is now the *jagadguru*, "guru of the world," who besides imparting esoteric teachings to a small inner circle, will also attract thousands of lay disciples and influence worldly events as well.

The fifth and final stage is the Tantric tradition, which stands on its own but has also influenced both Bhakti and Jñāna traditions. Here one

---

29. Bernard de Jouvenel, "Authority: The Efficient Imperative," in *Authority*, ed. Carl J. Friedrich (Cambridge, MA: Harvard University Press, 1958), 160.

30. But see Geoffrey Samuel, *The Origins of Yoga and Tantra: Indic Religions to the Thirteenth Century* (Cambridge: Cambridge University Press, 2008).

sees a climax in the deification of the guru—indeed, the guru is sometimes seen as even more important than the divinity. Detailed criteria for both guru and disciple often emphasize practical knowledge of ritual procedures, mantras, and the like rather than Vedic knowledge.

To sum up, one can discern two parallel lines of development. On the one hand, the importance of the guru grows from stage to stage: from teacher to metaphysical teacher, representative of the divine to the divine itself. On the other hand, the criteria for determining a true guru—and thus exercising institutional control over the guru—become increasingly vague. Likewise, from a purely institutional charisma, the charisma of the guru becomes progressively more personal.

## *Charisma in Indian Religious History*

Critiques of Steinmann's typology can take various forms.[31] The most obvious fault with his typology is that it makes the history of the guru institution and of Hinduism itself seem much less messy and entangled with other religions than it is in reality, particularly "on the ground" in the realm of daily, lived religion. It also fails to note the interplay between personal and institutional charisma that (as I endeavor to show) characterizes the Indian guru institution. However, the typology does demonstrate some of the openings toward charismatic innovation that the guru institution offers within a religion that generally idealizes an unchanging past.

According to Heinrich von Stietencron, in the Indian literary tradition, charisma is originally and primarily linked to the persona of the righteous (*dharma*-following) king, as a kind of radiating power and fortune that distinguishes him from his less fortunate peers.[32] Such a power was linked to Śrī or Lakṣmī, the goddess of fortune and consort of Viṣṇu, with whom the king was often equated. But the goddess of fortune is notoriously fickle (*cañcalā*), and this charisma may thus leave the king if he proves unworthy of the role of Viṣṇu by acts against the dictates of righteousness.

---

31. E.g., Broo, *As Good as God*, 74–75.

32. Heinrich von Stietencron, "Charisma and Canon: The Dynamics of Legitimization and Innovation in Indian Religions," in *Charisma and Canon: Essays on the Religious History of the Indian Subcontinent*, ed. Vasudha Dalmia, Angelika Malinar, and Martin Christof (Oxford: Oxford University Press, 2001), 18–19.

A second way of thinking about charismatic persons arose in the Gupta period in the fourth century CE with the revival of Brahmin influence after centuries of decline under Kṣatriya and Buddhist rule. The Kṣatriyas had institutionalized their charismatic kings into hereditary kingship, while the Buddhists through the monastic institution had to some extent succeeded in institutionalizing the charisma of the Buddha. The Brahmins had not been able to benefit from either process. By now linking divine presence and grace with religious leaders (the first instance seems to be Lakulīśa, a famous Śaiva teacher of the second century, who in the fourth century was deified and identified with Śiva himself) and by assuming leadership in various popular devotional (bhakti) groups, Brahmins managed to gradually regain much of their influence. The guru is no longer a simple teacher but someone close to the divine, even a mediator between man and God. Initiation (*dīkṣā*) is not only a rite of acceptance into a religious group but also a condition for or, indeed, the attainment itself of divine grace.[33]

Taken together, Steinmann and von Stietencron paint a picture of guruhood as an institution that initially performs a custodial function: to protect and preserve the sacred word of the Veda. Traditional Vedic scholarship should not be confused with a priestly type of vocation or biblical scholarship. Different from Christian priests who interpret and expostulate on the message of the Bible, scholars of the Veda function more like tape recorders.[34] Their job is to keep the supposedly eternal and unchanging Veda alive, without changing a single syllable. With the advent of the upaniṣadic ideal of personal spiritual enlightenment, and particularly with that of the popular devotional (bhakti) groups, the role of the guru grows, as does his or her influence on society at large.

## The Timeless Descending into Time

The concept of the divine descent (*avatāra*) is also useful to consider in this context. Just as the timeless Viṣṇu from time to time enters the temporal world through his descents as the divine fish (*matsya*) and in other forms, over time, other gods were thought to descend into this world to fulfill various tasks. In the Bhagavad-gītā (4.8), Kṛṣṇa gives "establishment" or

33. Von Stietencron, "Charisma and Canon," 21–23.

34. Michael Witzel, "Vedas and Upaniṣads," in *The Blackwell Companion to Hinduism*, ed. Gavin Flood (Oxford: Blackwell, 2003), 68–69.

"regulation" of *dharma* (*dharma-samsthāpana*) as one of the reasons for his own descent. While *dharma* in itself is considered timeless or eternal (*sanātana*), in this temporal world it may be lost and may therefore need to be reestablished or regulated. For such a task, a charismatic founder is needed.

Hinduism is sometimes divided into three very loosely defined sectarian clusters: the Vaiṣṇavas or worshippers of Viṣṇu (in one of his many forms), Śaivas or Śiva-worshippers, and the Śāktas or goddess-worshippers.[35] By no means does every Hindu identify with a particular group; many worship different deities according to pragmatic interests, while others worship none. Nevertheless, these *saṃpradāyas* are an extremely important part of Hinduism today, and they all have their founders, persons from whom begin *guru paraṃparās* extending through time down to the present moment.

Let us take the Śrī *saṃpradāya* as an example. This is an important and influential Vaiṣṇava *saṃpradāya*, found particularly in Andhra Pradesh, Karnataka, and Tamil Nadu in South India.[36] While the *saṃpradāya* is often said to stem from the famous Vedānta philosopher Rāmānuja (trad. 1017–1137), within the tradition itself he is not considered its original founder.[37] Rather, in a popular representation of Rāmānuja, he is preceded by six human teachers and three divine ones: Viṣṇu himself; Śrī or Lakṣmī, his consort; and Viṣvaksena, the commander-in-chief of Viṣṇu's army. Viṣvaksena "revealed" the doctrines of the Śrī Vaiṣṇava faith to Nammalvar, the first human preceptor in the line. Rāmānuja simply "structured" the teachings in "their present form."[38] Viṣṇu's timeless and divine truth descends into this temporal world, where this truth will require "structuring" and reassessment from generation to generation.

Because Hinduism does not have a single founder, there has never been a single, "true" Hinduism, whatever name we wish to give it. The

---

35. Robert Jackson and Dermot Killingley, *Approaches to Hinduism* (London: John Murray, 1988), 182.

36. For a general introduction to this *saṃpradāya*, see S. M. Srinivasa Chari, *Vaiṣṇavism: Its Philosophy, Theology and Religious Discipline*, 2nd ed. (Delhi: Motilal Banarsidass, 2002).

37. Arjun Appadurai, "The Past as a Scarce Resource," *Man* (n.s.) 16.2 (1981): 209.

38. Sri Rama Ramanuja Achari, *The Handbook of Sri Vaishnavism*, 6–7 (accessed 25 September 2012), www.srimatham.com/storage/docs/handbook-of-srivaishnavism.pdf.

astonishing plurality that arguably has always characterized Hinduism therefore requires mechanisms to establish eternal truths and assert the legitimacy of innovations of different kinds. One such mechanism is the institution of *guru paraṃparā*, "a line of authorized transmission of knowledge from fully trained teacher to tested student both of sacred scripture and its interpretation."[39] Even a universally recognized reformer such as Rāmānuja, then, needs to be situated in such a line of teachers to secure his authoritative status.

While Hindus may therefore resist labeling as "founders" persons such as Rāmānuja, these figures are nevertheless revered very much like founders of religions. There are many miracles associated with Rāmānuja's life, his writings are considered authoritative within the *saṃpradāya*, events associated with his life are celebrated yearly, and his tomb is ritually revered within the Sri Ranganathaswamy temple at Sri Rangam. In fact, within the *saṃpradāya*, Rāmānuja is commonly seen not only as a human but also as a being of divine descent—that of Adi-śeṣa, the divine snake on which Viṣṇu reclines.[40] Stemming from Rāmānuja are lines of disciplic succession (*guru-paraṃparā*), where the main qualification of the guru is being linked to Rāmānuja and his successors through appointment or lineal descent. Most gurus claiming their allegiance to Rāmānuja are descendants of Brahmin householder gurus that he appointed. Their charisma is thus almost purely institutional.[41]

## Tradition as a Source of Personal Charisma

While the institution of *guru-paraṃparā* is supposedly all about retaining sacred knowledge "as it is"[42] or unchanged from generation to generation, some action must still be taken to preserve it. According to Daniel Gold, a tradition can break down in two ways.[43] *Corruption* occurs when its ideals and actualities drift too far away from each other, so that the

39. Von Stietencron, "Charisma and Canon," 18.

40. Naimisaranya Das, *The Life of Ramanujacarya* (Los Angeles: Veda, 1989), 212.

41. This is mirrored in many other *saṃpradāyas* as well, such as that of the Caitanya Vaiṣṇavas (cf. Broo, *As Good as God*).

42. To quote Bhaktivedanta Swami Prabhupāda, *Bhagavad-gītā as It Is* (Los Angeles: Bhaktivedanta Book Trust, 1972).

43. Daniel Gold, *Comprehending the Guru: Towards a Grammar of Religious Perception* (Atlanta: Scholars Press, 1987), 90.

manifest forms seem tainted and no longer able to give access to the transcendent. *Collapse* occurs when the tradition is unable to adapt to changing external conditions, after which potential adherents no longer see the divine in the forms the tradition has hitherto offered, and thus lend it no practical support. According to Weber, rectifying such a situation is the task of a "sacred legislator," but every guru will need to guard against both of these two types of breakdown. Generally, no radical steps are needed. Every tradition will have its share of less-than-ideal manifest forms, but as long as it also manages to provide untainted, ideal examples for practitioners to emulate, such failings can always be pushed toward the margins.

Because of the common idealization of the past, even the most iconoclastic innovators will wish to reconnect to tradition. Commentary becomes the exegetical tool par excellence. While such commentary itself requires charismatic legitimization, sometimes, as in the different Vedānta traditions, it eventually becomes canon.[44] By adding layer upon layer of scriptural commentary, successive generations may slowly, even imperceptibly, update the teachings, while at the same time maintaining the link to an authoritative tradition. Even seemingly radical teachings can be advanced in a similar way. The remarks of Swami B. V. Tripurari, an articulate Western exponent of Caitanya Vaiṣṇavism, illustrate this point:

> One must distinguish between the form and the substance of tradition. Thus we find that the most prominent members of the lineage are involved in renovation of the tradition, revealing its truth in a way relevant to time and circumstance, such that those who are members in form only cannot appreciate them. To recognize reformers of the mission, practitioners themselves must also become essence seekers on a deeper level and thus remain vital in their practice. Failure to do so involves a break from the tradition despite superficial adherence to its external symbols.[45]

This approach opens the way for all manner of reinterpretation of tradition yet it is couched in the most traditional of forms: in a commentary

44. Von Stietencron, "Charisma and Canon," 16.

45. Swami B. V. Tripurari, *The Bhagavad Gita: Its Feeling and Philosophy* (San Rafael, CA: Mandala, 2001), 131.

on the Bhagavad-gītā, but in the course of arguing for the need of *guru paramparā* as well.

The authority of tradition can be taken much further. Sri Sri Ravi Shankar (b. 1956) is an internationally famous Indian guru who very consciously strives to present a message suited to contemporary sensibilities. This is how he is described as a "spiritual teacher" on his official webpage:

> As a spiritual teacher, Sri Sri has rekindled the traditions of yoga and meditation and offered them in a form that is relevant to the 21st century. Beyond reviving ancient wisdom, Sri Sri has created new techniques for personal and social transformation. These include the Sudarshan Kriya® [*sic*] which has helped millions of people to find relief from stress and discover inner reservoirs of energy and peace in daily life. In a mere 29 years, his programs have raised the quality of life for participants in 152 countries.[46]

Even here, where the main point is the efficacy of the Sudarshan Kriya breathing technique that was "created" (and duly registered with the trademark office) by the guru himself, it is emphasized that he has also "rekindled" traditions of yoga and meditation and offered them in a contemporary form. He is also said to have recited the Bhagavad-gītā as a four-year-old, without ever hearing it before, and to have completed both his traditional Vedic studies and a degree in modern science by the age of seventeen. In fact, even Shankar's creation of the Sudarshan Kriya is downplayed, when it is also said that it was "cognized" by him during a period of silence.[47]

While different in degree, these two examples underscore an important point for the understanding of religious innovation within Hinduism: to succeed, it almost always needs to be grounded in tradition, if only superficially. Even the most personally charismatic guru needs to draw upon the authority of "ancient wisdom" to justify new

---

46. The Office of His Holiness Sri Sri Ravi Shankar, "Biography," n.p. (accessed 18 February 2013), www.srisriravishankar.org/bio.

47. The Office of His Holiness Sri Sri Ravi Shankar, "Timeline," n.p. (accessed 18 February 2013), www.srisriravishankar.org/bio/timeline.

innovations. In the Indian context, being true to tradition is thus an important source of personal charisma.[48]

## *To Conclude: The Proverbial Cake*

What I have attempted to show is the manner in which Hindus through the ages have utilized the discourse of having no founders in a variety of creative ways. For Hinduism, having no founder is an important and powerful tool used both to boost its legitimacy and authority, as being eternal, unchanging, and superhuman, and also to create ample room for religious innovation. However, the idea of an eternal tradition also has a powerfully conserving function. We have thus seen how Hindu gurus are shaped by the interplay between personal charisma and the institutional charisma of a tradition, and also how charisma in an Indian context appears to be less disruptive than one might expect from Weber's typology.

As hardly any Hindus have more than an extremely superficial understanding of the Veda, many never having even seen a printed book, one might wonder how modern Hindus retain a sense of awe and reverence before the Vedic tradition. However, it is likely that the very vagueness of terms such as "Veda" or "Sanātana Dharma" is what makes them so attractive: they offer a tangible connection with a hoary past or even to an age beyond time itself, but one that is filled with so little content that over a billion human beings can agree on them. In this way, by having no founder yet being full of founders, Hinduism manages to have its cake and eat it too.

## *For Further Reading*

Dalmia, Vasudha, Angelika Malinar, and Martin Christof, eds. *Charisma and Canon: Essays on the Religious History of the Indian Subcontinent.* Oxford: Oxford University Press, 2003. An excellent collection of articles on Indian religious history, dealing in depth with many of the issues mentioned in this chapter.

Flood, Gavin. *An Introduction to Hinduism.* Cambridge: Cambridge University Press, 1996. A solid introduction to Hinduism, using a traditional framework but perceptively noting regional and sectarian variety.

---

48. Gita Dharampal-Frick, "Swadhyayaya and the 'Stream' of Religious Revitalization," in Dalmia, Malinar, and Christof, *Charisma and Canon*, 277.

Hiriyanna, Mysore. *An Outline of Indian Philosophy*. Delhi: Motilal Banarsidass, 2007. Originally published in 1932, but still one of the best general introductions to Indian philosophy available.

Lorenzen, David. *Who Invented Hinduism? Essays on Religion in History*. New Delhi: Yoda Press, 2006. A collection of well-written and provocative essays on, among other topics, the development of the modern understanding of "Hinduism."

Pechilis, Karen, ed. *The Graceful Guru: Hindu Female Gurus in India and the United States*. Oxford: Oxford University Press, 2004. Nine essays on historical and contemporary female Hindu gurus by leading scholars in the field.

Samuel, Geoffrey. *The Origins of Yoga and Tantra: Indic Religions to the Thirteenth Century*. Cambridge: Cambridge University Press, 2008. A genuinely multidisciplinary and thought-provoking approach to the development of religion in India. Samuel challenges many long-standing assumptions in the academic study of Hinduism.

Suthren Hirst, Jacqueline, and John Zavos. *Religious Traditions in Modern South Asia*. London: Routledge, 2011. A refreshing attempt at a new view of religion in modern South Asia, capturing the complexity of lived religion through engaging and well-chosen case studies.

Tripurari, Swami B. V. *Tattva-Sandarbha: Sacred India's Philosophy of Ecstacy*. San Francisco: Mandala, 1996. A well-written and engaging example of a contemporary Hindu commentary on a book commenting on a book commenting on yet another book commenting on the ancient Upanisads!

# 8

# *Crossing Boundaries*

## WHEN FOUNDERS OF FAITH APPEAR IN OTHER TRADITIONS

*Mark W. Muesse*

WHILE THE SIGNIFICANCE of any religious founder is surely greatest within the tradition he or she ostensibly inaugurates, let us not forget that those individuals who stand at the fountainhead of "their" religions often play important roles within traditions not their own. A brief survey of some of the major figures discussed in this volume reveals the wide range of functions these innovators and reformers serve for the adherents of other religions. In this chapter, we look at various ways they have been incorporated into traditions they did not found.

### *Jesus*

Because Jesus of Nazareth is associated with three major religious traditions, it is not surprising that he is a prime example of a "founder" who crosses the lines separating religions. Patrick Gray's chapter lays out the issues surrounding Jesus's status within Christianity, a religion he may or may not have founded, depending on what one means by "found." There is, however, little controversy concerning his centrality to the Christian tradition according to Christians and non-Christians alike. For Christians, Jesus is significant because he is inextricably connected to their ultimate salvation; Jews and Muslims, however, envision his significance in quite different ways; and the perception of many Asians concerning Jesus's role is very dissimilar from his place in Western monotheisms.

Although there is no doubt that Jesus was a Jew, Jewish sources tend to consider him as a messianic pretender who "had very little direct influence on the course of Jewish history or thought."[1] My own experience suggests that many Jews consider Jesus a Christian rather than a Jew and think of these as mutually exclusive categories. I videotaped a series of lectures entitled *Confucius, Buddha, Jesus, and Muhammad*, and after their release I received complaints from a half dozen Jewish friends and acquaintances who criticized my failure to include a Jewish sage in my study of great religious figures.[2] My response was that in fact I had omitted a *Christian* teacher, not a Jewish one. Most of them were not satisfied with that answer. Perhaps because Christianity became a Gentile religion so early in its history, many Jews have essentially discounted Jesus's Jewishness, a tendency certainly abetted by some of the earliest Christian documents, such as the Gospel of John, that try to distance Jesus from "the Jews."

The few Jewish texts that do mention Jesus are wont to consider him a practitioner of the magical arts who came into the world by means of an illegitimate birth and departed by way of a disgraceful death. The most important and best known of these texts is the *Sefer Toledot Yeshu*, or *The Generations of Jesus*, a medieval legend based in part on the Talmud.[3] It seems to have functioned primarily as an anti-Christian polemic for the Jewish masses rather than as a reflection of serious rabbinical Judaism. Because of its negative portrayal of Jesus, the *Toledot* was often cited by Christians to stir up anti-Jewish sentiment.

In more recent times, however, both Christian and Jewish scholars have sought to accent the Jewishness of Jesus. Geza Vermes's now classic *Jesus the Jew* was among the first works to argue explicitly that Jesus was a genuine *zaddik*, or Jewish saint, whose life and teachings make him an attractive spiritual exemplar (but not messiah) for Jews today.[4] Viewed within the context of first-century Palestinian Judaism, Vermes suggested, Jesus is properly regarded as fully Jewish and not the instigator of a new religion. The work of Vermes and other Jewish scholars signals a new openness to

---

1. Joseph Jacobs, "Jesus of Nazareth—in History," in *The Jewish Encyclopedia*, ed. I. Jacobs, vol. 7 (New York: Funk & Wagnalls, 1906), 160.

2. Mark W. Muesse, *Confucius, Buddha, Jesus, and Muhammad* (Chantilly, VA: Great Courses, 2010).

3. Morris Goldstein, *Jesus in the Jewish Tradition* (New York: Macmillan, 1950), 148–54.

4. Geza Vermes, *Jesus the Jew: A Historian's Reading of the Gospels* (Minneapolis: Fortress, 1973).

finding a place for Jesus within Jewish tradition, a place that few were willing to concede due to the long history of anti-Semitism in the West.

Whereas a positive assessment of Jesus in Judaism seems now only to be in its nascent stages, Islam has held him in high regard from the very beginning of Muhammad's ministry. Although the Qur'an explicitly denies Jesus's divinity, as does Judaism, the Muslim tradition generally considers him an authentic prophet (*nabi*) of God, indeed second only to Muhammad himself. Jesus's high status is based on the Islamic conception of a procession of prophetic intermediaries between God and humanity. Although only about two dozen are actually named in the Qur'an, tradition claims that God has sent 124,000 prophets to the nations of the world. All but a few of those identified are figures also found in the Bible, although most are not regarded as "prophets" by Judaism and Christianity. They include Adam, Noah, Abraham, Ishmael, Isaac, Joseph, Job, Moses, David, Solomon, John the Baptist, and Jesus. Although not named in the Qur'an, some Muslims also regard Confucius and the Buddha as prophets dispatched to humanity. Muhammad, of course, is the "seal of the prophets," the final and most important emissary of God, sent not just to a nation but to all humankind.

According to the Qur'an, however, Jesus was more than just one of the 124,000 prophets. He was also a "messenger" (*rasul*), one who brings not only the word of God but also a book. Furthermore, the Qur'an leaves no doubt that Jesus was among the greatest of all human beings. Like the New Testament, it affirms that he was born of a virgin and further declares that he was the only person ever born this way. The Qur'an acknowledges that Jesus performed many miracles and attributes to Jesus certain miraculous deeds that the New Testament does not mention, such as the ability to speak as an infant and to bring clay birds to life.[5] The Qur'an even uses the title "messiah" to refer to Jesus, although it is evident that the term does not mean the same to Muslims as it does to Jews and Christians.[6]

Yet the Qur'an (4:171 and elsewhere) is very emphatic that Jesus was not, and could not be, the son or incarnation of God. This is to go "to excess" in religion. The Qur'an's admonition rests on the doctrine of *tawhid*, the absolute oneness and singularity of God. Regarding Jesus as a son of God, as

---

5. The story of Jesus bringing clay birds to life is also found in the non-canonical *Infancy Gospel of Thomas*.

6. John Kaltner, *Ishmael Instructs Isaac: An Introduction to the Qur'an for Bible Readers* (Collegeville, MN: Liturgical Press/Michael Glazier, 1999), 243.

one of the trinity, or as a divine incarnation, in the view of Islam, violates the oneness of God and commits *shirk*, the greatest of all sins. Jesus is quoted as insisting that he is merely a human being devoted to the worship of Allah. His mission was not to die for the sin of humanity but to bear witness to the oneness of God and the necessity of submitting to the divine will. To be sure, Jesus was chosen and blessed by God and given a revelation to deliver to the Christians, the book known as the Injil, or the Gospel. The Injil, however, is not quite identical to the New Testament or the four gospels. Most Muslims believe that the original book delivered by Jesus was lost or at least corrupted by his followers, which might explain why Christians went "to excess" and ascribed divinity to their messenger. The Qur'an also indicates that Jesus served as a forerunner to a future messenger named Ahmed, whom it identifies as the Prophet Muhammad.

More surprising than Jesus' appearance in the Qur'an or as a character in Jewish folk traditions is his presence in some Asian religions. These religions generally lack a developed narrative about his life and regard him mainly as a figure of reverence, much like a saint in other traditions. For instance, in the city of Srinagar in India's northernmost province of Kashmir, there is a tomb that many believe to be that of Jesus, known locally as Yuza Asaf. Some who think of this shrine as the resting place of Jesus frequently connect it to the well-known (but widely discredited) idea that Jesus spent some of his adolescence and early adulthood in India and Tibet, where he was schooled in Buddhism and Hinduism. According to this legend, he later returned to Palestine to teach aspects of those religions in the Jewish idiom. The tale of Jesus's sojourn in South Asia was popularized in the nineteenth century by Mirza Ghulam Ahmad (1835–1908), founder of the Ahmadiyya Muslim Community, a sect that many mainstream Muslims regard as heretical. (The Ahmadiyya Muslim Community also proposed the idea that Confucius and Gotama Buddha were prophets of Islam.) Ghulam Ahmad declared the Kashmiri tomb, known locally as the Rozabal, to be the place where Jesus was buried after returning to India with his mother after surviving crucifixion. According to Ghulam Ahmad, Jesus fathered many children and died at the ripe old age of 120. Although the Rozabal is today maintained by Sunni Muslims, few believe the tomb is actually the grave of Jesus. Nevertheless, individuals of various traditions, notably Sufis and Hindus, occasionally visit the site as a place for prayer. For these lay practitioners, the tomb serves principally as an auspicious space where a saint is buried and not as the final resting place for an incarnation of God.

Relying on an East Asian version of the story made popular by Ghulam Ahmad, the small village of Shingo, Aomori in northern Japan also lays claim to being home to the authentic tomb of Jesus as well as his living descendants. In this iteration of the story, Jesus traveled to Japan at the age of twenty-one to study with a great sage near Mount Fuji and returned to Palestine twelve years later. There he was condemned for teaching heresy but escaped crucifixion by trading places with his younger brother Isukiri. Afterward, he was able to journey back to Japan where he married, became a rice farmer, fathered three children, and died at age 106. The site of his burial has become a pilgrimage (and tourist) site for many Shintoists and Buddhists, who offer prayers here much like their counterparts at the Kashmiri Rozabal. Not surprisingly, few of the 20,000 yearly visitors claim to be Christian, and the shrine appears to serve no function whatsoever in the faith of the very few Christians who inhabit the island.[7]

Dozens of other stories could be adduced to illustrate a highly positive image of Jesus from around the world. In India, it is not uncommon to see artistic renditions of Jesus in Hindu shrines or drawn in chalk or rice flour on the pavement or dirt paths. Unlike Jews and Muslims, Hindus generally have no difficulty regarding Jesus as an authentic incarnation of a god; their only hesitation comes with the Christian claim that Jesus is the only such incarnation. During the Taiping Rebellion in China in the nineteenth century, Hong Xiuquan claimed that Jesus was the inspiration for the uprising, which ultimately became one of the greatest military conflicts in world history. In ancient Manichaeism, Jesus was regarded as an "apostle of light" who may have been divine but was more of a forerunner to the Prophet Mani than the universal savior of humanity. Whether the figure of Jesus plays a significant role in non-Christian religions, such as Islam, or a very minor one, as in the case of Shinto and Buddhism, the world's assessment of Jesus seems to be overwhelmingly positive, whereas negative images, although not unknown, as in the *Sefer Toledot Yeshu,* are relatively rare.

## *Muhammad*

Such is not the case with Muhammad, especially in the Christian West, almost from the beginning of Islam in the seventh century. The main motifs of this negative representation are still familiar today: Muhammad

7. Franz Lidz, "Land of the Rising Son," *Smithsonian* (January 2013): 30–32.

was an opportunist who distorted the religion of the Christians for self-aggrandizement; he was a fanatic inspired by the devil who was not averse to using violence to promote his cause; and he was a sexual deviant, who violated every conceivable code of ethics governing sexuality.

From the outset, it appears that Christians misunderstood the role of Muhammad in Islam, perhaps not unlike the way early Muslims may themselves have misunderstood the role of Jesus in Christianity. In *The Song of Roland*, which dates to the tenth century and may be based on material from as early as the eighth, Muslims are portrayed as worshipping Muhammad as a god. Although that impression gradually diminished, the expression "Mohammedanism" as a designation for the religion itself persisted through the twentieth century. The belief that Muhammad was worshipped by Muslims may explain why he was often regarded as the Antichrist or labeled an "imposter," as if he were attempting to usurp the role of Jesus.[8]

In addition to the image of Muhammad as false messiah (or "false prophet" to use the language of John of Damascus, one of the earliest Christian interpreters of Islam), we find evidence that many Christians through the late Middle Ages regarded the Prophet as a heretic rather than the creator of a wholly new religion. This theme is not altogether hard to comprehend since, as R. Kevin Jaques notes, early Muslims saw Muhammad as preaching the ancient *islam* (submission to the will of God) of Abraham, Joseph, Moses, David, and Jesus. If Muhammad was regarded by his followers as falling in the same line as these other spiritual luminaries, as Christians saw Jesus, it would not be difficult to see why the Muslim Prophet was considered an apostate rather than the founder of another religion, like the Buddha. In Dante's *Divine Comedy* (1308–21), for example, Muhammad is depicted in the ninth ditch of Malebolge, the eighth circle of hell, reserved for schismatics. Muhammad is split in half, with his entrails spilling out, suggestive of the division he caused within religion.[9] The view of Muhammad as Christian heretic and schismatic is also implied in the legend that he was an opportunist who desperately wanted to be pope, presumably to satisfy his lust for power. According to this tale, Muhammad was a Christian cardinal who was disillusioned by

---

8. Edward W. Said, *Orientalism* (London: Penguin, 2003), 68.

9. *Inferno*, Canto 28. One of the ironies of Dante's portrayal of Muslim figures in the *Divine Comedy* is that while Muhammad himself is tortured in the lower realms of Hell, the Islamic philosophers Avicenna and Averröes are in Limbo among the virtuous pagans that include Socrates, Plato, and Aristotle.

his failure to attain the papacy and hence left Rome for Arabia, where he succeeded in gathering a community of followers who bestowed upon him a mantle greater even than that of the Holy Father.[10] As the idea that Muhammad was originally Christian suggests, many non-Muslims thought his message was not new but stolen from other sources. The similarities between the Qur'an and the Bible provided what was considered evidence for that claim. An old legend even suggested that Muhammad tried to make it seem he was actually receiving new revelations from God by training a dove to peck peas from his ears so that it appeared as if the Holy Spirit (symbolized by the bird) was whispering into them.[11]

A final characterization worth noting is the ancient idea that Muhammad was a lecher and sexual deviant. This is an especially important theme to flag simply because it still endures. Whereas the view that Muhammad was a Christian schismatic seems to have little currency today, depictions of his sexual appetite remain rampant. The number of the prophet's wives (eleven or thirteen, depending on how one counts) has long seemed scandalous to the Christian West, though similar objections were rarely raised against Abraham, Jacob, or even Solomon. Islam always defended the number of Muhammad's wives by arguing that most of them were women who were taken into his household after they had lost their husbands in war. These marriages were regarded, then, as acts of compassion rather than of prurience. While the sheer number of wives still seems problematic for many in our day, the real interest in Muhammad's sexuality appears to focus on his marriage to Aisha, to whom he was engaged when she was six. Although Muslim sources say this marriage was not consummated until Aisha was nine or ten, many non-Muslims still consider this age too young and are apt to label Muhammad a pedophile. This characterization appears in the notorious film trailer about the prophet that was released on YouTube, entitled *Innocence of the Muslims*, which some members of the Obama administration initially blamed for the attack on the US diplomatic mission in Benghazi, Libya, on 11 September 2012.

---

10. So widespread was the idea that Muhammad was a Christian schismatic that many Catholics began calling Protestants "followers of Muhammad" during the Reformation; see Lynn Hunt, Margaret C. Jacob, and Wijnand Mijnhardt, *The Book That Changed Europe: Picart and Bernard's Religious Ceremonies of the World* (Cambridge, MA: Belknap, 2010), 252.

11. Karen Armstrong, *Muhammad: A Biography of the Prophet* (San Francisco: HarperSan Francisco, 1992), 26.

Not until the twelfth century did the West recognize that Muslims did not worship Muhammad as a god, and more positive assessments of him began to sporadically emerge. William of Malmesbury in 1120 writes: "The Saracens and the Turks both worship God the Creator and venerate Muhammad not as God but as their prophet."[12] This notion was further advanced in the thirteenth-century *Estoire del Saint Grail*, part of the Arthurian cycle that describes how Joseph of Arimathea brings the Holy Grail to Great Britain. The author of this text suggests that Muhammad was a genuine prophet who intended to bring true Christianity to the Middle East until his pride caused him to fail. His skewed religion was nevertheless superior to the paganism he sought to displace.

Even more positive is Henri, the Comte de Boulainvilliers, who in a 1731 biography of the prophet argued that Muhammad was a forerunner of the Enlightenment and invented Islam to unify the world. In de Boulainvilliers' view, Muhammad's religion was based on reason, not revelation, which made it superior to Judaism and Christianity. The characteristic for which Muhammad is most appreciated during this age was his skill in statecraft. Jean-Jacques Rousseau, for example, praised the prophet in *The Social Contract* (1762) for his shrewd alliance of religion and governance.[13] The few groups that most significantly valued Muhammad's theology were the Deists and later the Unitarians, and both for essentially the same reason: Islam insisted on the oneness of God and denied the deity of Jesus. Here and there, one may thus catch a glimpse of admiration of the Prophet from non-Muslims, but this is the exception rather than the rule.

## *Buddha*

Like Jesus, and unlike Muhammad, the Buddha enjoys an overwhelmingly affirmative image in non-Buddhist religions. Most of these traditions are Asian, since, as Nathan McGovern notes in his chapter in this volume, the Buddha was not well known in the West until the modern period. To the degree that the Buddha was represented in the West, he was generally regarded as just another Hindu sage or deity. Still today among less informed Westerners, he is often considered a divine incarnation of a god or a jolly fat man whose statue is used by Buddhists as a lucky charm or

12. *Gesta Regum*, quoted in R. W. Southern, *Western Views of Islam in the Middle Ages* (Cambridge, MA: Harvard University Press, 1978), 35.

13. Hunt, Jacob, and Mijnhardt, *The Book That Changed Europe*, 253.

talisman. Of course, early Buddhists did not regard the Buddha as a god or a jolly fat man. The latter image derives from a popular East Asian folk saint named *Budai* (in China) and *Hotei* (in Japan). Over the years, he has come to be associated with the Maitreya Buddha, the Buddha of the next world-system, but he is most definitely not Gotama Buddha, the individual who brought the Dhamma to this world-system. Although these images of the Buddha are popular and misleading, they nonetheless present a rather benign view of the ostensible founder of Buddhism. One would be hard-pressed to find a portrayal of the Buddha anywhere that even approaches the negative image of Muhammad outside the Islamic world.

McGovern makes brief mention of the way the story of Gotama Buddha made its way into Christian hagiography, although the dynamics of this incorporation were not made evident until the modern period. The narrative is that of Josaphat and Barlaam, or as they are known in both the Eastern Orthodox and Roman Catholic churches, St. Josaphat and St. Barlaam. In the Christian version of the story, the wife of an Indian king by the name of Abenner gave birth to a son named Josaphat. Fervently anti-Christian, King Abenner had persecuted the Christians in his realm and determined to keep young Josaphat from their malevolent influence.[14] To prevent an encounter with this Christian menace, Abenner did his best to keep Josaphat confined to the palace. Yet despite his best efforts, Josaphat met a Christian hermit named Barlaam, was persuaded of the truth of Christianity, and submitted to baptism. Josaphat immediately forsook courtly life, renounced his throne, and lived out his days as a wandering Christian ascetic. Later, the story goes, King Abenner was himself converted and joined Josaphat as a forest dweller. Wilfred Cantwell Smith has shown how this tale derives ultimately from the story of the Buddha and was transmitted to the Christian West through Islamic and Manichaean sources. Through its Christian rendition, the story later influenced both Leo Tolstoy and Mohandas Gandhi.[15] Is it too much to say that the Buddha has become a Christian saint?

Early Western interpreters of the Buddha had difficulty separating him from Hinduism. Many of the first Christians to become acquainted with the Buddha were doing so at the time of the Protestant Reformation. For this reason it seemed evident to them that Gotama was a reformer of

---

14. According to tradition, Christianity has had a long presence in India, beginning with Jesus's disciple Thomas who brought the faith to the subcontinent in the first century CE.

15. Wilfred Cantwell Smith, *Towards a World Theology* (Philadelphia: Westminster, 1981), 6–9.

Hinduism rather than the founder of some new religion. Indeed, he was sometimes called, therefore, the "Luther of India." Although orthodox Hinduism regards Buddhism as a *nastika darshana*, a heterodox (sometime translated "atheistic") philosophy, many modern Hindus nevertheless wish to include Gotama as part of the Hindu traditions. Gandhi, for example, insisted that the Buddha was a Hindu, a claim that many Hindus today would still affirm.[16] The traditional belief that the Buddha was the ninth avatar of the god Vishnu, one of the cosmic deities of Hinduism, is often cited in support of this view. Many Hindus who claim the Buddha as one of their own, however, fail to recognize the ambivalence of this tradition. According to ancient Hindu texts such as the *Gita Govinda*, Jayadeva's twelfth-century love-song to Lord Krishna, the avatar Buddha takes earthly form to oppose the ancient Aryan practice of animal sacrifice. It is as a practitioner of *ahimsa* (non-violence) that the Buddha (and, by the way, Mahavira, the "founder" of Jainism) is principally remembered in Hinduism. Other texts and legends, however, reveal something of a sinister side to the Buddha as avatar. From this perspective, Vishnu descended as Gotama in order to teach false beliefs and lead demons astray. Although the ninth avatar is thereby associated with Vishnu's ever-compassionate pursuit of the good of the world, it is accomplished at the expense of making the Buddha and his followers seem deluded and perhaps even demonic. The adoption of the Buddha as an incarnation of Vishnu seems to have commenced at roughly the same time Hinduism gained in ascendancy in India and Buddhism began its decline.[17] Thus, the Hindu inclusion of the Buddha in the traditional list of Vishnu's ten avatars may in fact represent a part of Hindu efforts to eviscerate Buddhist power and appeal.

The Buddha is appropriated for minor roles in other traditions as well. The Ahmadiyya sect of Islam includes the Buddha as one of the prophets

---

16. Yet at the same time, one of Gandhi's opponents, B. R. Ambedkar, the great leader of the *dalit* (untouchable) liberation movement, led half a million outcastes to convert to Buddhism precisely because the Buddha was *not* a Hindu; see Urgyen Sangharakshita, "Milestone on the Road to Conversion," *Ambedkar and Buddhism* (New Delhi: Motilal Banarsidass, 2006), 72. One of the twenty-two vows Ambedkar gave to these dalit-Buddhist converts was: "I do not and shall not believe that Lord Buddha was the incarnation of Vishnu. I believe this to be sheer madness and false propaganda" (Hans Ucko, *The People and the People of God* [Münster: LIT Verlag, 2002], 101).

17. Ronald Inden, "Ritual, Authority, and Cycle Time in Hindu Kingship," in *Kingship and Authority in South Asia*, ed. J. F. Richards (New Delhi: Oxford University Press, 1998), 67, 55.

of Islam. In similar fashion, the Manichees referred to him as an "apostle of Light" (along with Jesus and Zoroaster), and the Baha'is, like some Hindus, consider him a manifestation of a god. And in a new twist on the image of the Buddha in Christianity, theologian Paul Knitter has recently entitled an autobiographical work *Without Buddha, I Could Not Be a Christian.*[18] Knitter does not portray the Buddha as an "anonymous Christian"—an individual who, in the phrase of Catholic theologian Karl Rahner, practices the teaching of Jesus without ever having heard of the Gospel and hence might be saved—but rather argues that a clear understanding of the teaching of the Buddha helps the modern Christian come to a better understanding of Jesus. In short, Knitter encourages Christians to study the Buddha to become more faithful to Jesus. Here, then, is a rare instance in which the "founder" of one religious tradition is said to illumine the followers of another.

## *Confucius and Laozi*

The Buddha has also long been considered as representative of one of the "Three Ways" of China and revered even by those Chinese who would not consider themselves "Buddhist." In his introduction to this volume, Gray mentions the famous painting usually entitled "The Vinegar Tasters," which depicts Confucius, Laozi, and the Buddha in what seems to be a friendly moment. Some regard the painting as more favorable to Daoism since, according to this view, Laozi smiles upon tasting the contents of the vat while Confucius scowls and the Buddha is expressionless. Whether the scroll in fact vindicates Daoism is certainly debatable, but what is incontestable is that for nearly two millennia the Chinese have considered Confucianism, Buddhism, and Daoism the dominant traditions of their culture and these individuals as the principal symbols, if not the actual founders, of those traditions.[19] Liang Cai and Gil Raz demonstrate the problems of these identifications during the formation of Confucianism

---

18. Paul F. Knitter, *Without Buddha I Could Not Be a Christian*, 2nd ed. (Oxford: Oneworld, 2013).

19. Others regard the image (and images similar to it) as suggestive of the ultimate *harmony* of Daoism, Confucianism, and Buddhism. A verse from the *Zenrin kushu* makes the point: "A Taoist hat, Confucian shoes, and a Buddhist robe combine the Three Houses into one" (Hung Ying-ming, *Master of the Three Ways: Reflections of a Chinese Sage on Living a Satisfying Life*, trans. William Scott Wilson [Boston: Shambhala, 2012], vi).

and Daoism, but it is clear that at some point in Chinese history, these three are taken to be the figureheads of the dominant Chinese schools. By the fifth century CE, at least one thinker had even posited that Confucius, Laozi, and Gotama were in fact the self-same individual and that differences in the interpretations and practices of his followers is what ultimately led to the establishment of three different sects.[20]

Although there is disagreement as to when Confucius first appears as a figure in Daoism and Laozi in Confucianism—due in large measure to the debates about what "Confucianism" and "Daoism" denote and their dates of origin—there is no doubt that both figures emerged at early points in the other's "religion." Confucius appears as early as the Daoist *Zhuangzi* (ca. third century BCE), and his role in the text seems rather ambiguous. The *Zhuangzi* clearly indicates a high regard for Confucius, or at least reports that many regard him highly. Yet Laozi (known as "Lao Dan" in the *Zhuangzi*) is often portrayed as the wiser and better philosopher.[21] An ancient legend even goes so far as to suggest that Laozi was in fact Confucius's teacher, a claim that gained wide currency and was incorporated in the 2010 film *Confucius*, directed by Hu Mai.[22] The ambiguity seems to reflect the Chinese ideal of the complementarity of Confucianism and Daoism (as well as the Daoist belief in its own superiority). In any event, it is clear that the figure of Confucius serves as a foil for Daoist viewpoints in many of the earliest Daoist writings.

There is not much to suggest that Confucius was well known in the West until the seventeenth century when Jesuit missionaries to China learned of him and gave him the Latinized name by which most of the world knows him today. The Christians who encountered Confucianism in the modern period were impressed by the way Confucian ethics seemed to parallel the teaching of Jesus. Italian Jesuit Matteo Ricci (1552–1610) was probably the first to translate Confucian writings into Latin, and it was through his work that Confucius became more widely celebrated by European thinkers, who were significantly impressed and influenced by

20. This perspective is argued by Gu Huan (390?–483?) in his *Treatise on the Barbarians and Chinese*; see Xinzhong Yao, *An Introduction to Confucianism* (Cambridge: Cambridge University Press, 2000), 226.

21. See, for example, *Zhuangzi*, chap. 4. Sima Qian's (ca. 135–86 BCE) *Shiji* also reports a story in which Laozi visits Confucius and upbraids him for his arrogance, ambition, pretension, and doubt.

22. John H. and Evelyn Nagai Berthrong, *Confucianism* (Oxford: Oneworld, 2000), 86.

his work. Enlightenment thinkers, in particular, were especially entranced by the teachings of Confucius as well as by Confucius as a symbol of free thought. In the Chinese sage, philosophers such as Leibniz and Voltaire saw an ancient figure from the East who independently established a philosophy similar to their own. Voltaire considered Confucianism to be a highly rationalistic system that could serve as an alternative to Christian morality. In his famous *Philosophical Dictionary,* Voltaire praised him as a sage who introduced no new religion and taught "nothing but the purest morality, without the slightest tinge of charlatanism."[23]

Just as Confucius served as a foil to Daoists, so the figure of Laozi served a similar purpose for Confucianists. But Laozi enjoys a career in other religions in ways that Confucius does not. Perhaps most significant is the claim that Laozi left China and traveled to India, where he met Gotama Shakyamuni and became the Buddha's teacher. A slightly different version of the story indicates that Laozi in fact was the Buddha.[24] The Daoist *Hua-Hu Jing* (*The Classic on Converting the Barbarians*) suggests that Buddhism was thus a version of Daoism. Written around 300 CE, the *Hua-Hu Jing* seems to have been concocted by the Celestial Masters to gain favor with Chinese emperors, who frequently sponsored debates between the representatives of the various schools.[25] In a similar tale, Laozi also appears as Mani, the founder of Manichaeism, a claim that was accepted by many Daoists but also by some Manichees, who still maintain a tiny presence in Asia.[26]

## *Moses*

Mark Leuchter's chapter indicates that there is no dearth of credible candidates for the "founder" of Judaism, if we find it necessary to choose one. Many of the potential contenders—Abraham, Moses, David, and Ezra—have been appropriated in numerous ways by the two major religious traditions that claim to maintain some continuity with ancient Israel, namely,

23. Voltaire, *Philosophical Dictionary,* trans. W. F. Fleming, in *The Works of Voltaire: A Contemporary Version,* vol. 4 (New York: E. R. DuMont, 1901), 82.

24. A Daoist tale from the early centuries of the CE even suggests that Laozi was born from his mother's side as she clung to the branches of a tree, precisely the same mode of birth ascribed to the Buddha by the *Buddhacharita.*

25. Holmes H. Welch Jr., *Taoism: The Parting of the Way* (Boston: Beacon, 1957), 152.

26. Samuel N. C. Lieu, *Manichaeism in Central Asia and China* (Leiden: Brill, 1998), 112–14.

Christianity and Judaism. Other than Jesus and perhaps Paul, Moses may be the most prominent Jewish figure in Christianity. In the Sermon on the Mount, the Gospel of Matthew portrays Jesus as the New Moses, a lawgiver who ascends a mountain to deliver his message. He comes not to abolish the Law but to fulfill it (Matt. 5:17). The second-century Christian apologist Justin Martyr refers to Moses as "our first prophet and lawgiver" and "our first religious teacher."[27] According to Justin, Moses' significance derives from his role as the medium through which the Law comes to the Jews. "Law," of course, is a central category in early Christianity, and Moses is often seen as its symbol. But "Law" is also an ambiguous category. To many interpreters, such as Luther, Paul regarded the Law as that which condemns us, the commandments of God that reveal to us our need of salvation.[28] To this extent, one might argue that Moses functions as something of a negative figure in Christianity. Yet Luther and other theologians never make this claim, since it is precisely the Law that demonstrates our need for Christ. The figure in the Christian tradition (albeit one later declared a heretic) who may come closest to viewing Moses in a disparaging light is Marcion, the second-century theologian who argued that the God of the Hebrew scriptures was decidedly different from the God of Jesus.[29] Marcion saw Moses as the revealer of a deity of wrath who requites human sinfulness with suffering and death, not forgiveness.

In Islam, Moses functions much as he does in Christianity, but perhaps less ambiguously. In the Qur'an, Moses is mentioned more times than any other individual, including Abraham. In many respects, the Qur'an suggests that Moses was a prototype for Muhammad just as he was for Jesus according to Matthew. For example, Muhammad leads the Muslims out persecution in Mecca to a new promised land in Medinah as Moses led the Israelites out of Egyptian bondage. And like Muhammad, Moses was a *nabi* and *rasul*, a prophet and messenger, one who brings a book of revelation, which in Moses' case was the Torah. Many Muslims maintain that the words of the Torah (Deut. 18:18–19) foretell of the coming of Muhammad, a messenger like Moses.

---

27. See Paul Blackham, "The Trinity in the Hebrew Scriptures," in *Trinitarian Soundings in Systematic Theology*, ed. Paul Louis Metzger (New York: Continuum, 2005), 39.

28. Martin Luther, "Preface to the Epistle of St. Paul to the Romans," in *Martin Luther: Selections from His Writings*, ed. John Dillenberger (New York: Anchor, 1958), 19–34.

29. Sebastian Moll, *The Arch-Heretic Marcion* (Tübingen: Mohr Siebeck, 2010), 144.

Moses is even credited with establishing the ritual of prayer five times daily. According to *hadith* and the prophet's early biographers, late one night, while asleep near the Ka'ba after a vigil of prayer, Muhammad was awakened by Gabriel and taken to a creature called the Buraq, a small milk-white horse with wings. Muhammad mounted the Buraq and flew, alongside Gabriel, to Jerusalem. There he met with Abraham, Moses, Jesus, and other great prophets and prayed with them at the site where the Second Temple had stood. Afterward, Gabriel escorted him to the heavens where he was given a vision of paradise and hell and received instructions on prayer. According to extracanonical Islamic sources, Muhammad was initially told by God to require the Muslims to pray fifty times a day. When Moses learned of this new command back at the Temple Mount in Jerusalem, he told Muhammad to return to heaven and get the number reduced. Fifty times a day was simply too much! Muhammad went back and got the number cut to ten times a day, but Moses thought even that was too much. Finally, Muhammad returned to heaven, and the number was reduced to five. Moses told Muhammad that five times was *still* too many, but Muhammad was too embarrassed to ask God to change it, and so he returned to Mecca and five times daily became the Muslim standard.[30]

## *Hinduism*

As Måns Broo's chapter makes abundantly clear, Hinduism has no founder. But in closing, it is instructive to look briefly at someone who serves as a figurehead of one of the many sects that comprise what goes under the umbrella term "Hinduism" for the similarities and differences one sees when he is placed among the founders of the major traditions. Whether or not the Kabir Panth ("the path of Kabir") can be exclusively called a "Hindu" community may be debatable, but the overwhelming majority of its practitioners are Hindu (although a small number would consider themselves Buddhist and Jain). Nonetheless, the devotees of this *sampradaya* would have no difficulty naming the founder of their spiritual path: the mystic poet Kabir (1398–1448). What makes Kabir's status as the inaugurator of this community so interesting for our purposes is

30. Noorah Al-Gailani and Chris Smith, *The Islamic Year: Surahs, Stories and Celebrations* (Gloucestershire: Hawthorn House, 2003), 90–94.

his own spiritual identity, philosophy, and practice, so much at odds with the notion of a religion in his name.

The identity of Kabir has long been the subject of debate. Both Muslims and Hindus now claim him as one of their own, although during his lifetime both Muslims and Hindus tried to silence him, sometimes violently. His legacy is also affirmed by the Sikhs, who include many of his poems in their scripture, the *Adi Granth*. Kabir's name is Muslim, one of the ninety-nine "beautiful names" of Allah. His poetry, however, seems to suggest a greater affinity for Hindu practices, such as his recitation of "Ram" as the name of God and his apparent belief in rebirth. Many scholars think that Kabir belonged to a caste of weavers from the holy city of Banaras who had recently (and perhaps cursorily) become Muslims.

No matter how he is identified today, Kabir leveled scathing criticisms at institutional religion in general and Hindus and Muslims in particular. In one verse, for instance, Kabir sarcastically condemns the Hindu ascetics who think renunciation and celibacy will bring them closer to the divine, and in others he berates the Brahmins and the Muslims with equal vigor.[31] While Kabir condemns the rituals and sacred traditions of his contemporaries, he invites them to turn inward to seek the divine in their hearts.[32] He has little use for scripture, ritual, temples, religious professionals and saints, and sacred images—the stock-in-trade of institutional religion. Yet today, he is regarded by his followers as the founder of a tradition in which most of these elements play roles. His *Bījak* has the status of scripture; he has become a saint; and his devotees divide into priests and laity, practice strict vegetarianism, and wear sacred Tulsi and Rudraksha beads. Many think of Kabir as one who preached the unity of Islam and Hinduism, whereas his writings actually seem to condemn both. Thus in Kabir we find a "founder" who would be, like many others discussed in this volume, uncomfortable with that role or title. This irony, however, may appear more evident in Kabir than in the others because he goes out of his way to condemn virtually every aspect of religious tradition. Here then is a despiser of religion who unwittingly "founds" one.

---

31. John Stratton Hawley and Mark Juergensmeyer, *Songs of the Saints of India* (New York: Oxford University Press, 1988), 50; cf. *The* Bījak *of Kabir*, trans. Linda Hess and Shukdev Singh (Delhi: Motilal Banarsidass, 1983), 69, 85–86.

32. *The* Bījak *of Kabir*, 73–74.

## *Conclusion*

Our broad examination amply attests that the idea of a religious "founder" is significant to outsiders even if the concept is problematic or even meaningless to those within the tradition primarily associated with these "founders." Confucius, the Buddha, Mahavira, and Muhammad all insisted that they taught nothing more than an ancient truth, yet to those who are not their followers, at least not in a primary sense, these religious figureheads are indeed the creators or inspirations of "their" traditions.

We can see religious founders functioning in other religions along a wide spectrum. At one end, we discover founders who serve as a foil to the teachings or teacher of another tradition. To many Christians in the West, Muhammad was the Antichrist, the one who represented everything to which Jesus was opposed: self-aggrandizement, false belief, power-grabbing, violence, and sexual license. We also find that these images were rarely based on a considered study of the Qur'an and *hadith* but rather represented what Gray calls a conflict by proxy, reflecting, for example, the Christian resentment of Islamic imperialism. Conflict by proxy also seems an apt description of the way the *Sefer Toledot Yeshu* depicts Jesus as a magician of the black arts and a messianic pretender.

In a less vitriolic manner, one sees the roles of Confucius in Daoism and of the Buddha as the ninth avatar of Vishnu functioning as symbolic contrasts to other religious viewpoints. In these instances, the "outsider" is well regarded yet also understood as inferior to the "inside" position. Confucius was a great sage, according to the *Zhuangzi*, but not as great as Laozi. The message is clear: however much Daoism shares with Confucianism, the Daoist approach is superior. The Buddha taught the practice of non-violence, according to some Hindus, but was also a teacher who misled the unsuspecting, according to others.

At the other end of the spectrum, we find figures who are seen as unambiguously positive. Both Christianity and Islam want to affirm the great value and sanctity of a procession of saints and prophets found in Hebrew scripture. Both also suggest that Moses was a prototype for their "founders." Islam even goes so far as to indirectly credit Moses with its daily prayer regimen. The Ahmadiyya sect of Islam wants to include the Buddha and Confucius in its understanding of God's prophets. Manichaeism and the Baha'i traditions make similar gestures toward inclusivity. In East Asia, we discover a broad tradition that sees Confucius, Laozi, and the Buddha as friends—or even that the three were really just one person—suggesting a harmony among the traditions they represent. Finally, we meet Christian theologians who suggest that there is not only harmony between Jesus and the Buddha, but that the latter illuminates the former.

In the middle of this spectrum lies the position of indifference, amusement, or mild appreciation or dismissal. Here we have the common understanding of the Buddha as a happy fat man or Confucius as an old Chinese with a Fu Manchu mustache who utters truisms or banal proverbs. What differentiates this region of the spectrum from its extremes is that the middle views have little serious impact on the religious world of those who see other founders this way. A Christian who thinks of Confucius as a thinker whose wisdom is only worth putting in fortune cookies is not apt to take Confucianism very seriously. If anything, such an image reinforces a sense of the superiority of one's own religion.

At the ends of this continuum, views about the founders of other traditions—whether true or not, informed or invented—can have important consequences. That Muhammad was represented in the West for centuries as an immoral, violent fraud has deeply influenced the way Christians and Jews have treated Muslims. On the other hand, when Muslims regard Jesus as a prophet teaching submission to God in the same manner as Islam and then encounter Christians who accuse Muhammad of heresy and sexual deviance, this cognitive dissonance has real consequences.

The chapters assembled in this volume have, as they should, predominantly focused on the role of religious "founders" from the point of view of their primary followers and devotees. But we should always bear in mind that the "construction" of founders or religious figureheads is a complicated process that often involves not only those within but also those without. And through this process, figures from other traditions become part of the world of other religions: the Buddha becomes a Christian hero and a Hindu deity; Muhammad becomes a heretical Christian cardinal; Kabir unwittingly creates a religion that goes by his name; and Jesus witnesses to the truth of Muhammad and becomes a saint for Sufis, Shintoists, and Buddhists.

# Author Index

# *Subject Index*


Aaron, 27, 30
Abbasid Revolution, 13
ʿAbd Allāh b. Thāmir, 140, 152
ʿAbd al-Mālik b. Hishām, 132
ʿAbd al-Muṭṭalib (Shaybah), 143, 144, 145, 146
Abenner (King), 183
Abhidharma tradition, 57
Abrahah, 145, 146
Abraham, 10, 15, 16, 24, 36, 187. *See also* Ibrāhīm
Abu al-Muzaffar al-Isfarayini, 128
Abyssinians, 145, 146
*Ācārya*, 165
Acts of the Apostles, 112
*Adi Granth*, 190
Ahab, 20n10
Ahijah, 32
Ahmadiyya Muslim Community, 178, 184–185, 191
Ai of Lu, Duke, 67
Aisha, 181
Akivah, Rabbi, 7, 37n40
Akṣobhya, 58
al-Ḥārith, 144
*al-Mabʿath*, 132, 139
*al-Maghāzī*, 132
Almond, Philip, 45, 46, 48
*al-Mubtadaʾ*, 132, 139
Ambedkar, B. R., 184n16
Amitābha, 58
Amos, 32
ʿAmr b. Luḥayy, 142, 143
*Anāgāmins* (non-returners), 57
*Analects*, 75, 86
*Annals of the Historian* (Sima Qian), 88–89, 90
*Annals of the Lord of Dao, Sage of the Latter Heavens of Shangqing*, 104
Anti-Catholic sentiment, 46
Anti-Semitism, 8, 126
Apologetics, 10
Apostolic succession, 121
"Archaelogy and Protestant Presuppositions in the Study of Buddhism" (Schopen), 50
Archaeology, 19, 50
Aristotle, 180n9
Asherah, 19
Aśoka (Emperor), 56
Assyrians, 28, 31
Astrology, 63
Augustine, 127
Avalokiteśvara, 57
*Avataṃsaka Sūtra*, 58
*Avatāra* (divine descent), 168
Averröes, 180n9

Knitter, Paul, 185
Konakamuni (Konāgamana), 56
*Kong Clan Anthology* (Wang Su), 66
Kṛṣṇa, 168
Kṣatriyas, 168
Kṣitigarbha, 57
Kublai Khan, 42
Kumārila Bhaṭṭa, 158

Lakṣmī, 167–168, 169
Lakulīśa, 168
Lamaism, 51
Lamotte, Étienne, 42, 49–50
Lao, Lord, 97, 98, 100, 110
Laozi
  appearances in other faith traditions, 185–187
  *Daode jing* and, 84, 86
  Daoism and, 88–97
  deification of, 93–97, 187n24
  family lineage of, 89
  first mentions in connection with Daoism, 88–93
  as founder, 4, 6, 7, 12, 85
  historicity of, 113
  humanity of, 96
  in Vidal's *Creation*, 1
  Western scholarship on, 9
Latter Prophets, 31, 36n36
Legal tradition of Judaism, 21, 25–30
Leibniz, Gottfried Wilhelm, 187
Levites, 29, 35
Leviticus, 30
Lewis, Mark, 78n59
Li, Lord, 104
Liberal Protestant theology, 3, 114
Lin Chi, 8
Littledale, R. F., 47n21
Liu Ying, 93
Lopez, Donald, 43, 44
Lorenzen, David N., 3
*Lotus Sūtra*, 58
Lu Xiujing, 105, 107
Lūṭ (Lot), 137
Luther, Martin, 7, 46, 48, 127

Maccoby, Hyam, 128
Machen, J. Gresham, 124
Mahāpadāna Sutta, 55, 56
Mahavira, 1, 184
Mahāyāna, 52, 55, 56, 58, 59
Mainstream Buddhism, 56, 56n42, 57
Maitreya, 56, 183
Malachi, 36n36
Mani, 4
Manichaeanism, 4, 179, 185
Mañjuśrī, 57
*Mantra-muktāvalī*, 162
Maoshan Daoism, 102
Marcion, 188
Marco Polo, 42, 43
Mark
  Gospel of, 116
  *Secret Gospel of*, 120
Marx, Karl, 125
Mary
  *Gospel of*, 120
  veneration of, 122
Mary Magdalene, 125
Massey, Gerald, 119n9
Masuzawa, Tomoko, 3, 3n6, 85–86
Mata Amritanandamayi Devi (Amma), 160–161
Matthew, Gospel of, 188
Mazdians, 140
McClintock, Sarah, 54
Mecca, 146, 147. *See also* Ka'bah
Melito of Sardis, 117
Mencius, 63, 70, 71, 72, 74, 74n45, 75, 79
Mendelssohn, Moses, 5n12
Merneptah (Pharaoh), 22
Micah, 32
*Mimamsaka* philosophers, 13

Persia, 31
Peter, 125, 129
  *Gospel of*, 120
*Philip, Gospel of*, 120
Philosophical Daoism, 7
*Philosophical Dictionary* (Voltaire), 187
Pilgrimage. *See Ḥajj*
Plato, 180n9
Polytheism, 19
Porphyry, 126
*Prasāda*, 166
Priesthood, 17, 25–30
Priestly Code, 29
Priestly Torah, 29–30
Prophets
  in Hinduism, 164
  in Islam, 132–133, 134, 148, 153
  in Judaism, 30–35, 36
Protestantism, 3, 46, 50–51, 60, 114, 121, 122, 138, 183
Proverbs, 17
Psalms, 19
Purāṇic period, 166
Purāṇic texts, 43
Pure Abodes (*śuddhāvāsa*), 57, 58
Pure Land Buddhism, 57, 58

*Qi* cultivation techniques, 88
Qin Dynasty, 11, 72–73
Qing Dynasty, 76
*Questions of Duke Transcendent*, 106
Qur'an, 5, 121, 126, 135, 138n16, 140, 142, 146, 177, 188
Quraysh, 141, 143, 144, 146, 147, 149
Quṣayy b. Kilāb, 143, 144

Rabbinic tradition, 15–17, 30, 37n39
Rahner, Karl, 185
Rāmānuja, 169
*Rasūl*, 136
Rationality, 122, 182, 187
Reformation, 7, 12, 46, 50, 121, 183
Religious Daoism, 7
Ren (Emperor), 84
Revelation, 122
Ricci, Matteo, 186
Righteousness, 70
Ritual, 64, 64n7, 65, 74, 140–141, 147, 149, 152
*Rituals*, 68
Roman Empire, 16n1
Rousseau, Jean-Jacques, 182
*Ru*
  Confucius and, 11, 63–74
  defined, 63
  as school of thought, 72
  versatile tradition of, 74–77
*Rūpakāya*, 58

Śabara, 158
Sacred legislators, 164, 171
Sacrificial rites, 98
Sade, Marquis de, 10n30
Said, Edward, 42n5, 50
Śaiva, 159, 169
Sakkapañha Sutta, 54
Śāktas, 169
Śākyamuni, 41, 52, 55, 56, 57, 58
Salmān the Persian, 140, 141, 148, 152
Salvation, 81, 105, 107, 138, 164
Sāmaññaphala Sutta, 54
*Saṃbhogakāya* (Enjoyment Body), 58
*Sampradāyas*, 156, 169, 189
Samuel, 32, 33, 34
Saṃyutta Nikāya, 39
Sanātana Dharma, 160, 163, 173
Sana'ā', 145
*Saṅgha*, 40–41
Śaṅkara, 166
Sanskrit, 44, 46n17, 46n19, 47
Sārah, 137
Satguru Sivaya Subramuniyaswami, 159, 161
Saul, 33
Schopen, Gregory, 42, 50–52
Schwartz, Benjamin, 65n11, 75